The City's End

JOSEPH PENNELL DEL.

THAT LIBERTY SHALL NOT
PERISH FROM THE EARTH
BUY LIBERTY BONDS

MAX PAGE

The City's End

Two Centuries of
Fantasies, Fears, and
Premonitions of
New York's
Destruction

Yale University Press New Haven & London

Frontispiece: Joseph Pennell, Liberty Bond poster, 1917

Published with assistance from the John Simon Guggenheim Memorial Foundation and from Furthermore: a program of the J. M. Kaplan Fund.

The author would like to express appreciation to the University Seminars at Columbia University for their support for this book through the Schoff Subvention Fund. Materials in this book were presented to the City Seminar.

Designed by James J. Johnson and set in Melior and Meta types by Tseng Information Systems, Inc.
Printed in the United States of America.

Library of Congress Cataloging-in-Publication Data

Page, Max.
The city's end : two centuries of fantasies, fears, and premonitions of New York's destruction / Max Page.
   p.   cm.
Includes bibliographical references and index.
ISBN 978-0-300-11026-5 (cloth : alk. paper)   1. American fiction—20th century—History and criticism.
2. New York (N.Y.)—In literature. 3. New York (N.Y.)—In art. 4. New York (N.Y.)—In motion pictures.
5. Disasters in literature. 6. Disasters in art. 7. Disaster films—History and criticism. 8. New York (N.Y.)—
Civilization. 9. September 11 Terrorist Attacks, 2001—Influence. I. Title.
PS374.N43P34 2008
813´.509327471—dc22
2007052370

A catalogue record for this book is available from the British Library.
The paper in this book meets the guidelines for permanence and durability of the Committee on
Production Guidelines for Book Longevity of the Council on Library Resources.

10   9   8   7   6   5   4   3   2   1

Contents

The City's End

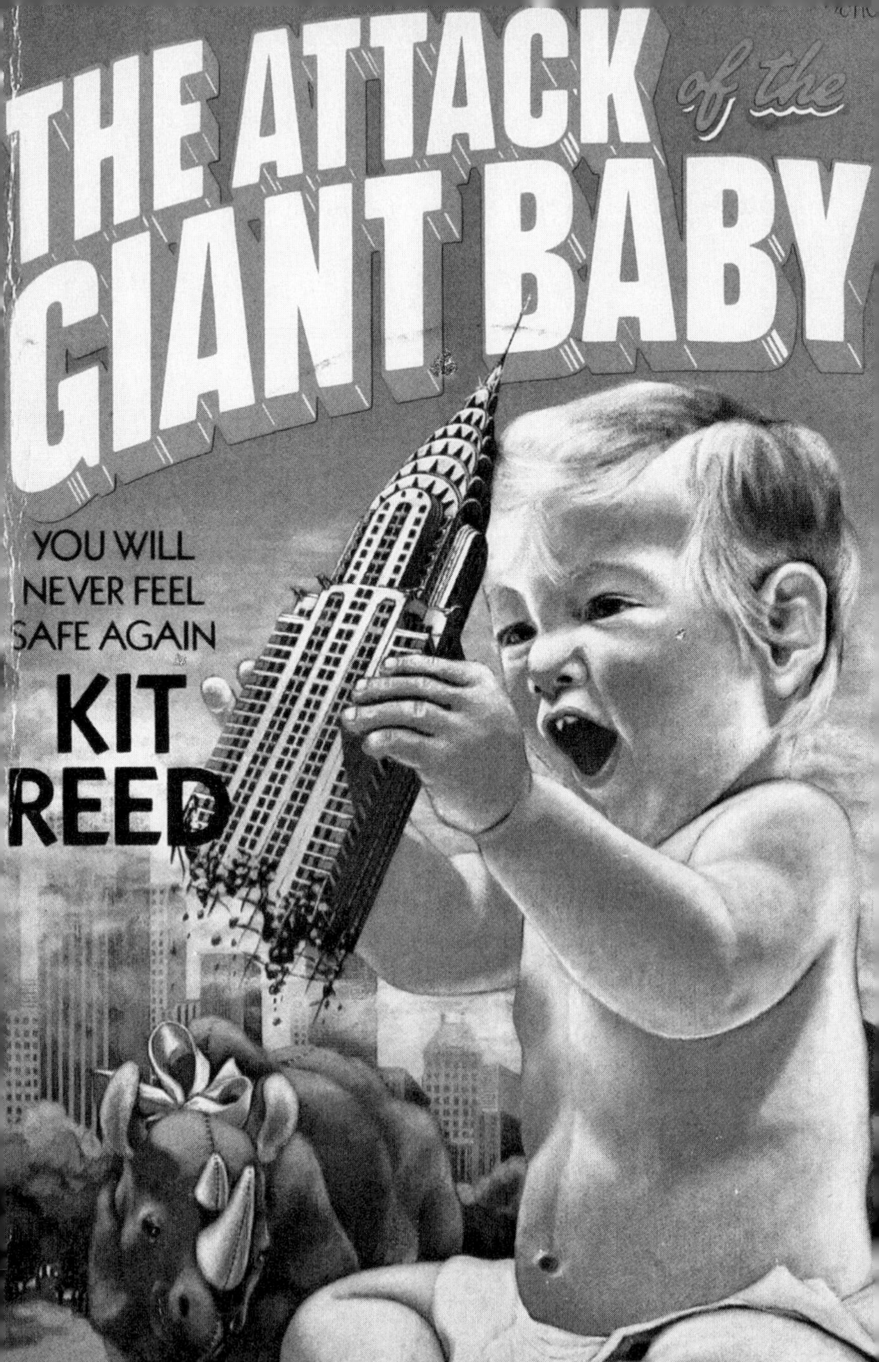
THE ATTACK of the
GIANT BABY
YOU WILL
NEVER FEEL
SAFE AGAIN
KIT
REED

one

Beauty and Terror

All my life, and it has not come to any more than this: beauty and terror.

—MARY OLIVER SPENGLER

SOON AFTER I GOT MY FIRST COMPUTER, AN AT&T 6300 (WITH A big fat 512 kilobytes of RAM, and a couple of five-inch floppy drives), I bought a copy of Microsoft's Flight Simulator software. Flight Simulator was at the cutting edge of graphics in 1987, even if those early versions are laughable today.

Sitting at my desk, I took off from Sikorsky Airport in Bridgeport and gently rose into the Microsoft sky so I could see both the Connecticut coast and Long Island out my left wing. On that first flight, I knew exactly where I wanted to head—New York City. By 1987 I had been smitten by a love of cities encouraged by Professor Vincent Scully, who urged us to think of "architecture as the city as a whole" and reminded us to "look up" when walking in the city. I had never lived in New York, had never spent more than a day or two there at a time. But when I graduated from college, I would move there, and I have written about it ever since.

As I floated along the coastline, I knew I wanted to see, if only on my green LCD monitor, those unforgettable images I had seen flying into JFK or La Guardia: the skyline of Manhattan, the great physical invention of the twentieth century.

I headed across the East River, past the Empire State Building, and, instinctively, downtown. The two towers beckoned. As I headed toward the World Trade Center towers—how good could Microsoft make them look?—I wanted to perform my own version of Philip Petit's famous tightrope walk between the towers in 1974. I suddenly thought: maybe I can fly in between the towers.[1] And if

Screenshot from Microsoft Flight Simulator, 1990 edition

I failed—well, failure might be even more thrilling. I had a hard time controlling my horizontal roll (those pesky arrow keys were poor substitutes for the joystick I never got around to buying), and suddenly, bang, I had crashed into the south tower.

The motorboat sound of my Microsoft Cessna stopped, and the plane exploded into a hundred pieces. The Trade Center towers stood unscathed, as if they were indestructible steel boxes. With graphics I thought remarkable, the pieces of airplane drifted gently to the ground, past the floors of the Trade Center tower, and landed in a heap in the plaza. And then came the greatest trick of all: in a split second the plane threw itself together and was whole again, ready for the next flight. No disaster, no scar.

Why was it so natural to want to fly into the World Trade Center? Why cause havoc, death, and destruction in this awe-inspiring city? Is it simply a late-twentieth-century American lust for "disaster porn"? An instinctual desire to go where the spectacle of destruction would be most exciting to watch? What draws someone to want to destroy New York? Why imagine the city's end?

The view of the World Trade Center from the cockpit in Microsoft's Flight Simulator software, 2004 version, and as modified by Aerosoft Manhattan scenery to include the World Trade Center towers, which had been removed from the versions of the program issued in the years after 9/11

Two contradictory phrases were spoken over and over again on September 11, 2001, and during the weeks and months following. On the one hand: "It was unimaginable." On the other: "It was just like a movie." The sight of the twin towers falling was, in fact, both: utterly incomprehensible and, at the same time, wholly recognizable. If the first phrase reflected our daily experience living in relative safety in the world's one remaining superpower, the second emanated from our well-trained popular-culture imaginations, shaped by what we see when we turn on the television, go to a movie, or play a video game. By the millions, we have read these books, watched these movies, played these games, and found an electric thrill in watching the skyscrapers of Manhattan topple. Despite repeated observation that the events of September 11 were unimaginable, our culture has been imagining and even rehearsing these events for decades.[2]

America's writers and imagemakers have pictured New York's annihilation in a stunning range of ways. Earthquake, fire, flood. Meteor, comet, Martian. Glacier, ghosts, atom bomb. Class war, terrorism, invasion. Laser beams from space ships, torpedoes from Zeppelins, missiles from battleships. Apes, wolves, dinosaurs. Environmental degradation, nuclear fallout, "green death." American culture has been obsessed with fantasizing about the destruction of New York. It is fascinating to explore the most common methods American culture makers have invented for the city's end—floods and fires, bombs and ice. Why has the watery death had such staying power, along with the image of the city left physically intact but stripped of its people by a mysterious disaster? The recurrence of similar modes of death across time stands out.

But what is ultimately more interesting, and what leads to the chronological organization of this book, is the social and cultural meaning of these images in the context of New York's historical development. At each stage of New York's advance over the past two centuries, visions of how the city would be demolished, blown up, swallowed by the sea, or toppled by monsters have proliferated in painting, graphic arts, cartoons, literature, photography, postcards, films, and computer software. These visions have been not only the purview of elite artists and novelists but a common narrative, inscribed in all popular forms of communication and culture.

Visions of New York's destruction resonated with some of the most long-standing themes in American history: the ambivalence toward cities, the troubled reaction to immigrants and racial diversity, the fear of technology's impact, and the apocalyptic strain in American religious life. Furthermore, these visions of the city's end have paralleled the city's economic, political, racial, and physical transformations. Projections of the city's end reflected and refracted the domi-

Meteorite!

Is bombardment from outer space pure science fiction? Not at all, according to scientists. The Earth is scarred by hundreds of impact sites. These include a crater carved by the meteorite probably responsible for the extinction of the dinosaurs 65 million years ago, and the vast area of Siberia obliterated by an exploding fireball as recently as 1908. No single death has been officially attributed to a space object—so far. How long will our luck hold?

Big hole
The Meteor Crater in Arizona provides unmistakable evidence that a huge object crashed into the Earth 50,000 years ago. To create such a pit, almost a mile wide and 575 feet deep, the meteorite must have been 130 feet wide, weighing 300,000 tons, and traveling at more than 30,000 mph.

Crash course

Asteroids, small planets orbiting the Sun, range from 600-mile-wide giants to tiny rock and iron fragments. When these objects hit Earth, we call them meteorites. The Earth collides harmlessly with small debris every day, nearly all of which is burned up in the atmosphere, but if a large object struck, it could lead to worldwide devastation. Scientists estimate the chances of impact with such a meteorite at once every million years. Even so, they now constantly monitor space, because it could come at any time. It is only a slight comfort that an incoming object could possibly be intercepted by nuclear weapons to keep it from colliding with Earth.

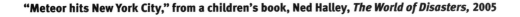

"Meteor hits New York City," from a children's book, Ned Halley, *The World of Disasters,* 2005

"Let's face it—the city's in our blood."

Danny Shanahan, cartoon representation of Godzilla and King Kong in Manhattan.

nant social issues. Each era in New York's modern history has produced its own apocalyptic imagery that explores, exploits, and seeks to resolve contemporary cultural tensions and fears.

In Joaquin Miller's 1886 novel *Destruction of Gotham,* a great fire engulfs the city as lower-class mobs attack the homes and stores of the wealthy. Only when Manhattan has "burned and burned and burned to the very bed-rock" is the apocalypse complete.[3] In Jacob Riis's *How the Other Half Lives,* a photographic chronicle of the slums of the Lower East Side, the journalist encapsulated the fears of many Americans in 1890 with his metaphors of the waves of radical immigrants flooding onto the beaches of Brooklyn.[4]

At the Dreamland amusement park on Coney Island, the immigrants' recreational paradise, a tenement stage set was ignited at regular intervals, giving those same immigrants a chance to safely witness the destruction of the tenuous world they inhabited on the Lower East Side.

In paintings by the futuristic artist Chesley Bonestell from the cold war

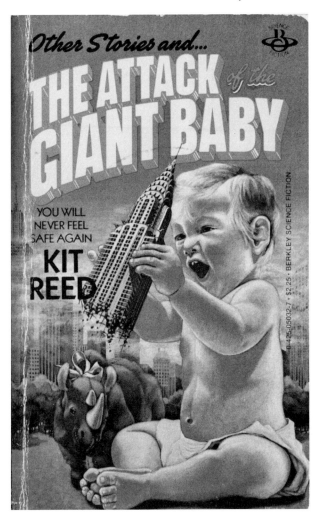

Jill Bauman, cover art for Kit Reed, *Other Stories and The Attack of the Giant Baby*, 1981

1950s, in popular magazines such as *Fortune* and *Collier's,* Manhattan is repeatedly devastated by atomic bombs. In the SimCity software of the 1990s, users could pick which disaster would strike New York, or just watch previous disasters play out before their eyes. And in movie after movie, Hollywood has found inspiration in destroying New York: through earthquake (*Deluge*), tsunami (*Deep Impact*), asteroid (*When Worlds Collide* and *Armageddon*), and monster (*King Kong* and the 1998 remake of *Godzilla*).

It seems that every generation has had its own reasons for destroying New York.

In this book I explore why American culture has so readily and so creatively narrated the city's end, long before 9/11 and after. Artists and writers of every era—each with their own world of cultural and social concerns—re-

Nicole Schulman, *No RNC,* poster protesting the Republican National Convention, August 2004

turned to New York, to destroy it, to entertain their audiences, and to define their stances on the social concerns of the day. New York's death is a story line that plays through every type of fiction American culture has produced. As varied as the media are, the narratives play in two consistent if harmonically different keys. One is the dark, minor key of alarm and warning, lessons and political arguments, fear and premonition of real disaster. The other is the key of celebration and entertainment, homage and love for the city. These two registers mark the two ends of the American ideological composition: a persistent embrace of progress and modernism, utopia and ascent, but also a suspicion of failure, and the harsh truth of the jeremiad. American identity has been built on a "culture of calamity."[5] That culture has been built on imagining our greatest city's end.[6]

There is an evolutionary reason why we enjoy the thrill of fear: the rush of adrenaline is followed, when the threat is gone, by a feeling that is not only relief but something very close to joy. The disaster movie, the bungee jump, the haunted house, the fires raging hourly at Coney Island, the panoramic view of a frozen New York in *The Day After Tomorrow*—we pay for all of these to give us that rush of fear, panic, and expansive relief.

But there is something more, beyond the desire of advanced society to recapture what was once a regular experience of heightened fear and response. Susan Sontag wrote in her 1966 essay "The Imagination of Disaster" that "we live under continual threat of two equally fearful, but seemingly opposed, destinies: unremitting banality and inconceivable terror."[7] Sontag was writing in the 1960s, under the fear of worldwide nuclear holocaust and William Whyte's nightmare of the deadened "organization man." The fears today are somewhat different. Rightly or wrongly, we don't fear nuclear world war the way we once did. But we have our fears of dramatic catastrophe—terrorism, West Nile virus, avian flu, global warming and the angry natural phenomena it is producing. And though we don't worry about the banality of everyday life, we do fear the insecurity of work, and the powerful, invisible forces of globalization. The workings of the global economy—moving capital and jobs dramatically around the globe according to decisions made on the Internet and in corporate headquarters—feel as inevitable and unstoppable as bad weather.

We destroy New York on film and paper to bound (in the frame of the screen or between book covers) the fear of natural and man-made disaster. And we destroy New York on film and paper to escape the sense of inevitable and incomprehensible economic transformations, by telling stories of clear and present dangers, with causes and effects, villains and heroes, to make our world more comprehensible than it has become. "Only a catastrophe gets our attention," says a character in Don DeLillo's *White Noise*. "We want them, we need them, we depend on them." The "incessant bombardment of information"—the "white noise" of our advertised, televised, noisy environment—calls out for a bracing disaster now and then.[8]

A disaster, even when mediated through images or words, still retains an authenticity that has been the quest of modern society for two centuries. Lurking behind Walter Benjamin's reflections about the discomforting loss of authenticity inherent in the rise of the "age of mechanical reproduction" is a worry about the loss of authentic experience, the surge of emotion and reaction that comes from confrontation with a unique work of art. The American historian Jackson Lears wrote about the nervous American aristocrats at the end of the nineteenth century. Troubled by the homogenization and regularization of

the industrial world that was leaving them behind, the elite rushed to sports, to the "wild" nature of the West, to the arts-and-crafts movement, and to foreign wars in order to rediscover—or invent—a vigorous, "strenuous life" amid the banality of industrially produced products and the paper pushing of the new workplace. As Slavoj Žižek has cogently argued, the fears not just of individuals but of societies are invested in the picturing of particular disasters.[9]

Even as commentators argued that the sight of New York's destruction would be insulting and even psychologically harmful, the images of September 11 continued to play in those same newspapers and television newscasts. The enjoyment Americans took in the dramatic, awesome sight of the twin towers collapsing was the guilty secret behind the self-righteous posturing about the need to be shielded from violent imagery. William Langewiesche, who narrated the story of the nine-month cleanup operation at Ground Zero in *American Ground: Unbuilding the World Trade Center,* noted that "the truth is that people relished this experience. It's obvious that they would never have wished this calamity on themselves or others, but inside the perimeter lines and beyond the public's

Two drawings of planes bombing Manhattan by an Italian teenager living under Mussolini in the mid-1930s

view it served for many of them as an unexpected liberation—a national tragedy of course, but one that was contained, unambiguous, and surprisingly energizing." This was the quiet, disturbing truth that lay behind the simple comment "It was like a movie!" People's hearts beat faster; they felt the rush of history, which on a daily basis seems to happen to someone else far away; they felt the thrill of witnessing something spectacular, extraordinary. They witnessed something they understood as beautiful and terrible.[10]

How utterly alive Americans felt as 9/11 unfolded. Powerful emotions everywhere—fear for the country, worry for our children, gut-level pain imagining the people in the towers. But equally important to that sense of "aliveness" was the instant recognition that we were living through a significant moment of history. I found myself on 9/11 shifting instantly from a terrified present tense to the future perfect—seeing myself in later years looking back to this moment. That might be why I picked up my new digital camcorder and filmed the television set as the towers burned.[11]

My goal here is to understand how the narratives of disaster—the stories Americans have told themselves—have helped resolve society's fears, and why New York has so often been called on to do the job. Popular images of New York have vacillated between looking at the "sunshine"—the gleaming wealth and culture of the city—and the "shadows"—the crime, the poverty, the moral traps of the city. New York's dual claim to being the American utopia and the American dystopia is the foundation of its continuing power in American culture. But it is one thing to imagine and portray the living city's crime and violence, its gangs, its isolated disasters; it is very different to imagine the city's utter devastation. The stories of New York's "regular" disasters are built on the notion that New York is forever a stage set or container for human drama.

What compels this book, instead, is the total disaster that means the end of New York. That does not necessarily mean that there is nothing left of the city, although some films and novels picture that. Often, the imagination of the city's end is suggested with the ruins of the most compelling landmarks. But the key is that the physical and social order is shattered beyond recognition. The invincible skyscrapers are destroyed; a lone survivor walks down a deserted Fifth Avenue; stragglers inhabit subway tunnels like caves; the Statue of Liberty is submerged, toppled, sunken, sawed off, with no community to repair or even mourn it.

There may be a rebirth awaiting in the near future—in many examples the people return and the city begins to rebuild; or the story ends with the sug-

Roaming a devastated and empty London in *28 Days Later*, 2002

gestion that the city resilient will rise again. But more often a new world—if there is one—is rebuilt elsewhere. New York—perhaps the world's most significant city—is no more. The people scatter to create new utopias, in Africa (in Ignatius Donnelly's *Caesar's Column*), Chicago (in Richard Foster's atomic bomb fantasy *The Rest Must Die*), on a Dutch estate across the Hudson (in Upton Sinclair's *Millennium*).

I focus on narratives told in traditionally fictional forms—the novel, the film, the painting. The division between "fiction" and "nonfiction" is, of course, hopelessly blurry. Many supposedly nonfictional accounts—a general who argues for more military spending in preparation for World War I, a government report on the effect of a nuclear attack, an anti–nuclear proliferation manifesto seeking to raise awareness of the threat of nuclear fallout—have employed elaborate narratives to make their cases. From the Sunday "funny pages" to the secretary of defense, everyone has been busy imagining New York's end.

The heart of this book is an argument that each era has found it useful to destroy New York in its own particular way, and for its own particular political, social, and cultural reasons. But why New York? And why New York so consistently for the past two centuries? Every great city breeds fantasies of its end, from those who love it as much as from those who hate it. London, the world capital of the nineteenth century, had more than its share of visions of its destruction, most imagining a return to nature for the center of the Western world. Tokyo, a victim of devastation in World War II, found itself repeatedly destroyed in the Godzilla films of the 1950s and onward. In the United States, Chicago's identity—reinforced with countless novels and films—is bound up with its great fire of 1871. Washington, D.C., the seat of power with landmarks as significant as New York's, has found itself attacked with great vigor in all the arts. In the second half of the twentieth century, as the center of popular culture and the weight of population moved westward, Los Angeles became inspiration for numerous visions of apocalyptic urban endings.[12]

But all of these remain "second cities" to New York, at least in their power to move artists and writers to imagine urban disaster. New York, as the preeminent city of the United States for more than a century, has retained its hold on the imagination of the culture. Despite its economic travails in the 1970s, and despite the rise of Los Angeles, New York remains the city to beat. To destroy New York is to strike symbolically at the heart of the United States. No city has been more often destroyed on paper, film, or canvas, and no city's destruction has been more often watched and read about than New York's. The historian and philosopher Oswald Spengler wrote that "the rise of New York" was "the most pregnant event of the 19th century." When Spengler wrote those lines, in the 1920s, New York was at its peak and, therefore, in his mind, at the end of its time. The "monstrous symbol" of the modern world, New York in the twentieth century was "the stone colossus that stands at the end of the life-course of every great culture."[13] But the Great Depression, which followed Spengler's prediction by just a few years and which seemed to have the potential to bring the city down, produced two of the city's greatest landmarks—Rockefeller Center and the Empire State Building, which were completed just after the stock market crash. Despite the long, slow economic decline of the city through the 1970s and the growth of many other world capitals, as well as American metropolises, New York still reigns supreme in our popular culture. It is hardly an accident that the attacks on the nation's capital (one effective and one foiled) on September 11 quickly sank from consciousness. As the French theorist Paul Virilio put it simply: "The destruction wrought on the Pentagon was of little consequence; what exploded in people's minds was the World Trade Center, leaving America out for the count."[14]

Cultural forms express and reproduce social experience. It is not shocking, then, that a leitmotif of American popular culture of the past two hundred years has been the imagination of New York's destruction. The United States is a deeply religious nation; students of American history need constantly to be reminded that the United States remains the most religious of Western industrialized nations. It has exhibited a strong apocalyptic strain that has not been hard to translate into popular culture.[15]

These visions of the city's destruction also stem in part from the cycles of destruction and rebuilding that have defined New York for residents, visitors, and observers from afar. A series of natural disasters, as well as what I have called the city's relentless creative destruction, have led Americans to believe that, despite the dominance of their greatest city in the nineteenth and twentieth centuries, New York was fragile.[16] The connection over time between the daily destruction that defined New York life and the fantastical imagining of the city's demise is complicated. It would be a far stretch to suggest that New Yorkers—and especially the thousands of writers, artists, and other culture producers who were born or lived in New York—were somehow inspired to dream up the city's terrible destruction because of a numbness caused by the city's relentless cycles of destruction and rebuilding. (A parallel and detestable notion—that the terrorist attacks had been brought on by the moral debasement of American life, centered in New York—was suggested in the days after September 11.)[17] But it is fair to say that New York's repeated destruction in popular culture mirrors its regular, physical destruction, and the two are mutually supportive. New York's destruction—whether it happens by the swing of the wrecking ball or by the purple flash of a Martian laser beam—is an inspiration, a reinvigoration of the city's image and its identity.

Each era has its own particular answer to the question "Why New York?" But there are also persistent reasons for New York's magnetic lure for the destruction fantasies over nearly two centuries.

Beyond New York's preeminence lies New York's physical form and the aesthetics of destruction. We have seen, especially in recent years, a genre of film and television appropriately called "disaster porn"—a salacious obsession with graphically portraying death, mayhem, and destruction, whether at the hands (or jaws, or weapons) of alligators, "extreme cops," or alien spaceships. On a recent train ride I saw a poster advertising the Weather Channel's program *Storm Stories,* which noted that this was "Tornado Week" and displayed the tagline "Every Survivor Has a Story." The very existence of the Weather Channel—charting every storm across the country and the globe, is a symptom of this age of anxiety.

No place looks better destroyed than New York. Godzilla pounding through Phoenix instead of the canyons of Manhattan would not have the same visual impact. Some of those who watched the disaster of 9/11 on television from afar found the sight of the World Trade Centers falling horrifying, and, if they would admit it, also frighteningly beautiful. We have continued to destroy New York in books, and on canvas, and on movie screens and computer monitors for many reasons. But we should not ignore the psychological and the sociological, the more abstract benefits this society has gained from watching New York destroyed repeatedly. New York remains a place apart, to many an island thankfully on the edge of the continent. To Americans beyond the city's boundaries, New York City is a touchstone, the symbol of the best and worst of everything, the barometer of the nation's health and sickness, poverty and wealth. Americans are married to New York, not always happily but always intensely and profoundly. New York is a target, of love letters and hate mail, sermonizing and spectacle.

The balance between love and hate has swung wildly in the works of artists and writers of different political and class stripes. But love and hate are two sides of the same coin. American culture has destroyed New York because it is so unimaginable for Americans not to have this city. It is a healthy playing-out of our fears onto the screen. As E. B. White wrote, "New York is to the nation what the white church spire is to the village—the visible symbol of aspiration and faith, the white plume saying the way is up!"[18] The white plume we saw on Tuesday, September 11, 2001, was the billowing debris of two massive towers falling down, taking with them thousands of lives. This was a conscious choice of the perpetrators—to make our fantasies and our nightmares horrible reality, to turn gleaming symbols of the city into burning sites of terror.

September 11 is not the endpoint of this book, or of the imagination of New York's end. The memory of September 11 may have shifted the tone and content of portrayals of New York's destruction. But the ongoing—perhaps unending—war on terrorism, and New York's continued importance in American life, at the very least ensure that our culture will continue to spin stories of New York's end.

We can go back to the very beginning of New York's history to find fantasies of the city's end. For much of the city's early history, its survival was not assured. European New Yorkers (and New Amsterdamians before them) feared Native

Americans' attacks from beyond its wall and uprisings from within by the slaves who made up a fifth of the population in the early eighteenth century. The city was traded back and forth between the warring British and Dutch over the course of the seventeenth century and suffered fire and invasion during the war between the colonies and their crown. New York, built on rock, was a frail edifice.

But fears of the city's end became national fears (or wishes) only in the nineteenth century. In this book I focus on the century and a half after the Civil War, when New York became the vast industrial and cultural metropolis we know. We begin, though, with two fantasies from the beginning of the nineteenth century, when New York was on the ascent, about to become the preeminent American city, and when the hints of future reasons for destroying New York were formulated.

Motivated by the "desire to promote the cause of Christianity," Nicodemus Havens, a workingman of the rapidly growing city of New York, recounted a premonition he had experienced one night in which a considerable portion of New York City was destroyed in divine fury by a powerful storm and earthquake on June 4, 1812. Having settled down to rest with his parents after a trying day at work, he was aroused by a "dreadful crash." Violent thunder, lightning, and the "trembling of the earth" surrounded Havens; he was carried away "with the most surprising velocity." The world as he knew it was turned upside down, and he saw the full scope of the coming catastrophe. Thousands hurried to find shelter but were unable to escape the "devouring tide." Unleashed by God's wrath, the earth's upheaval annihilated everything in its path. It seemed much more than a simple shifting of the earth's plates, more like a plague, with its "death-like touch" imparting a "contaminating influence." Both "the most stately edifices" and poor men's cottages were leveled as the earthquake demolished most of lower Manhattan and its inhabitants.

The new City Hall, opened the year earlier; Tammany Hall, the political headquarters of what would be the dominant political organization of the nineteenth century; the City Hotel; and the Park and Bridewell Theatres—all were left in ruins as streets were "swept from existence." The power of the natural disaster outstripped the weak creations of mankind: "Fabrics which had stood the test of ages, were no longer to be seen; all had been engulfed in the dreadful ruin." No "penetrating eye [could] discover the slightest vestige of the habitations of our many distinguished magistrates; they were completely invisible, not a stone was left to shew the stranger where they stood, nor an inhabitant to tell the mournful tale. Whole families were enclosed within its horrid grasp, and whole streets in this flourishing city, swallowed together." "So electric was the shock" that people were literally thrown from their homes in an instant. One man, "while in the act of shaving off his beard, was transported, house and all, from the lower end of Lombardy, into State Street."[19]

The veins of destructive force reached up through the streets of the city, which still clustered at the very bottom of Manhattan Island—from William Street and Maiden Lane to Liberty Street and Greenwich Street (on the site of the future World Trade Center) to Cortlandt and Vesey, and finally leaping over to Blackwell's Island and then to Brooklyn, where the earthquake "engulfed" some 1,675 ferry boats. New York was the epicenter of the disaster, but it was worldwide. In London everyone was killed almost instantly, "except six . . . men of the most remarkable piety, disseminating religion throughout the world." Paris, "which boasted the largest population in the world," was reduced to just eighteen thousand houses. Jamaica and Santo Domingo, Trinidad and St. Bartholomew—all were "partially separated from the earth." The effects of this dreadful occurrence, Havens recounts, "were felt in like manner throughout the world."[20]

Finally, after exactly five hours and twenty-three minutes, the "convulsion" subsided. The toll of this vision was precise: New York lost 1,408 houses and 125,000 people.

But horror often takes as its company physical and spiritual resilience. "After so awful a warning," Havens gladly recounted, the people became "more devout and pious in their religious avocations." They took immediate measures to no longer permit "political dissention . . . to influence the councils of the country," completely abolish military establishments, and erect "no less than nineteen thousand additional places of public worship in the short space of three weeks." That is the "wonderful" in the "Wonderful Vision of Nicodemus Havens, of the City of New York, Cordwainer, Wherein he was presented with a view of the situation of the world, after the dreadful fourth of June 1812 and shewing what part of New York is to be destroyed."[21]

Historians traditionally mark 1825 as the moment when New York became the preeminent American city. Or even more specifically: November 4, 1825, the day Governor DeWitt Clinton performed the simple act of pouring water from Lake Erie into the Atlantic Ocean at Sandy Hook, marking the official completion of the 363-mile Erie Canal. By linking the Atlantic Ocean to the Great Lakes, the canal made New York the dominant port for shipping into the inland

Thomas Cole, *The Course of Empire: Destruction* (fourth in a series), 1836; oil on canvas, 39 1/4 × 63 1/2 inches; negative no. 6048c; accession no. 1854.4. Collection of the New-York Historical Society

states. Once the canal opened, New Yorkers set to work. They traded and created, bought and sold with new abandon. What competition remained between Boston and Philadelphia and Charleston for economic and cultural preeminence disappeared. From that moment on, the "first city" of the country was clear.

The anticipation of the Erie Canal was all the greater because of the tragedies the city had been through in previous years. The city was hit with one of the worst yellow fever epidemics in 1822, reminding New Yorkers that their city and its people were eminently destructible. It followed the Panic of 1819, and the fresh memory of severe hardship during the War of 1812 and the embargo of trade with Great Britain. The city approached the opening of the Erie Canal with great hope—here was a public project that no one thought possible, which could yield decades of prosperity. There was also great skepticism. Each boom of the city had been matched with a bust. War, disease, and economic turbulence were the diet of this nascent metropolis at the beginning of the nineteenth century.

It may not be surprising, then, that as the canal, the most impressive public works project of its day, neared completion, other fantastical public projects would gather the imaginations of New Yorkers.

Sometime around 1824, most likely in legend, a butcher struck up a conversation with some of his colleagues in the neighborhood of Mulberry and Spring Streets, a bit north of the Centre Market, located on Grand Street between Orange and Centre. "Uncle John" De Voe and a colleague known only as Lozier began to talk about the impending disaster that was to strike New York at any time. It was clear, they said, that the "island is getting too heavy on the Battery end, where it is altogether too much built upon." It would, sooner or later, fall into the sea. Something would have to be done.

The hoodwinking of hundreds of workers on the Lower East Side became, in the words of the first chronicler of this legend, John De Voe—a relative of "Uncle John"—"one of the most perfect 'hoaxes' ever introduced to the public."[22]

Lozier, who quickly became the mastermind behind the scheme, spun out an elaborate and insane plan to saw the island in half at Kingsbridge and spin the lower half 180 degrees, so that the sinking part would now be attached to the middle of the island, thereby securing the great metropolis. The project required, of course, an enormous amount of manual—and gullible—labor. Recruited to the cause of saving the city and lining their own empty pockets, hundreds of workers—the word spread from the meat markets across the Lower East Side—invested in Lozier in the expectation of being paid back fivefold when the massive project took off.

Needless to say, as the historian Eric Robb Ellis noted a century later in reference to this urban legend, "Manhattan remained intact," as did the poverty of the workers. Only their skins were tougher.[23]

So many of the themes of the New York disaster genre can be seen in these two stories. In Havens's tale a natural disaster is a heaven-sent judgment on this, the greatest and most debased of cities. New York is the epicenter of a worldwide disaster, the necessary place that will illustrate a larger apocalypse. The key landmarks of the city are destroyed in succession, as if on an itemized list. And finally, there is a ray of hope suggesting that disaster is a necessary precondition for the city's renewal, spiritual and economic.

Economic motive is not far beyond the religious mission. After the tale, an advertisement notes that the pamphlet is "Sold at the Corner of Theatre Alley, Price 33 Cents per dozen . . . 6 single." And on the very page, the universal mark of commerce: "Copy Right Secured." Here was religious warning for sale, and for profit. And here was New York's dual mission combined in the dreams of a cordwainer, or shoemaker: cradle for visionaries, cranks, and creative people of all types, and the capital of capitalism, where those visionaries could make a buck.[24] The legend of Uncle John and his island surgery scam speaks to a booming, entrepreneurial city of enormous wealth and enormous poverty, a city of the gullible and the crafty. And a city that would find enormous attraction and profit in telling and selling the tale of its own end.

two

"Horrors Were Their Delight"

Terrifying and Thrilling Wars at Home and Invasions from Abroad

JOSÉ MARTÍ, THE CUBAN REVOLUTIONARY WHO LIVED IN NEW York at the end of the nineteenth century, took a pause from his writings about the failures of the United States and the need for revolutionary upheaval in Cuba to speak admiringly of New York City's resilience in the wake of the crippling blizzard of 1888. New York, he wrote, "like the victim of an outrage, goes about freeing itself of its shroud." The democracy of snowfall, covering Fifth Avenue as heavily as it did Mulberry Bend on the Lower East Side, had brought out a "sense of great humility and a sudden rush of kindness, as though the dread hand had touched the shoulders of all men."[1] Martí's written account was accompanied by thousands upon thousands of photographs taken by members of the nascent profession of photojournalism to document a defining natural calamity in the city's history. That blizzard, which stopped the movement of people and goods for days, suggested that New York's "restless renewals," as Henry James caustically defined the city's destructive essence, could still be stemmed and that New York, the great metropolis of the world, could ease its way into the twentieth century with something approaching calm.

The upheavals of the coming decades proved that dream wrong. Even as the city seemed to be beginning its march upward into the sky and outward to the world's markets, the city's end was imagined in ever more popular and dramatic ways. Three themes anchored the fiction of the city's destruction in this period. First was the metropolis as a spectacular victim of its own size and the rapidity of its growth. Second was the way internal corruptions destroyed New

York. Third was New York threatened from abroad. Altogether, the outpouring of disaster scenarios created a nervous foundation for a city reaching skyward.

In the post–Civil War decades, New York went through as great a transformation of its physical organization as at any time in its history. The rise of New York as the financial capital of a continent-wide—and increasingly worldwide—economic system brought tremendous increase in the wealth, and the poverty, of the city. As David Scobey has written, New York created an "uptown utopia" for its new bourgeoisie: Central Park and Riverside Park in Manhattan, Prospect Park in Brooklyn, the Metropolitan Museum of Art, boulevards, and, finally and most important, the Brooklyn Bridge. But the solidity and apparent unity of these built projects merely hid an increasingly divided metropolis and nation. The vision of a republic of artisans and farmers (an equality made possible by slave labor at the base of the American economy) was now gone. The problem of slave labor had become the problem of free labor. The monster being created was a city with extremes of wealth and poverty, which seemed destined to result in social explosion.[2]

This new financial system, dominated by a relatively few individuals and banks and working almost entirely in the world of the stock market and its invisible transactions, seemed both inscrutable and unstable. It controlled cattle ranchers in Texas as well as sweatshops on the Lower East Side, but it also seemed utterly invented, a wisp of smoke in the offices of J. P. Morgan on Wall Street.

At the same time, New York became even more than before a city filled with immigrants. Increasingly inspired by radicalism from Europe, and increasingly willing to live by that radicalism, immigrants joined unions and political parties and marched—and at times rioted—in the streets.[3] In the eyes of the city's elites, the immigrants represented the corruption and revolutionary ideals of Europe brought to American shores. But their presence also raised the fear of a different kind of invasion. As Europe headed toward war, and Americans debated getting involved, the image of New York being destroyed by foreign invaders became central to the debate over preparedness and America's entry into the war.

The combination of these transformations brought about one of the most unsettling times for the great metropolis, even amid its greatest growth. During the late nineteenth and early twentieth centuries, New York became the largest city of the Western world. But it was also the era when the divisions within, and the fear of attack from abroad, seemed most to threaten the city. The explosion of

New York disaster scenarios, in print and on canvas, showed the city at its most productive and fearful.

Sinking Under Its Own Success: The Creative Destruction of Manhattan

The legend of Uncle John De Voe's 1824 scam of New York's laborers proved an inspiration to future imaginers of New York's end. But while the prank set upon gullible citizens of early-nineteenth-century New York was primarily about the "lures and snares" of the new metropolis, the new version that surfaced in 1909 was squarely about the destructive nature of the modern metropolis.

In Thomas J. Vivian and Grena J. Bennett's short story "The Tilting Island," a chasm opens at 125th Street along a previously unknown geologic fault line in the crust of the island. Water, gas, and electrical mains burst, fires rage throughout the city, rivers of water flood the streets, the tracks of the elevated trains are mangled into twisting wrecks, subway tunnels cave in, and masses of people from both ends of the island flee the disaster. The renowned Columbia University geologist Heinrich Herman, returning from a saloon late at night when the fault opens, sizes up the situation quickly. The fault line, whose existence he had suspected, could have been forced open only by human action: the massive concentration of skyscrapers at the bottom of the island.

> "Ah, they could not have believed it," Herman exclaims. "Like Babel we have built. Who thought that we little things could have made an island, a whole island tilt? But we have massed on its end those buildings—twenty stories of steel, thirty stories, forty stories—that is the hand of man on the edge of the plate. . . .
>
> "Look at that congregation of mighty skyscrapers that crowds the lower end of the island. That mountain range of masonry with its towering peaks of copper and its titanic ribs of steel; that mass of millions of tons that has been superimposed on the fragile extremity of the island; that gigantic, horrific mass has broken down one of the outpost foundations of Manhattan and the island is tilting to its destruction!"

Herman and Dalton, a young reporter eager to get the story into the latest edition, head downtown to a second fault line at Cortlandt Street, to see whether it too will give way. If it does, then only the financial sector of the island will be lost and the rest of the island will be spared. Down on lower Broadway, they see that the "prow of Manhattan was dropping as though it would bury itself in the Bay." As

Skyscrapers toppling in the 1909 story "Tilting Island" in *Everybody's Magazine*

Dalton and Herman watch, the "huge mass of skyscrapers with their cyclopean walls, their glistening summits and their deep canyons of shade, quiver and rock and slide and topple into the harbor!"[4]

The story, reaching an audience of some 150,000 in *Everybody's Magazine,* played on the flip side of the city's remarkable economic and physical boom in the second half of the nineteenth century.[5] The invincibility of the city's banks and manufacturing base, its enormous size, its magnificent stone and steel buildings—all of these only seemed to invite the question: when will it all collapse? Indeed, there was something fundamentally unnatural about the metropolis that suggested that nature would have its final revenge.

But it was also the very process by which the city grew that gave rise to these disaster scenarios. Fertilizing the soil of imagination has been the sense that, as the poet James Merrill wrote so many years later in the century, "as usual in New York, everything is torn down." When Henry James returned from Europe to his home city in 1904, he declared that New York is, always has been, a "provisional city," defined by a "dreadful chill of change."[6] Thirty years later, in 1935, a long-awaited visitor came from Europe to inspect Manhattan. Like James, the Swiss architect Le Corbusier came to see how well the most modern of cities measured up. In Manhattan he found a perfect soapbox for pontificating about his vision of the modern city, a "radiant city" of residential and office towers, submerged highways, and wide-open park space. Accompanied by reporters and architects, Le Corbusier toured New York, walked the narrow streets of lower Manhattan, and glided to the top of the Empire State Building.[7] Summarizing the essence of the island, he echoed James, declaring ephemerality to be the city's most defining feature. "New York," wrote Le Corbusier, "is nothing more than a provisional city. A city which will be replaced by another city."[8]

Though they used the same words, there was little similarity between these two men. For Henry James the "restless renewals" of Manhattan were a nightmare. The city's mad, money-hungry speculation had brought down his boyhood home and replaced it with a loft factory, and his genteel Fifth Avenue was filled with garish mansions of the nouveau riche. But what Henry James had put forward as an indictment, Le Corbusier now offered as high praise. New York was "a city in the process of becoming." He celebrated the city for being "overwhelming, amazing, exciting, violently alive—a wilderness of stupendous experiment toward the new order that is to replace the current tumult."[9]

Those two comments, thirty years apart, remind us of the central tension in New York life: the tension between celebrating and lamenting the city's propensity to destroy and rebuild constantly and its desire to hold onto parts of its past. The constant transformation of the physical landscape is mimicked in its social and cultural life. Conversely, the city's cultural vitality has been inspired by the city's physical resilience in the wake of New York's unique hurricane—the wrecking ball.

The economist Joseph Schumpeter captured the essential process of capitalism—the never-ending cycle of destroying and inventing new products and methods of production—in his phrase "creative destruction." "Capitalism," wrote Schumpeter in 1942, "is by nature a form or method of economic change and not only never is but never can be stationary. This process of Creative Destruction is the essential fact about capitalism. . . . To ignore this central fact is like *Hamlet* without the Danish prince."[10] Manhattan promoted and experienced the process of creative destruction as no other place did. As the densest and most populous city in the United States for more than a century, New York has been the ultimate "creatively destructive city," building and rebuilding itself repeatedly. Although the areas that became boroughs of Greater New York with consolidation in 1898 would be dramatically remade in ensuing years, on the island of Manhattan the process of city building was at its most vibrant. In the process of developing the city's land to accommodate the five million people who would flow into the city over the course of the first half of the century, laying sewers and subways, demolishing slums, replacing smaller buildings with taller ones, New Yorkers created and confronted a city dominated by a destructive logic.[11] At the end of the nineteenth century and in the early twentieth, Manhattan experienced its greatest eras of transformation. In a generation, developers largely wiped away the city of brownstones and church spires and replaced it with the modern, skyscraper metropolis we recognize today. "New York is never satisfied with itself," wrote the editors of *Architecture* in 1927. "Its new buildings are scarcely occupied before they are torn down to make way for better ones. The great steel frames of its structures will never disintegrate from rust—they are scrapped before rust can start."[12] One line, often attributed to O. Henry, may have captured New York's essence most succinctly: "It'll be a great place if they ever finish it."[13]

The list of what was built and destroyed in this era is stunning. Individual monuments of American architecture and engineering fell regularly, often only a few years after being built: the first two Madison Square Gardens, Temple Emanu-El, and the first Waldorf-Astoria, to name just a few. Mansions of the wealthiest and most powerful Americans came down like dominoes in the 1920s, replaced by apartment towers and museums. But as stunning as the disappearance of important landmarks was the removal of the anonymous buildings that made up the very fabric of the city. Rows of brownstones and acres of tenements were demolished to make way for widened thoroughfares, skyscrapers, bridges, and tunnels.

Equally important, this era was a time of unprecedented cultural interpretation of the convulsions of urbanization. Artists and writers, city leaders and intellectuals all confronted the problems and opportunities posed by a city undergoing "cycles of demolition and construction."[14] For many, New York was the creative city par excellence, a place where new political ideals, as much as new artistic forms and architectural designs, could be pioneered. Avant-garde writers and artists began to define New York's particular sense of place as a

Joseph Pennell, *Caissons on Vesey Street,* 1924. Etching on paper, sheet: 15 7/8 × 10 1/4 in.; 40.3 × 26 cm; image: 13 15/16 × 9 3/8 in.; 35.4 × 23.8 cm. Smith College Museum of Art, Northampton, Massachusetts. Gift of Mrs. H. Lawrence Holcomb (Alice Krigsman, class of 1972), SC 1976: 46-3

vertigo created by the dynamism of a bustling commercial center packed with an overwhelming diversity of peoples. The physical transformation of the city was glorious because it gave visual form to the consciousness of its inhabitants. "The physical and architectural upheaval of the city," the cultural historian Ann Douglas has written, "was a symbol of its inner spirit . . . its protean ability to assume new shapes and discard old ones; the city changes before your eyes."[15] John Dos Passos, Dorothy Parker, and others gloried in what might be called a landscape of amnesia, where the past would hold no authority and would offer no restrictions.

A central theme of paintings, photography, and literature of this era was to come to grips with this vibrant, frightening, and confusing creative destruction. George Bellows documented both the thrill of the steam shovels making way for the new Pennsylvania Station, completed in 1910, and the plaintive decay of the "long tenement" beneath a new bridge. Some of the earliest films of the Edison Company and others depicted life in Central Park and along the elite Fifth Avenue, as well as the demolition of the Star Theatre as it was dismantled to make way for something taller. Some of Alfred Stieglitz's most celebrated images—such as *Spring Shower* (1902) and *Old and New New York* (1910)—contrasted the old and the new, or, more precisely, the replacement of the old with the new.

"To old New Yorkers," wrote a *Vanity Fair* editorialist in 1925, "the real melancholy comes, not from the fact that the houses are soon to crumble into dust, but that the old and well ordered social fabric . . . has itself crumbled and vanished utterly from view."[16] Nostalgia and a longing for a past city—though largely invented—anchored their efforts to secure a sense of place. Gutzon Borglum, the sculptor of Mount Rushmore, noted that the "cruel thought" about New York "is the transient character of her life. . . . Her greatest buildings are ephemeral." "How," he asked, "can a people so transient develop municipal spirit?"[17] For many of these citybuilders and reformers, the destructive aspects of the city's social and cultural life were reflected and perpetuated, but also could be solved, in the creation of new physical forms and in the protection of older landscapes.

Even natural disasters—the fires and storms and floods that plagued New York and other cities from their start—could be transposed into a comment about the city's frightful growth. Three odd and humorous imaginings of New York's end in the *New York Times* at the end of the nineteenth century and the beginning of the twentieth allow us into the anxious minds of city people.[18]

In 1891 the *Times* reported on a "Lurid Prophecy: What a Colored Preacher Predicts Will Happen in New-York." "A preacher named Jones has created a whirlwind of excitement among the colored Baptists of the city," wrote the reporter, "by prophesying that a certain section of the New-York City is to be destroyed, with all its inhabitants, by 'fire and brimstone' from the nether regions."[19] Apparently after revealing this dire prediction, the preacher said that he had "shook the dust of New-York forever from his feet." The "colored people," it seems, had taken stock in Mr. Jones and his prophecy because he had "gained a reputation by foretelling incidents which have actually come to pass," including the Charleston earthquake and the Johnstown flood. "He has a great influence over New-York's colored Baptists, and it is reported that when he foretold its impending doom some of his followers fled from the city. . . . In Fordham he aroused such an intense state of excitement that several of the frightened believers fled, leaving their personal belongings behind."

A decade later, in 1902, a lecture announcement in the *New York Times* declared "Warning! New-York will be destroyed!" A "Warning Lecture" was to be given at the Metropolitan Lyceum organized around the question not of whether New York would be destroyed but of how: "Will it be by fire, earthquake, cyclone, or tidal wave?" Holding on to the older belief that disaster was God's wrath visited upon humans, the ad notes that "God has counted the saloons, theatres, brothels, gambling dens." "The cup of sin is almost full," the ad notes, quoting erroneously from Ecclesiastes (viii, 11). "God warned Babylon. God warned Sodom. Babylon paid no attention. Sodom gave no heed. Where is Babylon now? The Dead Sea covers its ashes. . . . God is warning New-York. Will you listen?" The name of the lecturer was not given, but the paper suggested sarcastically that he "seems to have a good opinion of himself." "If it is really God warning New York," the newspaper contended, "the lecturer will need to show good credentials as his chosen messenger. . . . Most experts do not regard the case of New York as yet hopeless. The new administration means to knock the bottom out of the cup of sin and prevent its getting any fuller, and so fire, earthquake, cyclone and tidal wave may be staved off until Tammany gets into power again."[20]

Not only religious leaders were sounding alarms—scientists were worried also. Similar skepticism greeted the predictions of Rudolf Falb, an astronomer who had determined the date of the end of the world: November 13, 1899. The *American Register* noted that a comet last seen in 1866 would reappear in 1899 and collide with the earth, causing a "great catastrophe." "Forewarned is forearmed," notes the reporter. "We shall have nearly six years in which to settle our sublunary affairs."[21]

A year later, in 1903, the *New York Times* reported on a private letter sent to the paper from Mexico City detailing how a recent rumor about the destruction of New York got started. News of a "terrible earthquake and cyclone in New York" that destroyed half of the city and killed one million people spread quickly in Mexico City during the month of April. The author of this "private letter" telegraphed New York to confirm this news, and received word that there was "not a word of truth in it. . . . It seems that two Spaniards who live [in Mexico City] and who had been on a visit to Europe returned to New York that day. They are known among their friends [there] as 'Earthquake' and 'Cyclone' and are besides great eaters. One of their friends in New York telegraphed to a friend [in Mexico City]: 'Earthquake and Cyclone arrived; have swallowed up half New York.'"[22]

On May 30, 1907, the *New York Times* reported that Horace Johnson of Middle Haddam, Connecticut, "known throughout New England as an accurate weather prophet," had predicted that all of Manhattan would be destroyed by a great earthquake "sometime in August."[23] The earthquake, Johnson predicted, would sink half of the island into the East River and the other into the North River. Thousands would die and, not inconsequentially, the property damage would be "incalculable." The article gives Mr. Johnson credit for predicting the great blizzard of 1888, as well as the recent earthquakes in San Francisco and Puerto Rico. He'd known about it for many years, but waited to announce the upcoming disaster—just three months away—"until he has made absolutely certain that it will take place."

Responses were immediate, no doubt because of the recent San Francisco earthquake. Anna Olcott Connelin responded the next day—from the safety of Brooklyn—urging that the *Times* "investigate further so that people may consider the possibility of escape from so horrible a catastrophe." If in fact Mr. Johnson has no credibility and there is no further evidence then "is it not cruel to disseminate such black forebodings by the words of an alarmist"? Another letter writer—"Constant Reader"—wondered about the believability of Mr. Johnson's prediction about the "total destruction of New York City next August by a terrible earthquake which would pitch half the town into the East River and the other half into the Hudson. . . ." Given that the prophet, "Old Horace," had also predicted the blizzard of 1888 and the San Francisco earthquake, the "Constant Reader" wanted to know if the *Times* had been able to ascertain if there was any truth to his recent prediction.[24]

A few days later, another Brooklyn resident (who noted that several of the nervous letter writers were from Brooklyn and thus out of immediate danger, and that apparently "New Yorkers themselves do not seem to care"), insisted that it wouldn't make any difference. Even if this prediction could be proved to everyone's satisfaction, New Yorkers "would stick to their doomed little old New York and go down with it." Furthermore, human nature—or American nature—being what it is, there would undoubtedly be others who "discover another big stone in the ocean on which it would not be possible to raise food enough for a mouse" and busy themselves about building tunnels and bridges, operating ferries to get there (and "cheat each other in thousands and one different ways"). They would choose, "generation after generation . . . to live on that stone" and "suck the richness of the country soil, with the help of expensive railroads and other transportation systems." "Old Horace's telling to the New Yorkers that their vanity bubble will burst in August will not do more good than the preaching of

Jonah to the Ninevites." This was signed by "The Spirit of Truth." The editors, in an apparent nudge at the negativity of the letter writer, titled his letter "Cannot Crush the New York Spirit."[25]

The stories and their reactions are fascinating. First, the 1891 prediction is striking because it reveals the power of these New York disaster scenarios to be believable to large numbers of people. Immediately, we think of Orson Welles—discussed in chapter 3—and the hysteria caused by a fictional account of New York's and world's end. But the newspaper mocks the preacher, and the gullible parishioners, for holding on to older notions of God's wrath as it is predicted would be visited on New Yorkers. Similarly the 1902 notice of a doomsday lecture at the Lyceum Theater is mocked by the paper as an example of an ancient, anti-modern, and superstitious kind of prediction of the world's end.

The responses to the predictions in 1907 of an earthquake reveal other popular notions. Two of the letter writers accept that such a disaster is completely possible, even inevitable at some point, but wonder about the truth to this particular claim. The next sounds like the Woody Allen figure of his day: he is sure disaster is coming but feels it simply won't make a difference. That is, it won't change anything about New Yorkers or about people. Cities are a product of a corrupt human race and they will, resiliently, rebuild on some other "big stone." New York—the society it represents, if not the actual buildings or even the island itself—is here to stay.

What is striking is the humor—perhaps the nervous humor—of these articles. The threat from angry mobs of oppressed immigrant revolutionaries. The fear of a German siege of the city. These—discussed below—were the serious fears of observers of the American scene wrestling with the modern metropolis. But threaded through the era—in newspaper accounts, in short stories—are these ironic twists on the modern jeremiads. By 1900, the city seemed so powerful, so indestructible. And yet, it also seemed to be utterly fragile—the buildings as well as the social structure which they housed. That tension produced the nervous, chuckling harmonics of popular culture.

But citizens did not need "lurid prophecies" or predictions of earthquakes to know that, from within and without, threats loomed.

Enemies Within

A vivid image by Thomas Nast was published on September 24, 1869, in the aftermath of the latest stock market crash that punctuated New York's history throughout the nineteenth century. It depicts a devastated Wall Street. All the buildings on either side of the street are in ruins. Only Trinity Church, financially secure in its vast landholdings on the west side of Manhattan, is intact. The street is block-aded with dead bulls, and a sign that reads "This Street is Closed for Repairs."

The symbolism of New York's destruction was already endlessly mal-leable. Nicodemus Havens feared God's wrath, expressed in the form of a "con-tamination." No such fear with Thomas Nast. The destruction was wholly human-made. The collapse of 1869 was due to the manipulation of the gold market by Jay Gould and Jim Fisk for their own profit. The resulting collapse was invisible; it was made visible and understandable through Nast's images.

Born in Landau, Germany, in 1840, Thomas Nast moved to New York City as a boy. At fifteen he became an illustrator for *Frank Leslie's Illustrated Newspaper,* and then, in 1861, joined *Harper's Weekly* (where he stayed until 1886) and gained a national reputation. During the period when he was the most visually effective critic of the Tweed Ring (between 1864 and 1873) he lived in Harlem, eventually buying a house near Fifth Avenue and 125th Street. Nast was a staunch Republican, and thus a supporter of municipal reform and im-migration restriction, as well as a critic of the Catholic Church and loose mone-tary policy. He is largely credited with spearheading the relentless attack on the Tweed Ring and helping to bring it down.[26]

The Tweed Ring was a corrupt group of politicians associated with the Tammany Hall political organization that dominated politics in New York City for much of the 1860s; the height of their power was between 1866 and 1871. During those years, the Ring, led by "Boss" William Marcy Tweed (leader of the 7th Ward and beginning in 1863 the head of Tammany Hall; later state senator), controlled the city government, the county government, the judicial system, the governorship, and the Board of Audit. The Ring members used this power to enrich themselves and their loyal supporters, while draining city funds. In 1871 the Ring began to unravel and Tweed was eventually convicted on 204 of 220 counts. He was placed in the Ludlow Street Jail (now the site of a high school in the Lower East Side), from which he escaped, only to be recaptured. He died there in 1877.

The final act of corruption was centered on a piece of architecture. The Tweed Courthouse was first planned in 1858 but was built between 1862 and 1870. The total cost of the project grew twentyfold—by 1870, $13 million had been ap-propriated, much of it siphoned off by Tweed and his Ring. Nast pursued the reve-lations of corruption mercilessly, offering one cutting cartoon after the next. For example, in an 1870 cartoon he called the courthouse "The Unfinished Diamond Palace." In the cartoon, the pediment over the entrance is inscribed "More," and

Thomas Nast, "Something That Did Blow Over," *Harper's Weekly,* **1871**

in front of the building lie "cartloads of money." Revelations about the exorbitant expenses associated with the construction of the courthouse, many of which were made public by people like Thomas Nast, helped bring down the Ring.[27]

Ever since, the Tweed Courthouse has served as a reminder of the ever-present danger of municipal corruption. Indeed, that legacy became the courthouse's best protector: future administrations resisted the demolition of such a costly building, lest they be accused of wastefulness. On July 7, 1889, a *Times* editorialist wrote: "The city of New York still suffers, for years to come will continue to suffer, the penalty of the official wrongdoing of the past. The enormous municipal plunder of the Tweed ring and the continuance of the political methods that made it possible fill the people with distrust and fear whenever there is any great public work to be done. This feeling has been a terrible check upon the progress and improvement of the city, and the chief obstacles in the way of securing for its authorities full control over its local interests."[28]

Nast recognized as well as anyone that New York's economic preeminence had made it the epicenter of particularly virulent forms of American vice. The irrational exuberance of a booming city was injected with the accelerant of greed, yielding vast wealth and poverty, as well as devastating periodic collapses, all united by the predictable hum of corruption among a nascent city government flooded with demands and cash. The Civil War draft riots of 1863, the greatest urban revolt in American history, and the growing numbers of immigrants and their increasing political power, inspired several novels that portrayed, in graphic fantasies, the descent of New York into a catastrophic war between classes and races.[29]

Joaquin Miller's 1886 *Destruction of Gotham* was a blistering condemnation of American society and a prediction of its coming end. The "argument of this story" is made clear by Miller in the opening pages: "The great city lies trembling, panting, quivering in her wild, white heat of intoxication, excitement, madness—drunken and devilish pursuits of power, pleasure, and gold. . . . It is the old story of the destruction of one whom the gods love. Never grew a city so great, so suddenly great. . . . She is madly, desperately drunk." At the core of the internal corruption is the "desperate pursuit of wealth." The publisher's endorsement—included at the end of the book—also made the point: "This is a most graphic story of the times, showing the conflict between the upper and lower strata of society in New York, ending in a great disaster to the city itself."[30]

Miller grew up on the Oregon frontier in the middle of the nineteenth century, lived with Native Americans, and later became known as a significant poet of the West with his *Song of the Sierras* (1871). He wrote *The Destruction of Gotham* after a world tour to market himself as a literary figure, taking advantage of the populist moment at hand, with its powerful animus toward the financial and industrial capitals of the eastern seaboard.[31]

As in other novels of the time, the signal that the city is sinking into dissolution is the fate of its women: what happens to them and what they become. *The Destruction of Gotham* opens with a young woman arriving by ferry, inevitably to be taken in by evildoers and to become a prostitute. "It is estimated," writes Miller, "that every day hundreds of young women enter New York never to return."[32] News reports of drunken women in the city's prisons are a clear indication of New York's decline: the city—all cities perhaps, but this city at this time in history in particular—will destroy women and womanhood.

The end of the city happens not by earthquake or flood, but by fire. "It was literally a burning island now. The very earth was on fire. The oil, the gas, the rum, the thousands of filthy things which man in his drunken greed had allowed to accumulate on the face of the island appealed to heaven for purification." And the fitting symbol for a city increasingly based on the trade of information—stocks and words alike—is the melting of type in newspaper offices. As Manhattan turns into a "burning island," "a river of lead was flowing from Franklin Square out and on and on, and out and into, and down to the deep mud

Laurence Schwinger, 1948
illustrations for Garrett Serviss's
1911 story "The Second Deluge"
and Frank Lillie Pollock's 1906
"Finis," both reprinted in
Fantastic Novels magazine, 1948

and muck of the river." It is impossible for the story of New York's end to be reported (as in "The Tilting Island," where the newspaper offices on Park Row are
tipping into the sea) because the news type has melted. That would be the city's
ironic ending—a death unreported.[33]

So deep is the corruption that it is sunk into the city's soil. It is not simply
in the skyscrapers (which topple over in a "vast sheet of flame" on the people
below) or on Wall Street or in the apoplectic meals at Delmonico's (though all
these places are mentioned in the catechism of destruction). It is so thoroughly
soaked into the city's life that only a fire will purify the land again: "And so the
flame laid hungry and hard hold of the face of the earth!"[34]

The fear of immigrants and the specter of cultural mixing and miscegenation was a powerful theme. In *How the Other Half Lives,* Jacob Riis worried,
along with his elite benefactors, about the "resistless flood" of immigrants they
feared would overwhelm New York.[35] This fear—which ultimately spawned a
wide eugenics movement as well as anti-immigration legislation—took novelis-
tic form. In *The Second Deluge* Garrett P. Serviss imagined the "flower of mankind" selected to board a modern-day Noah's Ark crafted to survive the great
flood. Writing in 1911, Serviss, a popular astronomer, details the consequences
for New York of the earth's collision with a "watery nebula." The selection process, based on the precepts of theoretical eugenics, places a premium on men
of science and morally sound women. The ark, prepared by Cosmo Versal, the
man who foresaw the coming deluge, will ferry the survivors around the world
in hopes of one day repopulating the earth and restoring civilization.[36]

A flood of biblical proportions ensues, sweeping away most of New York's
landscape and submerging what remains. The image of water—New York's life-
blood and its defining natural feature—finally overcoming the banks of Manhattan Island and submerging the city makes for a powerful effect:

> In this unearthly light many tall structures of the metropolis, which had as
> yet escaped the effects of undermining by the rushing torrents in the streets,
> towered dimly toward the sky, shedding streams of water from every cornice.
> Most of the buildings of only six or eight stories had already been submerged,
> with the exception of those that stood on high grounds in the upper part of the
> island, and about Spuyten Duyvil. . . . Every few minutes one of the great struc-
> tures would sway, crack, crumble, and go down into the seething flood, the
> cries of the lost souls being swallowed up in the thunder of the fall. And when
> this occurred within sight of neighboring towers yet intact, men and women
> could be seen, some with children in their arms, madly throwing themselves
> from windows and ledges, seeking quick death now that hope was no more.[37]

Cover and "City of
Ruins" illustration
from John Ames
Mitchell, *The Last
American: A Fragment
from the Journal of
Khan-Li,* 1889

The impact of the biblical flood is not fully realized until the twenty-fourth and penultimate episode, when the survivors construct a diving bell to explore the "necropolis" in the depths of "Her Ocean Tomb." Though there is no sight of the millions of people who were "swallowed up in this vast grave," some of the skyscrapers—at least their impressive steel skeletons, "immensely strong, and well braced"—remain. The survivors, after a long sojourn around the submerged world, set about creating a "New America" in conjunction with a group that had survived by forming communities on Pike's Peak in Colorado. In the end, they create a world "far superior, in every respect, to the old world that was drowned."[38] That hopeful future—after a far more horrific end of the city—is echoed in the greatest of these apocalyptic novels, Ignatius Donnelly's *Caesar's Column*.[39]

Caesar's Column (1890) imagines New York City in 1988 when the city is destroyed by the Brotherhood of Destruction—a vast organization of destitute proletarians bent on overthrowing the corrupt, Jewish-led oligarchy that has exploited them for generations. Barricading lower Manhattan, the "gloomy, dark, ragged, sullen multitude" loots the "great moneyed institutions" of the financial district, and then proceeds to the "wealthier parts of the city," where the rioters murder the condemned "aristocrats" in their homes. Led by the Italian immigrant Caesar Lomellini, the Brotherhood quickly defeats the oligarchy but subsequently descends into chaos. Amid the burning remnants of the once great city, scattered corpses of a quarter million of New York's prominent citizenry lay slaughtered on the streets.[40]

The focus on New York is unmistakable and crucial to the impact of the novel. The geography of the city is carefully drawn, derived in part from a half-century of "sunshine and shadows" literature, which contrasted the poverty of the "East Side" with the wealth of Fifth Avenue. The action of the novel concludes in Union Square, and the choice is deliberate. In 1882 some ten thousand workers had paraded up Broadway in the first Labor Day celebration, cementing the square's reputation as a place of parades and protest. (Labor Day would become a national holiday in 1894). A bustling center of commercial and political life (Tammany Hall bordered the square), Union Square brought travelers, businesspeople, and immigrant factory workers together in one place. The most powerful passages in an otherwise didactic and tedious *Caesar's Column* are the ones in which Donnelly describes the conditions of New York's masses before the revolution, and the bloody, animal-like ravages of the postrevolutionary city in chaos.

When the masses finally rise up in fury, it is as if a violent natural force has been unleashed: "And then all the avenues were open," Donnelly wrote. "And like a huge flood, long damned [*sic*] up, turbulent, turbid, muddy, loaded with wrecks and debris, the gigantic mass broke loose, full of foam and terror, and flowed in every direction. A foul and brutal and ravenous multitude it was, dark with dust and sweat, armed with the weapons of civilization, but possessing only the instincts of wild beasts." Donnelly declared: "The mighty city, with its ten million inhabitants lies prostrate, chained, helpless, at the mercy of the enraged *canaille*."[41]

It is the final act of barbarism that draws Welstein to Union Square. "The shops had all been broken into; dead bodies lay here and there; and occasionally a burned block lifted its black arms appealingly to heaven. As we drew near Union Square a wonderful sight—such as the world had never before beheld— expanded before us. Great blazing bonfires lighted the work; hundreds of thousands had gathered to behold the ghastly structure, the report of which had already spread everywhere."[42] There, in the middle of the square, which had by then become a center of labor activism, political meetings, and the publishing industry, stood a skyscraper of bodies, piled above the tallest buildings of the day, as a "symbol and memorial" of Caesar's triumph. Welstein, looking out over this column, writes an epitaph for the column: "This Great Monument Is Erected by Caesar Lomellini, Commanding General of The Brotherhood of Destruction, in Commemoration of the Death and Burial of Modern Civilization." With that, Welstein and his small group decide that they must finally flee in a balloon and allow the final consumption of the city to take place. As the small group floats away from the city, they look down below at a tableau of destruction: "The mighty city lay unrolled below us, like a great map, starred here and there with burning houses. Above the trees of Union Square, my glass showed me a white line, lighted by bon-fires, where Caesar's Column was towering to the skies, bearing the epitaph of the world."[43]

Despite the human degradation in the late-nineteenth-century city it describes, *Caesar's Column* is a utopian story. But it is utopian in the same way the American jeremiad of the Puritan era was. Donnelly's was a warning, a horrific, didactic, sermonizing warning of what America—and New York—would look like a century hence if it continued on its course of inequity, division, and moral emptiness. As Sacvan Bercovitch has argued, the jeremiad of Puritan ministers—which involved a detailed accounting of the community's failings, a visceral portrait of the fate awaiting a sinning community, and a call to return to first principles and behavior—persisted long after the Puritan era.[44] Indeed, the jeremiad became a central American narrative form, developed and perpetuated throughout the nineteenth century and into the twentieth. The catastrophic imagery of Donnelly's *Caesar's Column,* as well as Miller's *Destruction of Gotham* and so many other novels of the late nineteenth century, follow the jeremiad narrative form.

In this way, *Caesar's Column,* much less well known today than Edward Bellamy's *Looking Backward*—a story of a Bostonian, Julian West, who wakes up after a hundred years to find his city had become a socialist utopia—was in the mainstream of American literature and culture. Utopia was imagined from a state not of grace but of depravity. Dystopian cities could not long remain so—they would inevitably end in catastrophe. There was little middle ground. Utopia and catastrophe were two sides of the same coin in Donnelly's book, and in so much of the urban literature of the late nineteenth century. Bellamy's *Looking Backward* had sparked the new wave of utopian literature when it was published in 1888. Bellamy's book has come to be the one "utopian" novel to represent the literally hundreds of others written in the late nineteenth century. We will see echoes of this approach—utopia achieved not progressively but catastrophically through the "cleansing" action of apocalypse—throughout the twentieth century.

Donnelly's work emerged out of his own life and out of his times. Born in Philadelphia, he considered himself an urban dweller. When he moved westward (hoping to profit as a land speculator), he envisioned establishing a new city at Nininger, Minnesota. But the Panic of 1857—the product of stock manipulation in New York's stock exchange—left him overwhelmed with debt. He plowed the land of his future city and planted wheat. The urbanite and land speculator remade himself as a farmer and a westerner, resentful and bitter toward the East and its cities. The future of America, he began to realize, would be a battle "between the few who seek to grasp all power and wealth, and the many who seek to preserve their rights as American citizens and freemen." He moved in the world of the Grange, then the Greenback Party, and ultimately the Populist Party, after serving in the state legislature in the 1880s.[45]

Donnelly aroused his share of skepticism with his more outlandish writings, including *The Great Cryptogram,* published two years before *Caesar's Column,* which aimed to prove that Francis Bacon was the author of Shakespeare's works, or *Atlantis: The Antediluvian World,* which purported to prove the existence of the lost continent.

Donnelly's most famous bit of writing is not *Caesar's Column* but the preamble to the Omaha Platform, which articulated the central beliefs of the Populist Party at its national convention on July 4, 1892. "We meet," Donnelly wrote, "in the midst of a nation brought to the verge of moral, political, and material ruin." After a life begun in a city, Donnelly ended as a virulent hater of cities, or at least of eastern cities and the capital they allegedly leached from the rest of the country. He endorsed William Jennings Bryan, the Democratic presidential candidate who came to Omaha to receive the Populist Party's endorsement. At the convention Bryan took the wide-ranging and radical platform of the Populists and distilled—many would later argue gutted—it into a single issue: whether the financial system would be based on the tight-money gold standard (favoring cities and laborers who liked their dollars to go further because of its scarcity) or the looser silver standard (favoring farmers who depended on cheaper debt and believed more plentiful money meant more buyers for their produce). Bryan won the crowd over by his "Cross of Gold" speech, making this arcane issue a morality tale that pictured desolate cities, ruined by the loss of their source of life, the countryside: "You come to us and tell us that the great cities are in favor of the gold standard; we reply that the great cities rest upon our broad and fertile prairies. Burn down your cities and leave our farms, and your cities will spring up again as if by magic; but destroy our farms and the grass will grow in the streets of every city in the country."[46]

In a prefatory remark to *Caesar's Column,* Donnelly makes his purpose clear, lest the horrors of the story suggest a violent intent. "It must not be thought," he writes, "because I am constrained to describe the overthrow of civilization, that I desire it. . . . Neither am I an anarchist." To whom is the book directed? "I seek to preach into the hearts of the able and rich and powerful the great truth that neglect of the sufferings of their fellows . . . [will] eventuate in the overthrow of society and the destruction of civilization."[47]

Donnelly, a man of the nineteenth century, died on the first day of the twentieth.

Threats from Abroad

In 1916 Walter Harrison Cady undertook a pair of paintings very much at odds with his previous work. Born in Gardner, Massachusetts, in 1877, Cady had developed a fruitful career as an illustrator for the *Brooklyn Eagle* and, later, as an artist and cartoonist for *Life* magazine. He also drew for a variety of other magazines, such as *Saturday Evening Post* and *Ladies' Home Journal.* Something like an early Norman Rockwell, Cady specialized in drawings for children's books, graduating to gentle sketches of New York life and a series on the port town of Rockport, Massachusetts.[48]

But with war raging in Europe and with America being lured into the battle, Cady produced a pair of ink drawings in his characteristically detailed style. The first, titled *The Unready Nation,* pictures the Statue of Liberty proudly framing the white spires of lower Manhattan's skyscrapers, with steamboats and sailboats dotting the harbor. The second image, *The Grave of Liberty,* shows a desolate scene—Lady Liberty toppled, her flame just peeking out from the water, and the skyscrapers crumbling. The bridges are gone and the ships sunk.

Cady's images were followed by Joseph Pennell's marketing posters for Liberty Bonds, which were designed to spur a tentative nation to become militarily powerful. Pennell, born in Philadelphia in 1860 and one of the most important etchers and illustrators in the country, was widely published in such British periodicals as *The Graphic, Pall Mall,* and *The English Illustrated* and later produced widely seen images of American cities and their proud new skyscrapers. *St. Paul's, New York* is typical. It shows the construction of two skyscrapers on lower Broadway, just below City Hall Park, with St. Paul's Church wedged down below, in between. Pennell embraced the city's creative destruction and tried to portray the tension between the old and the new. The images are carefully balanced: viewers are both in awe of the new skyscrapers rising on a grid of steel and respectful of the landmarks that have anchored the city. Pennell understood New York's paradoxical need both to build and to destroy; this understanding made his images for World War I a few years later all the more powerful. War, of course, would offer none of that vibrant tension. Cady's Liberty Bond poster from 1917, which pleaded, "That Liberty Shall Not Perish from the Earth Buy Liberty Bonds," is a searing image. The black-and-white print is colored with flame reds and oranges. The Manhattan he so carefully depicts is awash in fire, with fighter planes above dropping more bombs to expand the disaster. Hardly a building can be made out. The Statue of Liberty in the foreground still stands but has been decapitated; the flame of the torch is lost in the firestorm. The poster is especially powerful in light of the rest of Pennell's work. While his other images capture the tensions in the city of constant destruction and construction, they are ultimately a part of the larger culture's romance with the city and its skyscrapers. The war posters, in contrast, are devastating in their vision of a city literally gone up in smoke.

Having spent almost three decades in England, including the first years of World War I, Pennell well understood the ravages of war. His images of New York, especially those after the war, are certainly tinged with regret, and the sense that destruction is ever present. *Caissons on Vesey Street,* the final print before his death in 1926, depicts construction equipment in lower Manhattan,

Walter Harrison Cady (1877–1970),
The Unready Nation and *The Grave
of Liberty*, 1916

near the Hudson River. Towering in the background is the Woolworth Building. But there is something oddly disturbing here: the smoke and clouds of dust from construction have almost completely obscured the building's first thirty stories. It is almost as if a bomb had exploded at its base.[49] In fact, the building looks as if it is teetering ever so slightly, suggesting the frailty of even this, the tallest skyscraper in the world. And there may have been echoes of the bomb explosions of war, which Pennell found intoxicating.

New York and the Military Preparedness Debate

The burning and occupation of New York by the British in the Revolutionary War remained in communal memory as New York's one great experience of invasion. In the 1860s, when New York was battered by fires and threatened with attack in the Civil War and with class and racial unrest, the fear of invasion from beyond American shores had subsided. But by the end of the nineteenth century, and especially in the World War I era, fear of invasion from abroad and weakness within had supplanted the dread of immigrant and labor revolt that had seemed to dominate imaginings of New York's end.[50] To make their loud and usually unified argument—that the United States, the greatest economic power in the world, was utterly unprepared to withstand a military attack—writers returned repeatedly, and almost exclusively, to scenarios of New York being destroyed or threatened by a sneak attack.

One of the earliest of these works was Arthur Vinton's *Looking Further Backward* (1890), written as a parody of Bellamy's vision of a cooperative society. *Looking Further Backward* is written as a series of lectures given by Professor Won Lung Li, "successor to Julian West" (the hero of Bellamy's utopian novel), in Boston in 2023—in the years after China has conquered the "American Barbarians." It is the tale of how the United States was so easily subdued. The answer, of course, is that the cooperative society of Bellamy's vision had been achieved, and had left Americans utterly unprepared—militarily and constitutionally—for threats from abroad.[51]

Bellamy's cooperative world had, in the Chinese professor's words, led to a "loss of individualism." With no sense of personal responsibility, people ignored serious threats from abroad. "No man any more has any care for the morrow," Won declares, "either for himself or his children, for the nation guarantees the nurture, education and comfortable maintenance of every citizen from the cradle to the grave." The "Nationalistic system"—as Won calls Bellamy's ideas about peaceful cooperation, disarmament, and economic equality—sapped citizens of their energy to fight and sapped the nation's commitment to protect itself. The Chinese find easy work in conquering the United States, as each city, first in the East and later in the West, offers little fight. Washington "had fallen without the firing of a shot"; Chicago and Boston surrender quickly. Philadelphia doesn't resist, but "with characteristic slowness," debates "her inevitable surrender."[52]

Only New Yorkers resist. A great riot breaks out in the city and kills a million people; a retaliatory bombardment by the Chinese ensues. The city, unlike the others, which are preserved by their surrender, is "promptly reduced to ruins." "The horror of the catastrophe appalled the world," writes Vinton, but it proved the "folly of those nations which had dreamed of war as a thing of the past." As a final indignity, the survivors of the bombardment—some fifty thousand workers—are chained together and forced to clear the streets of debris before being "marched in their chains on board the transports which then left with them for France."[53]

The preparedness debates of the 1910s were on one level about the very real disparity between America's economic might and its relative military weakness. But as the historian David Kennedy has argued, the rhetorical battles in the press and in Congress were about far more. In a way, they were about everything. The question of whether and how America would "prepare" for its own defense and its potential involvement in the European war became a vehicle for debates about American society more generally.[54] At base, this was a contest between political and economic liberalism on the one hand—the heart of the so-called Progressive movement—and conservative business politics on the other. Powerful preparedness lobbies, including the National Security League (bankrolled by entrepreneurs such as Cornelius Vanderbilt, Henry Clay Frick, and Daniel Guggenheim), used this debate as the opening salvo of a more conservative political movement. Pacifists and liberal progressives approached the war in Europe with great optimism. If the United States could stay out of the war and remain "unscathed," it could become the great power in the wake of Europe's self-immolation.[55]

The program of liberal Progressivism quickly disintegrated in the "quickening tempo of war": education for immigrants turned into repression and wholesale restriction by the late 1920s. Woodrow Wilson, for example, warned Congress in 1915 of foreign-born "creatures of passion, disloyalty, and anarchy." The right wing, including eugenicists, found in the preparation battle a means by which to advance their dreams.[56]

War also gave conservative business leaders an opening to rationalize American society and industry. Germany was hated, but also respected. The image of a rationally organized, highly militaristic, and efficient German society was for many conservatives a model to copy. As we will see, many of the fantasies of New York's destruction are at the hands of the German navy—miraculously rebuilt after the loss of the World War and stunningly efficient and stealthy.[57]

Earlier literary nightmares of the masses rising up were transformed into images of fearful immigrants at war with their adopted country. Narratives that combined a critique of American society as weak, even effeminate, with a call for greater military might drew a powerful response. Wilson, who had long been championed by the American left and its pacifists, slowly turned to greater investment in the military and, of course, eventually led the country into what was to be an idealistic war. The effect of this betrayal on the "liberal spirit" was "withering."[58]

A number of novels and journalistic accounts used didactic stories of New York's invasion as a means by which to call for greater investment in the military. Here is a lieutenant of engineers, writing in 1885:

> A hostile fleet lying in the upper bay of New York would have within reach of their guns about two billion dollars' worth of destructible property in New York City alone, and including Brooklyn and Jersey City, over two and a half billions. These guns would be of the largest calibre, many of them capable of throwing 16- and 17¾-inch shells charged with 75 pounds of explosive gelatine. Should the enemy resort to a bombardment in order to enforce his terms, the result would be terrible beyond description. Even when we read of the havoc wrought by a few pounds of dynamite in the public buildings of London, we have but a slight idea of the completeness of demolition which would result from the explosion of 75 pounds of nitro-gelatine in the interior of such a building as the New York Produce Exchange. There are within gunshot of this room eight buildings, the assessed value of which for 1885 was over twelve millions of dollars. Every one of these might be totally wrecked by just eight happily directed shots. . . .
>
> But the effect produced by shells alone would be insignificant in comparison with the sweeping destruction resulting from the fires caused by their explosions. No fire department, however efficient, could check the progress of the flames, extinguished at one point only to break out at another, even should the men attempt such a hopeless and dangerous task. New York would be doomed.[59]

The most famous story of New York's destruction is H. G. Wells's 1908 portrayal of a German air attack in *The War in the Air.* "This here Progress," says Tom Smallways, a simple farmer in Bun Hill, south of London, as he watches airships rising before him, "it keeps on." But of course the argument of the book—what Wells called a "fantasia of possibility"—is less sanguine about that principle: progress does "keep on," not toward a better world but toward a new kind of war that will decimate the world. By time the world—or at least all the great cities—has been bombed into ruins, the people left in preindustrial poverty, Wells can only write that the great war "'didn't ought ever to 'ave begun.' . . . Somebody somewhere ought to have stopped something, but who or how or why were all beyond his ken."[60]

Wells, one of the most prophetic of science fiction writers, saw that aviation would become the primary tool of wars (although he acknowledged years later that he had made an "extraordinary mistake" in predicting the dominance of airships, and not airplanes).[61] In his preface for the 1921 edition, Wells makes explicit the argument of *The War in the Air,* as well as what motivated him to write it. He writes,

> The main idea is not that men will fly, or to show how they will fly; the main idea is a thesis that the experiences of the intervening years strengthen rather than supersede. The thesis is this; that with the flying machine war alters its character; it ceases to be an affair with "fronts" and becomes an affair of "areas"; neither side, victor or loser, remains immune from the gravest injuries, and while there is a vast increase in the destructiveness of war, there is also an increased indecisiveness. Consequently, "War in the Air" means social destruction instead of victory at the end of war. It not only alters the methods of war but the consequences of war.

Wells goes further to suggest that although many had mocked the imaginary flights he took when the book was first published in 1908, his warnings had been quite prescient. Indeed, though the catastrophe of the Great War finally had ended, "the militarist process" continued apace and "national and imperialist rivalries march whole nations at the quickstep towards social collapse." Wells's preface to the 1941 edition states simply, with a tone of resignation, "Is there anything to add to that preface [from 1921] now? Nothing except my epitaph . . . 'I told you so, You *damned* fools.'"[62]

In Wells's book, during the first decades of the twentieth century, the powerful nations of Europe, North America, and Asia secretly develop and amass large forces of "flying machines." Amid a background of technological advancement, nationalist fervor, and international rivalry, each prepares itself for the contingency of war. A belligerent Germany is the first to attack, and conducts a massive airship raid and bombardment on New York. With the "Navy

Yard on the East River," City Hall, "two of the great business buildings on Wall Street and Lower Broadway," and the Brooklyn Bridge destroyed, the municipal government capitulates and raises the white flag. Abandoned by city leadership, New York's citizens resist German occupation and launch an insurrection. The German air fleet attempts to quell the rebellion by destroying the city but is interrupted when an American force of flying machines counterattacks. The conflict soon escalates into a full-scale world war that ultimately results in the destruction of modern civilization. When the destruction of the world's most important cities is followed by financial panic, famine, and pestilence, civilization is left in a state of regressive feudalism.

Wells's argument comes to a head, of course, in New York. Though all of the world's cities will eventually be destroyed in this world war, the story of New York's end is literally and symbolically at the center of the book. Wells famously, or apocryphally, said, on first viewing the Manhattan skyline, "What a ruin it will make!"[63]

As in many other didactic military preparedness novels, Wells shows New York utterly unprepared for the attack. Just as in the opening passage of *War of the Worlds,* Wells describes New Yorkers as taking "no heed of war, save as a thing that happened far away, that affected prices and supplied the newspaper with exciting headlines and pictures." New Yorkers "felt as secure as spectators at a bullfight."[64] The novel describes a world war that condemns every major city to destruction. Indeed, at the end of the novel, it is not even clear whether the war is even over. And yet Wells, a British author, chooses to focus the most detail on New York. The attack on London is not described but is simply reported in passing after the long narrative of New York's destruction. Reports follow of the bombing and burning of Berlin, Paris, San Francisco, and Hamburg. "All de vorld is at vor!" says a German soldier. In the last pages, the reader is offered a quick history of how the world has devolved into premodern civilizations of scavengers and small farmers.[65] The logic of focusing on New York is made clear with Wells's opening lines of the chapter "How War Came to New York": "The City of New York was in the year of the German attack the largest, richest, in many respects the most splendid, and in some the wickedest, city the world had ever seen. She had long ousted London from her pride of place as the modern Babylon, she was the centre of the world's finance, the world's trade, and the world's pleasure; and men likened her to the apocalyptic cities of the ancient prophets."

The initial attack on New York lasts but a few minutes, with bombs hitting key landmarks in lower Manhattan:

"The Martians appeared to be marching toward Windsor": illustration from
H. G. Wells, *War of the Worlds,* 1898

Below, the immense buildings, tremendous and fine as they were, seemed like the giant trees of a jungle fighting for life; their picturesque magnificence was as planless as the chances of crag and gorge, their casualty enhanced by the smoke and confusion of the still unsubdued and spreading conflagrations.

[A German airship] crumpled up like a can that had been kicked by a heavy boot, her forepart came down in the square, and the rest of her length, with a great snapping and twisting of shafts and stays, descended, collapsing athwart Tammany Hall and the street towards Second Avenue.

As the airships sailed along they smashed up the city. . . . Below, they left ruins and blazing conflagrations and heaped and scattered dead men.

Wells drew a portrait that could have been transported to the morning of September 11, 2001, without a single word changed: "Lower Manhattan was soon a furnace of crimson flames, from which there was no escape. Cars, railways, ferries, all had ceased, and never a light lit the way of the distracted fugitives in that dusky confusion but the light of burning. . . . Dust and black smoke came pouring into the street, and were presently shot with red flame."[66]

In *America Fallen! The Sequel to the European War* (1915), J. Bernard Walker, a onetime editor of *Scientific American,* offered what he hoped was a realistic account of how a defeated kaiser would launch a surprise attack on the United States.[67] Slipping into New York's harbor in the cover of night, submarines attack the Brooklyn Navy Yard and within a short time have taken over New York's meager defenses at Sandy Hook and Fort Hamilton. The invaders issue a demand for $5 billion in twenty-four hours. The mayor offers $1 billion; in response, bombs rain down on the city. The kaiser's men attack Manhattan, but not to destroy it; they want only to frighten the population and leadership into submission. Carefully choosing their targets—especially the Woolworth Tower, then the tallest skyscraper in the world—the Germans seek to destroy the confidence of New Yorkers. One man in the Woolworth Building finds himself on stairs leading straight into the sky—the side of the building has been blown away. From there "he heard the roar of the 12-inch shells, as they hurled past the tower to fall upon the doomed city, and the observation platform would enable him to watch the stupendous spectacle of its destruction." The Equitable Life Building, a gargantuan building that, ironically, had burned down in 1912, was hit, as was the city's own new skyscraper, the McKim, Mead, and White Municipal Building just behind City Hall. Each of the city's new signature corporate towers—the Singer Building, the City Investing Building, the Adams Express, and the Western Union Building—was hit.[68]

The terrifying onslaught sends mobs into the streets, crushing hundreds.

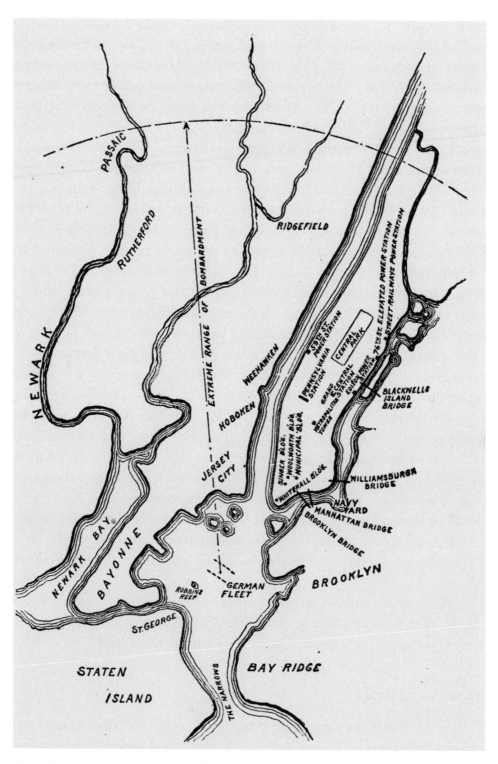

"Map Showing How Guns of German Fleet Covered the Whole Of Manhattan," from J. Bernard Walker, *America Fallen! The Sequel to the European War,* 1915

If the invasion from beyond were not enough, the inherent destructive power of New York's concentrated populace would wreak havoc. New York's crowds, in Walker's description, create a "fatal accumulation of pressure." And using new technology, a German plane circles the city and the pilot considers sheering the cables of the Brooklyn Bridge, across which thousands are fleeing. Slicing the bridge's cables would kill fifty thousand. But the pilot chooses not to: "The purpose of the bombardment was to damage—not destroy." Within a few hours, the city has succumbed. "The roar of the bombardment had ceased," Walker writes, "and save for a few shell holes in the taller buildings, there was nothing to indicate that, for one full hour, Hell had vented its fury upon their noble city."[69] The mayor as well as the financiers agree to meet the demands of the invaders.

Walker's scenario was replicated, to a remarkable degree, by a number of other writers. In a 1915 article General Francis V. Greene evoked the German invading army marching across Long Island in a few days, unstopped by America's meager army. Unless a huge army—a quarter of a million or so strong—were created and marshaled, Manhattan would be taken with relative ease. Again, Greene imagined not destruction of the city (except that New Yorkers destroy the bridges in the hopes of stopping the invaders) but a ransom. The goal would be a bond for $5 billion, as in Walker's book.[70]

The decision in these accounts to leave New York relatively unscathed does not appear to be out of concern for frightening readers with visions of New York's end. Rather, it is a further critique of the city's, and nation's, preparedness. New York does not even need to be destroyed for the city and nation to give in. The buildings will stand, but the leadership will crumple. Barely a shot needs to be fired to make the city succumb. There is a sense here of an emasculated city, incapable of putting up even a modicum of defense. New York, awash with people and money, with its awe-inspiring skyscrapers, is nonetheless a weak city.

These novels and newspaper stories end in uniform desolation. The Germans move on to other cities in the country, leaving behind an economically defeated, and psychically if not physically destroyed, New York.

Darkness and Dawn

In *Caesar's Column,* the skyscraper at the heart of the city is not a building of commerce, or a symbol of the great city's economic might and architectural innovation. It is, instead, a column of death, thousands of bodies piled high. In *Darkness and Dawn,* one of the most remarkable of all disaster novels about New

Madison Square Garden returned to a state of savage nature in George Allan England,
Darkness and Dawn, 1914

York, the skyscraper is virtually all that remains of civilization and is the refuge of the last two people in New York.[71]

In George Allan England's 1912 story of a mysterious disaster, a man and a woman—Allan Stern and Beatrice Kendrick—wake up in Stern's engineering office near the top of the Metropolitan Life Insurance Tower thousands of years in the future. Humankind has been destroyed, while they have survived in a chemical hibernation, the lone survivors.[72] What follows is their exploration of the destroyed city, their struggle against the half-animal, half-human beings that have taken over the city, and their efforts to reconstitute civilization on the ruins of the past.

Allan and Beatrice first look out over the city from near the top of the tower, awed by the sight of the great metropolis of their time in ruins. "Dead lay the city, between its rivers," writes England. Over in New Jersey, an old-growth forest has taken over, with "some skeleton mockery of a steel structure" jutting through. Ellis Island is overgrown; the Statue of Liberty has lost her torch. Instead, her arm, a "lolling mast of steel" is "thrusting up from the desolation, like a mute appealing hand raised to a heaven that responded not." "It's just as though some cosmic jester, all-powerful, had scooped up the fragments of a ruined city and tossed them pell-mell into the core of the Adirondacks!" Allan cries. "It's horrible—ghastly—incredible!"[73]

They begin with a tour from above. The solid landmarks of the world metropolis are utterly transformed. Broadway has become, in Allan's joking words, "quite a respectable Forest of Arden," while the heart of the journalistic world on Park Row consists merely of "steel cages." The bridges have all fallen or buckled, with the Brooklyn Bridge's towers, those first great skyscrapers, "two isolated castaways on their island in the sea of uttermost desolation." The Flatiron Building across Madison Square from the Metropolitan Life Tower was a "shattered pile of stone and metal." "Nature has got her revenge at last on man," Allan declares. All that is left is a "mausoleum of civilization."[74]

Allan, searching for food and tools—and, ultimately, weapons—soon explores the city on foot. He finds the city "had entirely ceased to be." He ponders, "If the builders could have foreseen this they wouldn't have thrown quite such a chest, eh? And *they* talked of engineering!" He explores the subway stations, Penn Station, the wharves, walks down the middle of Fifth Avenue (a walk taken by many lone survivors of New York disaster scenarios throughout the twentieth century), and visits what were, in his most recent memory, chaotic, bustling piers. At Penn Station he reaches his nadir of depression when he sees, beneath that grandest of monuments, the disintegrated tracks, the jumbled remains of locomotives and luxurious Pullmans with weeds growing rank upon them. . . . The sunlight beating down through the caved-in roof of the Pennsylvania station "concourse," where millions of human beings once had trod in all the haste of men's paltry, futile affairs, filled him with melancholy. . . . "*Sic transit gloria mundi!*" he murmured as with sad eyes he mused upon the down-tumbled columns along the facade, the overgrown entranceway, the cracked and falling arches and architraves. "And *this,* they said, was builded for all time!"[75]

Though the exploration of well-known landmarks in ruin occupies the first half of the book, for many readers *Darkness and Dawn* was primarily a romance. Indeed, it was marketed as a "Book of Thrills" by its publisher. "Romance, Mystery, Adventure" trumped "Disaster, Struggle, and Socialism" in the selling of the book. It was, the copywriters insisted, "a type of novel that will always be popular." A reviewer called it, without irony, a "romance of a depopulated New York."[76] Romance represents the resilience of humanity. Out of the rubble comes both romance and confidence. It does not take long for Beatrice to recover from the incomprehensible shock of what has happened to feel a "strange new thrill of confidence and solace. . . . Though the whole wide world had crumpled into ruin, yet he would find a way to smooth her path, to be a strength and refuge for her."[77]

The despair the two feel quickly yields to the quest for survival. And in that quest, traditional hierarchies of race and gender are reasserted. For many late-nineteenth-century apocalyptic writers, one of the signs of the decay of society was the decline of the patriarchal family and the rise of what will later be called the "new woman." *Darkness and Dawn* opens with the suggestion of a new type of woman who will beget a new civilization: after all, young Beatrice Kendrick was the lone assistant to Allan Stern. She worked in the tallest office tower in the world, part of the new class of professional women taking part in the corporate headquarters economy of New York, and taking center stage in American culture.

And yet the budding romance—which begins with neither of them clothed, like Adam and Eve—and the relationship that slowly develops are built on traditional gender roles. The building block of the new civilization, if it is to exist, will be the solid foundation of traditional gender roles and traditional marriage. Allan explores the city, recapturing his more physical abilities after a lifetime of scientific experiments in the tower. Beatrice quickly adopts women's traditional roles, creating "a real home out of the barren desolation" of their shelter in the Metropolitan Life Tower. Despair banished, those first days become, for Allan, the "happiest of his life, for the understanding between this beautiful woman and himself at such times became very close and fascinatingly intimate."[78]

The pinnacle of this growing romance, and the embrace of their obligation to re-create humanity, must be achieved through what can be seen as nothing less than a violent battle of the races. What Beatrice hopes are arriving human survivors, coming across the river to Manhattan, turn out to be a combination of white society's worst fears: not just "savages" but a combination of every racially inferior group. "What race are they descended from? He could not tell." Allan, a scientist, detects a "trace of the Mongol in the region of eye," while also describing them as members of tribes using flints and spears, as "black . . . no bigger than apes" and prone to "voodooism." "These things," Stern is sure, are "lower than any human race ever recorded, far lower than the famed Australian bushmen, who could not even count as high as five." Or perhaps they are Neanderthal men. They are, to be sure, a bundle of fears: of racial miscegenation, corruption, and foreign invasion.[79]

While time has moved forward several thousand years, it is clear that evolution has gone in the opposite direction. White, civilized, urban society has devolved into the mixed-race half-animals that now threaten the last two survivors of civilized society. England emphasizes a theme of the *Last Americans* and other similar novels, such as Van Tassel Sutphen's *The Doomsmen,* which suggests that, after New York had ruined itself, no other society could advance beyond where New York had left off at the beginning of the nineteenth century.[80] New York's end, though deserved because of internal corruption or weakness in the face of invasion, meant the end of the progress of civilization. In *Darkness and Dawn,* something much worse has happened: human society has not just stalled in the wake of New York's end; it has devolved back toward its animal roots. New York was the font of new ideas and inventions; it was also the dam holding back the devolving instincts of human society.

Ultimately, it is new technology—the steel skyscraper, the symbol of the city, and a new type of explosive—that will protect the two survivors and allow them to prevail. Madison Square, or "Madison Forest," as they have come to call it, has become a "regular voodoo hangout," threatening their quiet home in the Metropolitan Life Tower. Using the latest destructive technology—Pulverite— Allan is able finally to destroy the hordes that occupied the square.[81] In a city that has been ruined slowly by time, the effect of the Pulverite bombs is dramatic and instant. Allan drops seven bombs from the tower onto the throngs in Madison Square and yields an "indistinguishable mass of ruin and of death. . . . The forest, swept as by a giant broom, became a jackstraw tangle of destruction." Allan, ex-ultant in the success of this new destructive weapon, declares, "Gods! Gods we are now to them—to such of them as may still live. Gods we are; gods we shall be forever! The great white gods of terror!"[82]

The victory leads them not to new confidence in resettling the city but in a wish to flee. And like the white suburbanites who already were fleeing cities to escape the flood of suspect races, Allan and Beatrice decide to head across the Hudson, leaving the city to the enemy, if there are more of them. The city will remain the source of their survival—"the latent resources of this vast ruin haven't been even touched yet!"—but the city will now be, as it would be for millions in the coming generation, a place to visit. Finding a boat near the "grim ruin" of Grant's Tomb in upper Manhattan, they row across the Hudson to the former estate of Harrison van Amburg, the billionaire of his time. His concrete home—"built for all time"—will become their new home, and the birth of a new civilization.

The novel ends with a clarion call that will be echoed in the utopian visions of the 1920s: "The race of men, our race, must live again—shall live! . . . Once more shall cities gleam and tower. . . . A kinder and a saner world this time. No misery, no war, no poverty." That this vision is built around a deep-seated racism and a longing for traditional gender roles indicates its profound limitations.[83]

three

Utopian and Dystopian Fantasies of the "Stone Colossus" in the 1920s and 1930s

Finally, there arises the monstrous symbol and vessel of the completely emancipated intellect, the world-city, the centre in which the course of a world-history ends by winding itself up. A handful of gigantic places in each Civilization disfranchises and disvalues the entire motherland of its own Culture under the contemptuous name of "the provinces." The stone Colossus "Cosmopolis" stands at the end of the life's course of every great Culture. The culture-man whom the land has spiritually formed is seized and possessed by his own creation, the City, and is made into its creature, its executive organ, and finally its victim.

—OSWALD SPENGLER, 1926

IN AUGUST 1920 THE FIRST COMMERCIAL RADIO STATIONS BEGAN regular broadcasting. Out of Pittsburgh came the radio reports of KDKA, in time for the November Harding-Cox presidential election.[1] They were also in time to broadcast the news of September 16, 1920, when a bomb went off on Wall Street, killing forty people and shocking New York and the United States with an attack "unprecedented in horror."[2] New Yorkers had feared something like this. The end of World War I had brought military peace, but not peace at home: in 1919 hostile labor strikes, widespread race riots, and a series of bombs mailed to prominent individuals set the country on edge. A massive crackdown on immigrants and "radicals" by Attorney General A. Mitchell Palmer fomented suspicion of foreigners, which was only exacerbated in New York by the trial of the Wall Street bombing suspects, who were alleged to have discussed plans to encourage a mass uprising of immigrants in the city. The bombing ushered in a decade of attacks on immigrants, culminating in the imposition of quotas beginning in 1924.

The threat to New York, so feared and yet unrealized in World War I, became reality with the 1920 bombing. It both heightened the celebration of American finance capitalism and deepened the critiques. The advent of radio broadcasts, which would soon become national, so that someone in California could hear the very same news report or orchestra concert as someone in New York, was a dramatic shift. It marked the beginning of a mass society that Progressives had been predicting and worrying about for two decades.

Both of these developments—the new technology and this new threat to the heart of American might—inflamed fantasies of New York's end. So many of the scenarios of New York's destruction in the 1920s and 1930s were bound up with apprehensive questions about new technologies, especially radio, television, and film: what powerful, invisible forces would control the words and images Americans absorbed? What would instant communication mean? And, perhaps most important, whom could you trust? This last question had particular resonance in the 1920s and 1930s, when the solid bases of community and the efficacy of American civilization were doubted. In the wake of World War I, skepticism about the effects of modern Western civilization on the world brought the entire question of civilization—its contradictions, its dangers, its prospects—front and center.

The stock market crash and the resulting Great Depression seemed to justify the critiques of American civilization. The labor and political movements of the 1930s gave rise to utopian visions, but in fact the city found itself under siege from both natural and man-made attackers. Only Superman's arrival at the end of the thirties, in the face of Hitler and the start of World War II, brought a defender strong enough—even if only in dime-novel fiction—to protect the city and American civilization.

In the 1920s a utopianism born of a robust critique of American civilization can be seen in two fictional imaginings of New York's end.

Du Bois's "The Comet" and Sinclair's *Millennium*

In a little-known short story by W. E. B. Du Bois, a comet's tail sweeps past New York and kills the city's population with a burst of deadly gas. Everyone, save two: a poor black man and a rich white woman.

"Danger!" declare the newspaper headlines on the day of the disaster. "Warnings wired around the world. The comet's tail sweeps past us at noon. Deadly gases expected. Close doors and windows, Seek the cellar!" Assigned to the underground vault of the bank in which he works, Jim, a black messenger, is the only man to survive the catastrophe. (His first terrified thought on finding the guards outside the vault dead is, "If they found him here alone—with all this money and all these dead men—what would his life be worth?")[3]

Scouring the city for survivors, Jim is free to wander up Fifth Avenue (the most popular promenade for postapocalyptic New Yorkers) and enter the "gorgeous, ghost haunted halls" of a "famous hostelry" that "yesterday . . . would not have served me." Everywhere he finds people dead but the city's buildings intact. "The stillness of death lay everywhere and everywhere bowed, bent, and stretched the silent forms of men," writes Du Bois. "In the great stone doorway a hundred men and women and children lay crushed and twisted and jammed into that great, gaping doorway like refuse in a can—as if in one wild, frantic rush to safety, they had crushed and ground themselves to death."

Jim soon comes across Julia, the daughter of a rich white Metropolitan Life Insurance executive, and she accepts his invitation to seek out their families together, first in Harlem and then at the Metropolitan Life Insurance tower on Madison Square. "Yesterday, he thought with bitterness, she would scarcely have looked at him twice. He would have been dirt beneath her silken feet." They roam the city and find only "silence and death—death and silence." "They hunted from Madison Square to Spuyten Duyvel; they rushed across the Williamsburg Bridge; they swept over Brooklyn; from the Battery and Morningside Heights they scanned the river, Silence, silence everywhere, and no human sign. Haggard and bedraggled they puffed a third time slowly down Broadway, under the broiling sun, and at last stopped."[4]

As they search for any remaining survivors, and are drawn to one another, their sense of despair ebbs away.

> Yet as the two, flying and alone, looked upon the horror of the world, slowly, gradually, the sense of all-enveloping death deserted them. They seemed to move in a world silent and asleep,—not dead. They moved in quiet reverence, lest somehow they wake these sleeping forms who had, at last, found peace. They moved in some solemn, world-wide *Friedhof,* above which some mighty hand had waved its magic wand. All nature slept until—until, and quick with the same startling thought, they looked into each other's eyes—he, ashen, she, crimson, with unspoken thought. To both, the vision of a mighty beauty—of vast, unspoken things, swelled their souls; but they put it away.[5]

And in this, what would seem to be the first relationship of a new world, they throw out old assumptions. For Jim, Julia is "neither high nor low, white nor black, rich nor poor. She was primal woman; mighty mother of all men to come and Bride of Life." For Julia, Jim was "glorified. He was no longer a thing apart, a creature below, a strange outcast of another clime and blood, but her Brother Humanity incarnate, Son of God and great All-Father of the race to be." Their sexual union is the consummation of a new world: "Their souls lay naked to the night. It was not lust; it was not love—it was some vaster, mightier thing that needed neither touch of body nor thrill of soul. It was a thought divine, splendid."[6]

But the next day as they continue the search for Julia's father, he finds them in his office in the Metropolitan Life Insurance Tower. As it turns out, "only New York" was hit by the comet's gases. In an instant, the world of yesterday returns: They turn to Jim. "It's a nigger Julia! Has he dared . . . ?" Others yell, "A nigger? Where is he? Let's lynch the damn . . ." Julia defends Jim but is escorted away and doesn't protest. Jim is given a few dollars for his troubles and sent on his way. A crowd that has formed laughs that in "all New York, just a white girl and a nigger!" The story ends as Jim turns at the sound of his wife's voice, and they embrace.[7]

"The Comet" is a spare but powerful rumination on what it would take to create a new world. Du Bois suggests that racial division is so powerful that it would take something like this—a catastrophic, tectonic shift in society—to make new race relations possible. In "The Comet," the New Woman also has a place she has not had in other New York disaster stories. Julia leaves her Upper East Side apartment and eagerly opens her eyes, not only to Jim but to her city, to her sexuality, to the possibilities for her self. In *Darkness and Dawn* from just a few years earlier, and in many other postapocalyptic, utopian novels, the role of women remains steadfastly traditional. They might have moments of heroism, but they remain subservient.

And yet racism is so powerful—indeed, resilient as a rubber band—that when the island world is repopulated, prejudice snaps back and the brief view into a different world is instantly closed off.

Just a few years later, in a 1924 novel, New York was again destroyed by a freak accident, leaving the city physically intact but only a few survivors alive. The new civilization created out of the disaster looked radically different from Du Bois's. Upton Sinclair, the author of *The Jungle* (1906), based *The Millennium* on an unproduced play he had written in 1907.[8]

In the New York portrayed in *The Millennium* the gulf between wealth and poverty has dramatically widened. A select group of the world's most wealthy and powerful capitalists gather for the grand opening of the hundred-story-high Pleasure Palace built in the middle of Central Park solely for enjoyment by the city's elite. During the festivities, the de facto emperor of America's financial aristocracy, Mr. Lumley-Gotham, learns that a government scientist has developed a source of "energy greater than any known upon earth" called X-radiumite. If mixed with air, however, X-radiumite would result in "the annihilation of all animal life upon the surface of the globe." Conspiring with his son-in-law, the Secretary of State, Mr. Granville, Lumley-Gotham orders the scientist arrested and the X-radiumite seized. When the scientist is backed into a corner, he threatens to drop the jar. Fearing for their lives, Granville, Lumley-Gotham, and a select group of friends and family climb aboard an airplane and head for the safety of the skies. From the air they witness the "blinding light" of the explosion, and six hours later they land to find that not a single living thing has survived.

As they explore the city (in conveniently undamaged cars filled with seemingly bottomless gas tanks), they see thousands upon thousands of piles of dust — all that remains of New York's inhabitants. It is a portrait of a neutron-bombed city, thirty years before that weapon had been invented. "'Dead! You drive down Broadway — it's like a string of graveyards. There are cars, cabs, motorcars — not a soul in them. Little piles of dust on the sidewalk — piles in the shops — piles in the cars. But not a sound! Not a fly alive!'" As with Du Bois's story, the actual destruction of the city is largely passed over, a mere vehicle for the author to get to his main point: imagining how a new society would be built.[9]

While Du Bois sees black Jim and white Julia quickly freed from the supposedly unbreakable bonds of racism, Sinclair offers a madcap morality tale about how capitalist corruption reasserts itself in the smallest of communities and in the most bizarre of circumstances. The eleven survivors regroup and attempt to set up a small community in the abandoned Consolidated Hotel. A succession of power struggles ensues among these previously pampered individuals who now must eke out a subsistence living. While cans of food remain in the stores of the annihilated city, the elite survivors find them inedible and crave the food pills that had been developed for the august Lumley-Gotham. The struggle over this commodity, and the means of its production, sends this society rushing through the Marxian stages of history, from a state of nature, to slavery, feudalism, and onward to capitalism. The former butler, Tuttle, ultimately emerges on top but turns out to be the most violent and oppressive dictator of all. Throughout, Sinclair derisively portrays the one-man church in this new society, in the form of the Lord Bishop of Harlem, and the one-man state (Granville) as lapdogs to whatever leader is in charge.

But one subset of the group escapes this maddening cycle. Billy Kingdom, the young pilot who has flown the survivors to safety at the start of the story, and his paramour, the daughter of Lumley-Gotham, decide to flee to the country to found a new civilization. As in *Caesar's Column* and *Darkness and Dawn* before it, and *The Rest Must Die* in the 1950s, the new utopia is built not within the remains of old New York but in a new place—in this case a Hudson River estate dating back to the Dutch settlers. In Sinclair's novel, Billy and Helen flee, but not far: to the grand Dutch estate of the Lumley-Gothams in the Pocantico Hills of New York, across the Hudson. Somehow, it seems that the lands of the oldest Gotham money—the original estates of the Dutch landed gentry from the seventeenth century—are free from the class divisions of Manhattan in the twentieth century. Amid the splendor of these estates a new socialist community is created. As the coup de grâce of the old regime, the great Mrs. Lumley-Gotham declares near the end that she is a changed woman: "'I,' said the great lady, proudly, 'am an organizer of the I.W.W.'"[10]

As in "The Comet," only the destruction of New York's people—its social and political structures—can lead to a new form of society. Du Bois's story ends much more unhappily, with the world of yesterday immediately returning, with renewed venom, while Sinclair and other socialist writers (such as George Allan England), leave the reader with a vision of a hopeful future. But both seem to suggest that leaving the city is the only answer. So out of the destruction of New York comes a better society, at the cost of abandoning the city.

The End of the Dream

Du Bois and Sinclair sustained a long-standing critique of New York that held that the city's internal contradictions—vicious racism in a polyglot city, great wealth and great poverty, and a near standstill brought on by sheer human congestion—would bring it down. The dark tension in the air—between celebrating the city's rapid growth in the building of the great skyscraper metropolis, and fearing what the development would lead to—pervaded American culture.

These critiques were echoed by visitors from abroad, who found their animus toward the West confirmed and fueled by New York. The city, in their eyes, was filled with rootless cosmopolitans, lustful and obsessed with material possessions, vicious, and at base, inhuman. Sayyid Qutb, one of the key thinkers of modern Islamic fundamentalism, lived in New York between 1948 and 1950, before returning home disgusted by the city and its nation. Qutb wrote, "If all the world became American it would undoubtedly be the disaster of humanity."

Qutb was repelled less by the city's "decadence," by the Kinsey Report, by dancing and sexual promiscuity, than by the "crass materialism that smothered charity." Most of all, just as the Spanish poet Federico García Lorca had been twenty years earlier, Qutb was disgusted by the "evil and fanatic racial discrimination." For these critics, the city's end would represent the victory over American and even Western values. Numerous young intellectuals have visited New York and returned home to become revolutionaries, writing apocalyptic visions of New York's downfall as the stand-in for the downfall of modern capitalist values.[11]

These visions seemed to come true on October 29, 1929. García Lorca walked Wall Street on Black Tuesday in 1929 and imagined the destruction of Manhattan by "hurricanes of gold" and "tumults of windows." In his memoir of his time in New York, *Poet in New York* (1932), García Lorca noted that the "terrible, cold, cruel part is Wall Street. Rivers of gold flow there from all over the earth, and death comes with it. There, as nowhere else, you feel a total absence of the spirit: herds of men who cannot count past three."[12] New York, he said in an interview the year before, "is something awful, something monstrous. I like to walk the streets, lost, but I recognize that New York is the world's greatest lie. New York is Senegal with machines."[13] The painter José Clemente Orozco spent eight years in New York City and was taken less by the soaring skyscrapers than by the sight of "hard, desperate, angry men, with opaque eyes and clenched fists."[14] His painting *Los Muertos* (1931) is a dizzying image of skyscrapers bending and falling and cracking like breadsticks. It seems almost an illustration of what Jimmie Herf, in John Dos Passos's novel *Manhattan Transfer,* might be thinking when he imagines "a grooved building jutting up with uncountable bright windows falling onto him out of a scudding sky."[15]

This became a creative motif of the stock market crash—falling skyscrapers as metaphor for falling stocks. The relatively unknown paintings of James Rosenberg capture this same sense of desperation and fury. A bankruptcy lawyer in New York, Rosenberg was especially attuned to the trauma of the stock market crash. Though he had made his first images on paper in 1919, watching the World War I victory parade pass his office on Fifth Avenue, he found his true source of inspiration on one of the most disastrous days in American history. On October 29 and in the months after, Rosenberg etched a half-dozen lithographs depicting the "debacle which led to depression and World War II."[16]

Rosenberg had a varied career in public and private life. He negotiated the reorganization of the Maxwell Motor Company into the Chrysler Corporation, and he consulted on the International Match Corporation case, one of the largest bankruptcies in American history at the time. During the 1930s he be-

James N. Rosenberg,
Oct 29 Dies Irae, 1929

came increasingly involved in Jewish affairs and in fighting anti-Semitism at home and abroad. He wrote a book, *We Jews and Antisemitism,* and advocated for an official statement on genocide from the United Nations.

But he was also a painter. Beginning in 1919 he began a half-century of painting as well as art collecting. Though not widely known, his work is owned by many of the major art institutes, including the Art Institute of Chicago, the Metropolitan Museum of Art, the Philadelphia Museum of Art, and the New York Public Library.[17] He painted a series of images of war. But his best-known images are those capturing the horror of the great stock market crash.

Following George Bellows's images of the city's upheaval, Rosenberg suggests the collapse not only of the stock exchange but of the entire city. Most of the images share similar elements.[18] Ghost-like figures, squashed together, make up the bottom of the lithographs. They scream and cry, battling each other in the canyons beneath the skyscrapers.[19] What were often treated—by Joseph Pennell, for example—as the solid, heroic buildings of the great metropolis, are here teetering, dangerous objects, made completely unstable. A cluster of church spires is featured in each piece—these too are ready to topple. Black crows—or vultures—fly overhead. Ironic messages—often the titles of the works—are written into the images: *Mad House, November 13, 1929, The Shambles Nov 1929,* and *The Call for Margins.*

So began the 1930s.

Beasts and Bad Weather: Hope and Despair in the Great Depression

In 1935 the Russian émigré Louis Lozowick painted the glorious skyline of New York, heroic as ever amid the Depression. The tilting, crashing skyscrapers of James Rosenberg were gone. To this World War I soldier who had settled in New York in 1924, New York's skyscrapers remained objects of reverence. In *Storm Clouds Above Manhattan,* the sun's rays push through the clouds, creating a halo above lower Manhattan. It is a Renaissance image, the sun's beams shining on the modern Madonna, the Manhattan skyline. And yet, there is in Lozowick's painting a tense ambiguity: the sun's rays may be bursting through the clouds, dispersing the gray to create a blue sky, or they may be the last desperate attempts of the sun to give light before being blocked by gathering clouds. In the midst of the heavenly sunshine we feel a sense of brooding gloom. A decade later, after Hiroshima and Nagasaki, it would have been hard not to imagine that Lozowick had anticipated the cloudburst of an atomic weapon above the city. He caught a tension at the heart of the 1930s, between the despair of economic deprivation and oncoming war and the hopefulness offered by the New Deal and the progressive visions of American artists and writers. Some have seen in novels and films of the 1930s a continued optimism, a celebration in fantastical images of the city that would continue the progressive vision of Futurism and Modernism.[20] But fantasies of New York's end played out equally on a far darker narrative.

The rumblings of the 1930s brought the first and greatest of monster invaders, King Kong. But in the same year, 1933, the ultimate savior of the city, Superman, was invented.[21] Growing audiences for film in the decade saw both *Deluge* and *S.O.S. Tidal Wave,* which featured New York as susceptible to natural disaster as at any time, with the consequences much more dramatic and horrific in a city of skyscrapers. The end of the decade brought Stephen Vincent Benét's

James N. Rosenberg, *The Call for Margins,* 1929. Lithograph printed in black on buff wove paper, sheet: 15 3/4 × 11 1/8 in.; 40 × 28.3 cm; image: 13 1/8 × 10 3/8 in.; 33.3 × 26.3 cm. Smith College Museum of Art, Northampton, Massachusetts. Gift of James N. Rosenberg, permission granted by Anne Geismar. SC 1951: 182

Louis Lozowick, *Storm Clouds Above Manhattan*, 1935

musings on the city destroyed by a dramatic new weapon and left as a ruin, as well as the most famous fictional attack of all on the city, Orson Welles's *War of the Worlds.* The hopefulness of the early part of the decade—that the country would emerge from the Depression quickly and that the country would stay out of battles on distant continents—was soon shattered.

The Empire State Building was that classic New York invention: an impossible dream achieved in record time. With hundreds of workers on round-the-clock shifts, welding together steel that seemed still warm from the furnaces in Pittsburgh, the tower went up floor by floor, more than one every week. A speculative venture that wouldn't become profitable until almost twenty years after its completion, the Empire State Building nonetheless soothed the despair of the Great Depression, becoming the permanent symbol of the city. As E. B. White wrote, it "managed to reach the highest point in the sky at the lowest moment of the Depression. The Empire State Building shot 1250 feet into the air when it was madness to put out as much as six inches of new growth."[22] That view was like a magic potion: once you took it in, you could never be the same. Some were inspired to greatness while others were driven to destruction by the view from the top of the skyscraper. The Swiss architect Le Corbusier came to New York for the first time in 1935 expressly to look down from the Empire State Building. What he saw made the city look like a set of toy blocks and crystallized his vision for violently remaking cities.

Like nearly every other New Yorker (more than one million people looked out from the observatory in the first year of the building's existence), F. Scott Fitzgerald was lured to the top, for a literal uplift during the depth of the Depression—and ruined by the experience. "Full of vaunting pride," he wrote in his 1932 essay "My Lost City," "the New Yorker had climbed here and seen with dismay what he had never suspected, that the city was not the endless succession of canyons that he had supposed but that it had limits. . . . And with the awful realization that New York was a city after all and not a universe, the whole shining edifice that he had reared in his imagination came crashing to the ground."[23]

In April 1931, a month before it opened, the skyscraper inspired its first depressed New Yorker to jump to his death. Within the year, it also had inspired fantasies of the building's own end. "Somehow we know by instinct that outsize buildings cast the shadow of their own destruction before them," wrote W. G. Sebald just before 9/11, "and are designed from the first with an eye to their later existence as ruins." Those who attempted suicide understood. The magnet of death and the thrill of desire have been partners in the life of the Empire State Building since the moment it was created.

Americans like to focus on the Empire State Building as a hopeful symbol amid the decade's despair. But American culture wasted no time in taking aim at this beloved target.

The Empire State Building opened on May 1, 1931. Less than two years later it was threatened by a climbing ape from the South Pacific. *King Kong* tells the story of a massive primate brought to New York to serve as the latest money-making freak show, a tradition dating back at least to P. T. Barnum. Kong, who had ruled atop the highest peak on Skull Island, bursts out of a Broadway theater and crashes through the city, upending an elevated train on the way to his destination: the tallest structure on Manhattan Island. Kong's legendary climb to the top of the Empire State Building is an unintended consequence of Manhattan's 1916 zoning law: because of the required setbacks on skyscrapers as they rose from the street, the skyline had come to appear vaguely mountain-like, with jagged peaks visually analogous—at least in the ape's eyes—to his mountaintop roost.

The film, like many later "monster movies," suggests the dangers of toying with nature. In *King Kong,* the greed of New York entrepreneurs leads to a

Still from *King Kong*, 1933

King Kong falls to his death from the Empire State Building in *King Kong*, 1933

disaster when the monster is literally "misplaced"—taken out of his place and brought to New York. That greed leads to the tragedy of the ending, where Kong is killed as he swats at airplanes from the top of the Empire State Building. He falls to his death on 34th Street, a destructive creature misunderstood and mistreated. The city—or, more precisely, the craving of some New Yorkers for the almighty dollar, wherever it can be made—is responsible for the death of the great ape.

But this tragic film is also a powerful celebration of the city. The Empire State Building in *King Kong* is, by its analogy to a mountain peak in the eyes of Kong, raised to the level of a natural wonder—it is our mountaintop. King Kong, a frightening and destructive attacker who defeated all challengers on Skull Island, is brought down by human technology, the airplane and its guns. He cannot conquer the tallest peak here.[24]

If *King Kong* represented the persistence of hope in the face of disaster—the city in the end defeats the invader, even though the ape never wished to destroy the city—*Deluge,* a film from the same year, revels in the city's complete destruction, then leaves it behind. Subtitled *A Romance,* the British writer S. Fowler Wright's 1928 novel uses a worldwide disaster to set up a story of a love triangle in a postapocalyptic world.

The novel, set outside London, only alludes to the death and destruction wrought by worldwide earthquakes and tidal waves. But the American film version, written by John Goodrich and Warren B. Duff and directed by Felix E. Feist, transfers the story to the United States and opens with a tense sequence culminating in several minutes showing the total wreckage of New York City. It is the first great filmic interpretation of New York's end.[25]

Special effects—a relatively new term—were created with miniature sets by Ned Mann, Billy Williams, and Russell E. Lawson. So tirelessly created (and expensive, consuming much of the film's $171,000 budget), and so effective, the effects of *Deluge* were used repeatedly in future years as stock footage for other disaster films, such as *S.O.S. Tidal Wave* (1939) and the *King of the Rocketmen* serial in 1949. A miniature New York was constructed at the Tiffany Studios, with skyscrapers built up to six feet high around a twelve-foot Empire State Building.[26]

The film opens with the wide-eyed scientists noting the drop in barometric pressure, followed by frantic telephone conversations between scientists on opposite coasts, and, as in "The Comet," a crush of people around a newsboy, who hawks a *New York Journal* extra declaring "Earth Doomed." Reports of disasters all over the world filter in. New York, of course, is last to go. But when

Building the set for *Deluge*, 1933. The newspapers announce the end. The waters rise . . . and the city falls

it does, it is spectacular: the Statue of Liberty is swallowed by waves; a skyline full of skyscrapers topples; ocean liners are heaved into the avenues; the Times Square subway station is leveled; and, at the end of the ten-minute sequence, the just-completed Empire State Building, viewed from its base, simply crumbles. What King Kong couldn't do, nature does in seconds with the ripples of earth-quakes and floods. The end result is complete devastation of the city: every single building cracks, crumples, and falls to the ground.

The destruction of New York is extraneous to the main plot. The hero, Martin Webster, listens to the radio with his wife, Helen, and their two small chil-dren, in a suburb of New York, and then awaits the disaster. During the course of what appears to be nothing more than a strong storm, Martin is separated from his family and finds himself alone on a newly created island. Claire Arlington, a star swimmer who had been planning a swim around Manhattan Island when the disaster hit, ends up on a nearby island, only to find herself set upon by two men who battle over whom she belongs to. Claire escapes the way she knows best, by swimming away. She ends up on Martin's island. Both alone—he presumes his wife and children to be dead—they soon fall in love. Some (including a *New*

York Times reviewer of the book in 1928) might suspect that, as in other utopian novels we have discussed, the death of New York would ultimately herald a better world. But the bulk of the novel is focused on the savagery unleashed by the death of civilization, symbolized by those collapsing skyscrapers. Desperate men nearby discover Claire and Martin and threaten to take Claire as their concubine. At the last instant before being caught, they are rescued by settlers in a nearby town that has survived and is trying to re-create civilization. Claire and Martin are brought back to the town, only to find that Martin's wife and children are alive.

Ultimately, Claire herself makes the decision of who will have Martin. She rushes back to the shore and swims off across the water, probably to oblivion, with Martin watching. Only now, at the very end, is it suggested that perhaps under Martin's leadership (free of his unintentionally adulterous affair), civilization might be rebuilt, even improved. By the end of the film, we have moved far beyond the terror of the city's destruction. But so worried were the filmmakers about the effect of those first ten minutes that the film opened with the kind of disclaimer that Orson Welles would use a few years later: the story, it insisted, came from the "author's imagination," suggesting that it was not based on real science. And the filmmakers also offered a different kind of solace. Quoting the Bible, the film reminds viewers that after the Great Flood, God promised Noah that never again would he destroy the world by water.[27]

Burning City: The Apocalyptic Poetry and Prose of Stephen Vincent Benét

Stephen Vincent Benét is no longer required reading in high school English classes, but he was once one of the most widely read American poets and fiction writers. Celebrated for his historical works *John Brown's Body* (1928) and "The Devil and Daniel Webster" (1936), Benét for a brief moment spoke to a particular mood in American life: a celebration of America's colonial beginnings, a patriotism leavened with warnings, and use of clear, easily accessible language.

Never a favorite of literary critics, especially among the New Critics of the mid-twentieth century, Benét has largely slipped from popular view, although his epic poem *John Brown's Body* has remained in print most of the eighty years since its initial publication. Benét has been called the author of "passable verse journalism," but little more.[28]

He wrote for a broad audience and on popular themes in part for purely financial reasons—he simply did not believe he would be able to support his family by pursuing writing of a purely literary bent. By all accounts he was dedicated to his wife and three children, so this seems more than a rationalization. But more important, the rise of totalitarianism and fascism called him to action. With little apology, he embraced his role as a storyteller for American democracy and for Franklin Roosevelt's New Deal. He saw his writing as a small contribution to the war effort. He wrote radio scripts with overtly patriotic stories—such as "They Burned the Books" and a series entitled *Dear Adolf*—as well as essays and poems. "If what I am writing today . . . will hurt my eventual reputation as a writer," he wrote, "very well, then let it. I can't just sit on my integrity as a writer, like a hen on a china egg, for the duration." The artist, he insisted, must "state his belief. . . . For neither his freedom of speech nor his liberty of action will automatically preserve themselves. They are part of civilization and they will fail if it fails. And he has a responsibility to his own art and that is to make it great. I doubt he can do that by blacking himself out."[29] That Benét wrote overtly patriotic literature in the 1930s—many would call it propaganda—is one reason he was later disdained. He died at age forty-four on March 13, 1943, before he could the see the Allied victory in World War II, and before he could return to writing poetry.

In the year Benét published "The Devil and Daniel Webster," a tribute to American democracy set as the story of a Faustian bargain, he published a volume with a very different tone. *Burning City* is a compilation of poems previously printed in such magazines as *Atlantic Monthly,* the *New Yorker,* and the *New Republic,* warning of the impending storm of war and fascism, and what it might mean for American life. The book's cover features the New York skyline encircled by flames; other black-and-white woodcuts in the book suggest the city ruined. New York, destroyed in a variety of ways—termites, rogue machines, sterility brought on by war, climate change, destructive materialism—is the vehicle by which Benét warns of what the future might bring. He suggests that American life—the glorious traditions and heroes, the brotherly battles exemplified in *John Brown's Body* and "The Devil and Daniel Webster"—might be ruined by the ideologies and the machinery of death battling in Europe, as well as by weaknesses at home.

In "Notes to Be Left in a Cornerstone" Benét offers a letter to future generations who might "gaze upon our ruins with strange eyes." An ode to New York, the poem takes the form of a conversation between a former inhabitant of the city and a living person far in the future. "I have gone to the museum and seen the pictures," says the living speaker. But the dead one responds that one cannot know the city that was from its pictures:

But the maps and the models will not be the same.
They cannot restore that beauty, rapid and harsh,
That loneliness, that passion or that name.

. . . .

But the skin is not the life but over the life.

. . . .

It is long ago this all was. It is all forgotten.[30]

This theme—of the city, its people, and its entire physical landscape lost to the future but for some images and artifacts—surfaces again and again in Benét's work. "Notes to Be Left in a Cornerstone" offers no clue as to the means of the destruction of the city, or how long it took. The final section of *Burning City* is much more direct and fantastical, imagining three specific "nightmares" of New York. In "Metropolitan Nightmare" the city has become mysteriously warmer and more humid, bringing the beginnings of a rainforest landscape. The city slows down in the heat ("Even the Communists didn't protest"). Greenery starts to grow from cracks, making its way up the Brooklyn Bridge, out of buildings. No one appears to notice, as the entire city seems self-satisfied in its prosperity:

There wasn't any real change, it was just a heat spell,
A rain spell, a funny summer, a weather-man's joke.

But the true "nightmare" comes when a young reporter is sent to explore why there seem to be so many termites in the city. At the Planetopolis Building (shades of Metropolis and the *Daily Planet* building of *Superman,* which would appear in just a few years), the reporter sees a "dark line creeping across the rubble"—the busy termites. But it is not wood they are eating. These evolved termites have developed a taste for a more substantial diet: "He pried from the insect jaws the bright crumb of steel. . . . It will be the smallest insect that will bring down the city, which at the moment is sauntering along, laughing at its tropical weather fluke. The smallest creature has quietly invaded and will bring down the greatest of cities."[31]

In "Nightmare Angel," the narrator is greeted at night by an angel who speaks "in a professorial-historical-economic and irritated / voice" about the decline of past civilizations, and the potential decline of this one. At the end of the poem a new angel approaches with a gas mask around its face and declares:

"You will not be saved by General Motors or the pre-fabricated house.
You will not be saved by dialectic materialism or the Lambeth Conference.
You will not be saved by Vitamin D or the expanding universe.
In fact, you will not be saved."[32]

ONE   THREE

Charles Child, illustrations for Stephen Vincent Benét, *Burning City*, 1936

"Nightmare Number Three" is perhaps the most gruesome of the visions, as the narrator reflects on how the machines that made American life so prosperous and comfortable rose up to destroy the very civilization that created them, with "the Madison Avenue busses leading the charge" and the Duesenberg that "pinned three brokers to the Racquet Club steps." Benét is less concerned with the process of destruction—we learn about the termites only in "Metropolitan Nightmare," and the inevitable cannibalism of the machines appears in the last lines of "Nightmare Number Three"—than with what would be lost, and the blindness of the inhabitants to their own complicity.[33]

While Benét surely wrote propaganda, his New York disaster literature had a jeremiad quality, highlighting the failings of society, and calling it back to its original values in order to fight against the true evil abroad. *Burning City* ends with a poem, "1936," that is an overt warning of the impending war in Europe. Ghosts, whom the narrator assumes are the dead soldiers of the First World War, march through battlefields and burrow in the trenches "as they had of old." When the narrator yells, "Must you march forever from France and the last, blind war?" they respond: "Fool! From the next!"[34]

The results of that inevitable "next" war seemed already to be on Benét's mind as he wrote *Burning City*. The next year he published what would become one of his best-known short stories, "By the Waters of Babylon," which seemed clairvoyant about the destructiveness of weapons of the future.

"By the Waters of Babylon" is a classic story of a young man drawn to the big city by its mysteries and possibilities. But it is set in a postapocalyptic future, after the city has been destroyed and the few refugees from the disaster have fled to live a savage existence in the Catskills. The story takes place several generations later, and the city has become a place of legend, the "Dead Place" and the "Place of the Gods." Among the tribe, it is forbidden to go east to the Place of the Gods since the "Great Burning," when the "fire fell out of the sky."[35]

The young man, though, like so many others from beyond New York, is drawn to the city. "If I went to the Place of the Gods, I would surely die, but if I did not go, I could never be at peace with my spirit again. . . . My hunger for knowledge burned in me." He is not disappointed. The island is beautiful: "No wonder the gods built there. If I had come there, I also would have built." As he ventures through the city, he uncovers the remains of buildings, and names on pediments partially broken off: "ubtreas" is the first one, with a statue titled "ASHING," whom the young man assumes must be one of the gods. This is of course the statue of Washington in front of the Subtreasury building on Wall Street. He eventually heads north, along the "god-road," better known as Fifth Avenue, and into the Metropolitan Museum of Art. In the middle of the night he awakens to see that the lights of the city have miraculously turned on: "Everywhere there were lights—lines of light—circles and blurs of light—ten thousand torches would not have been the same. . . . They had turned night to day for their pleasure—they did not sleep with the sun."[36]

He imagines the fate of the inhabitants during the Great Burning: "It was fire falling out of the sky and a mist that poisoned. It was the time of the great Burning and the Destruction. They ran about like ants in the streets of their city— poor gods, poor gods! Then the towers began to fall. A few escaped—yes, a few." But the land remains poisoned, as if, in later parlance, it were radioactive. What he recognizes through this vision, and as he walks through the city, is that the inhabitants had been "neither gods nor demons," but men. "It is a great knowledge, hard to tell and believe." While he falls in love with the place, he also recognizes why his forefathers had proscribed the Dead Place. It was better, he agrees, that truth should come little by little. Perhaps, he muses, "in the old days they ate knowledge too fast." He will reveal the truth about the place slowly, and only slowly re-inhabit the place. "It is not for the metal alone we go to the Dead

Place now—there are the books and the writings." In a hopeful end, the young man insists that "we shall go the place of the Gods—the place newyork—not one man but a company. We shall look for the images of the gods and find the god ASHING and the others—the gods Licoln and Biltmore and Moses. But they were men who built the city, not gods or demons. They were men. I remember the dead man's face. They were men who were here before us. We must build again."[37]

Benét has often been classified as a science fiction writer. But like the work of Du Bois, Benét's poems and "By the Waters of Babylon" are not first and foremost fantastical tales but moral lessons taught through apocalyptic imagery.

The New York "nightmares" of Stephen Vincent Benét in *Burning City* were conjured to give a sense of the possibilities of disaster facing the United States. Just a year later—or about the time "By the Waters of Bablyon" was published—news from Europe brought even more evidence that would lead artists and writers, as well as politicians, to imagine an invasion of the United States. The bombings by the Germans and Italians of Spanish cities in September 1937 were stunning evidence of the brutality and efficacy of warfare in the air, as H. G. Wells had warned decades before.

Benét and so many other artists of the time, including O. Louis Guglielmi, were powerfully affected by the air raids and civilian casualties inflicted on the Spanish population during the country's Civil War. The war was one of the main reasons Benét felt it necessary to begin writing as a defender of democracy. It also inspired Guglielmi to produce two images of what would later be called "social surrealism" to raise awareness of the international threat of fascism.

In November 1938, just after the German annexation of Austria, in the very month of Kristallnacht, and, incidentally, immediately after Orson Welles's *War of the Worlds* broadcast, Guglielmi first exhibited *Mental Geography,* a warning about the threat of fascism. The painting shows, in realistic detail, the Brooklyn Bridge after a bomb attack. The two towers have begun to crumple; the web of cables is unraveling; the roadbed in the foreground has collapsed. A woman sits astride a beam, with a missile in her back, watching the bridge falter. A suit of armor—a common symbol of fascism among artists in the 1930s—falls toward the river, entangled in the cables. But on the remaining part of the bridge, between the two tumbling towers, a harpist continues to strum, perhaps trying to evoke the long history of literary celebrations, including that of Hart Crane, who had used the imagery of the harp to evoke the Brooklyn Bridge's glory.[38]

Guglielmi, like many of the Social Surrealists openly political, was explicit about his goals for this image: "Headlines, eloquent loudspeakers of fascist destruction scream out of the bombing of another city, another moment of human achievement, a debris of mutilation. A hundred dead, a thousand violated bodies. Valencia, Madrid, Barcelona, Guernica. Yesterday Toledo, the Prado—Tomorrow, Chartres—New York—Brooklyn Bridge is by the process of mental geography a huge mass of stone, twisted girders and limp cables."[39] He later expanded on his interpretation of his own painting in order to emphasize the warning: "In *Mental Geography,* painted during the Spanish Civil War, I pictured the destruction after an air raid; the towers bomb-pocked, the cables a mass of twisted debris. I meant to say that an era had ended and that the rivers of Spain flowed to the Atlantic and mixed with our waters as well."[40]

Mental Geography, though painted by an artist aligned against fascism as well as against capitalism and militarism of all sorts, is linked to the military preparedness writers and artists of the World War I era. The warning inevitably was also a call to arms on the part of the United States, which remained neutral even as Guglielmi painted.[41]

The painting achieves its effect in large measure because of the detailed portrait of one of the most famous of American landmarks after an attack. We see the exterior masonry, the interior bricks, and the steel skeleton of the bridge— the clothing of this great landmark has been ripped. Previous writers and artists called on the same disaster scene. Compared with the kind of human destruction that would take place by air attacks in future years, the surrealist fantasy of *Mental Geography* is almost quaint. The rest of the city appears in fine shape; the sun is shining; nothing else is amiss. Damage to the bridge looks more like an urban renewal project than an effect of war. Guglielmi also seems to be suggesting, with his harpist and the mother and child amiably standing on the bridge, that America continues to be ludicrously satisfied with its relative safety and security. Stephen Vincent Benét had suggested something similar in his wake-up "nightmares": America has not recognized the disaster in Europe and the threat to itself.[42]

New York and Orson Welles's *War of the Worlds*

A year after Stephen Vincent Benét's "By the Waters of Babylon" was first published, and just days before Louis Guglielmi's *Mental Geography* was first exhibited, came a Halloween prank that got a little out of control.

Adapting H. G. Wells's *War of the Worlds,* Orson Welles and the writer Howard Koch produced a version of the story in which the Martians chose to

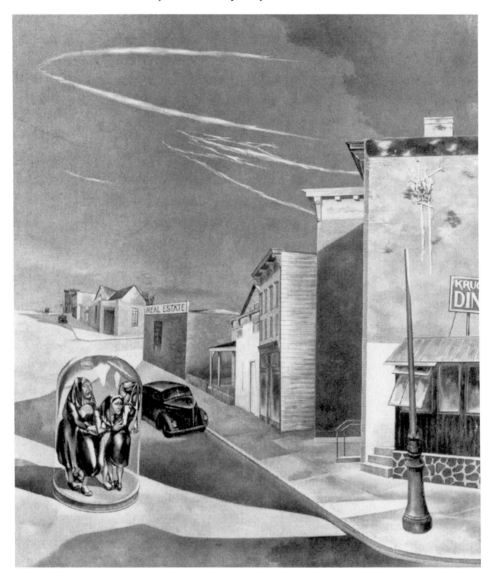

O. Louis Guglielmi, *Terror in Brooklyn*, 1941. Oil on canvas mounted on composition board, framed: 39 1/2 × 35 3/4 × 1 1/4 in. (100.3 × 90.8 × 3.2 cm). Whitney Museum of American Art, New York; purchase 42.5. Photograph © 1996, Whitney Museum of American Art, New York. Photography by Sheldan C. Collins, N.Y.

begin their assault on Earth in North America. Aware of his competition in the Sunday evening time slot—the enormously popular *Chase and Sanborn Hour,* featuring Edgar Bergen's dummy Charlie McCarthy—Welles and his Mercury Theatre staff looked to do something novel to draw away as many listeners as possible. The fiction of Charlie McCarthy's humanity was transparent; everyone

Orson Welles rehearsing the radio broadcast of *War of the Worlds*, 1938

knew that he was a dummy voiced by Bergen. In contrast the "news" reports on Welles's *War of the Worlds* were meant to sound genuine. Welles had decided to "electrify fiction," as one critic wrote in the heady days after the panic.[43]

The first Martian in the Welles production lands in Grovers Mill, New Jersey, a real place randomly chosen by Koch. But it quickly becomes clear, as the Martians emerge from their "cylinders," that their real object is, as we might expect, New York City. Just as the original *War of the Worlds* culminated in the destruction of London, Welles's *War* is a New York disaster play. The script describes a total invasion—the "Martian cylinders" have been reported falling outside Buffalo, Chicago, and St. Louis. A U.S. Army commander declares early on that the "evident objective is New York City." And sure enough, the Martians assemble across the Hudson River on the New Jersey Palisades and pound through the water, as the radio reporters watch from the roof of New York's soon-to-be-toppled skyscrapers.[44]

Down below there is chaos on the streets—the secondary disaster that always follows in New York destruction fantasies. "The streets are all jammed," the radio reporter tells his listeners. "Noise in crowds like New Year's Eve in city."

> Now the first machine reaches the shore. He stands watching, looking over the city. His steel, cowlish head is even with the skyscrapers. He waits for the others. They rise like a line of new towers on the city's west side. . . . This is the end now. . . . Black smoke, drifting over the city. People in the streets see it now. They're running towards the East River . . . thousands of them, dropping in like rats. Now the smoke's spreading fast. It's reached Times Square. People trying to run away from it, but it's no use. They're falling like flies.

And then, to heighten the sense of realism, the dispatch from the roof of the Broadcasting Building stops midsentence as the Martians' lethal smoke arrives. Welles masterfully used Americans' growing reliance on and trust in the radio to heighten the drama, and the fear. It is obviously difficult to portray the end of the world on radio. But to give a sense of the snuffing out of New York, Welles in an instant severs that invisible thread keeping people tied together.[45]

The sound of news reports of the Martians—a sign that civilization remains, proof of the invisible network that Americans were increasingly confident of, despite depression and oncoming war—was snipped in a moment. It is hard for us to imagine today, with multiple instant means of communication, the power of severing a radio broadcast. The end of the "news" report represented the end of the city and the world. As the reporter declares: "We will continue broadcasting until the end." All across the country, on CBS's nationwide network of stations, people heard the play and believed that the destruction of New York was under way, and that was just the beginning. As one women in Indianapolis succinctly put it: "New York destroyed; it's the end of the world. You might as well go home to die. I just heard it on the radio."[46]

The final minutes of the broadcast featured the account of one of the few survivors, a Professor Pierson from Princeton who describes New York after the apocalypse—it is a city that has lost its skyline. "Next day I came to a city vaguely familiar in its contours, yet its building strangely dwarfed and leveled off, as if a giant had sliced off it highest towers with a capricious sweep of his hand." He makes his way, for the sake of impact of those near and far, who would have known the landmarks, through an empty Times Square, "past silent shop windows, displaying their mute wares to empty sidewalks . . . past a shooting gallery, where a row of empty guns faced an arrested line of wooden ducks, and

into Central Park." H. G. Wells's creatures succumb to the tiniest of living creatures—bacteria—on the top of Primrose Hill, overlooking the city. Welles's Martians meet their end in Central Park, on Frederick Law Olmsted's parade mall
leading to Bethesda Fountain.[47]

But the hopeful ending of the story was lost on many listeners. The panic
that Welles described in his fictional account was soon reality on the streets of
New York and cities across the country. People rushed to train stations, took to
their cars, and flocked to churches. Hospitals saw a surge in people arriving for
treatment of shock and hysteria. Welles certainly did not intend to promote the
panic that would lead to thousands fleeing their homes, and to a country bewil-
dered by its own ability to turn fiction into fact. Nor could he even have imagined
such a result. But he did intend to frighten. As Welles himself said at the end of
the program:

> This is Orson Welles, ladies and gentlemen, out of character to assure you that
> the *War of the Worlds* has no further significance than as the holiday offering it
> was intended to be. The Mercury Theatre's own radio version of dressing up in
> a sheet and jumping out of a bush and saying Boo! Starting now, we couldn't
> soap all your windows and steal all your garden gates, by tomorrow night . . .
> so we did the next best thing. We annihilated the world before your very ears,
> and utterly destroyed the Columbia Broadcasting System. . . . That grinning,
> glowing globular invader of your living-room is an inhabitant of the pumpkin
> patch, and if your doorbell rings and nobody's there, that was no Martian . . .
> it's Hallowe'en.[48]

But it was already too late. In the aftermath, there were calls for Welles to
be fired, for new regulations to be put in place by the Federal Communications
Commission to prevent a future panic. Educators weighed in and wondered
whether their negligence had contributed to the "panic pulse of the world's
people today."[49]

And, of course, many cashed in. Within days, Universal Studios announced the immediate release of *Mars Attacks the World,* unapologetically trying to capitalize on the furor and publicity surrounding the Welles radio show.
Although Welles, fearing lawsuits, solemnly declared that night that "I don't
think we will choose anything like this again," he quickly recognized that all
publicity is good publicity. He fanned the flames of interest in the story. In the
coming years, it would be replayed and turned into a play, a comic book, a 1953
movie, and a 2005 film by Steven Spielberg.[50]

Orson Welles's adaptation of the H. G. Wells story is, of course, not nearly

Cover of *War of the Worlds* record, Longines Symphonette Society SY-5251

as important as the reaction of the audience. The most thorough study of the panic remains one published in 1940 by Hadley Cantril of Princeton University. It is as revealing about the attitudes and fears of the late 1930s and the 1940s as it is about the nature of the panic. Cantril is not content to follow the received wisdom that the poor and uneducated were, as always, susceptible to influence, especially via new forms of mass communication and new, invidious forms of brainwashing. It was true that the bulk of those who believed the broadcast were less educated than those who understood it to be fiction. And it was true that radio had created a mass audience that trusted its news reports far more than those of newspapers to be unbiased.[51]

Cantril, however, points to the "social setting" of 1938 that made Americans not just susceptible to believing the report but prone to reacting hysterically. The effects of a nearly decadelong depression, with its consequent social instability, and the fear of war had conspired to make people ready not only to believe that a catastrophe was coming but almost to welcome it and surrender to the hysteria it engendered. "The thrill of disaster," Cantril writes, is a "temporary change or escape from . . . troubles. . . . Because of intense worries or anxieties he has, he may consciously or unconsciously welcome the cataclysm." One interviewee put it quite bluntly: "I was looking forward with some pleasure to the destruction of the entire human race." This view was more common than we might expect. Many "had a feeling that we were already ghosts granted temporary visas for an earthly stay," wrote Alice V. Keliher, a leader of the Progressive Education Association, soon after the show.[52]

Fear was everywhere. As Heywood Broun wrote in a November 2, 1938, article in the *New York World-Telegram* which Cantril quotes, "I doubt if anything of the sort would have happened four or five months ago. The course of world history has affected national psychology. Jitters have come to roost. We have just gone through a laboratory demonstration of the fact that the peace of Munich hangs heavy over our heads, like a thundercloud."[53] Louis Lozowick's 1935 *Storm Cloud Above Manhattan* now had its moral.

Americans needed better education and greater "critical ability" in the face of radio's power to influence. But, Cantril insisted in the end, they also needed "greater educational opportunities and greater economic security which would promote emotional insecurity." Americans must, he declared, "be less harassed by the emotional insecurities which stem from underprivileged environments." While some took the panic of *War of the Worlds* as evidence of the need for greater preparedness, as in the disaster scenarios of World War I, others, like Cantril, saw in the panic a call for greater social spending. *War of the Worlds* was proof of the need for the New Deal, which was faltering by the late 1930s.[54]

What Cantril missed is that, for New Yorkers and Americans reared on several decades of repeated New York disasters, real and imaginary, and legitimately anxious about an attack by Hitler, an invasion of New York was not far beyond the realm of possibility. Indeed, a number of the people Cantril interviewed assumed that the reporters had mistaken Martians for Hitler's army. But they believed the gist of the "news" they were hearing. "Don't you know New Jersey is destroyed by the Germans," reported Sylvia Homes of Newark afterward. "It's on the radio." Samuel Tishman of Manhattan ran into the street to join hundreds of others who were convinced that the "city was being bombed."[55]

The mention of recognizable place names contributed to the realism of the radio play and thus helped to account for the panic, among both New Yorkers and people far from the city. CBS censors made some changes to lessen the reality—the "Hotel Park Plaza" was substituted for the "Hotel Biltmore," for example—but this did little to undercut the accurate descriptions of the Manhattan besieged by the Martians. The play was still centered in New York, and the battleground included such landmarks as the Holland Tunnel, Broadway, Fifth Avenue, and Times Square. Listeners far from New York were less likely to panic than those nearby, but many people as far away as Mississippi or California broke down in fright. New York was known and owned by all, and listeners could take its devastation to mean only that they, wherever they might be, were next.[56]

Academic and political fascination with "the people"—their beliefs, their fears, what bound them together—was enhanced by the *War of the Worlds* fiasco. It is no accident that as the United States entered into World War II and then the decadelong cold war, this play—or rather the story of the panic in reaction to the play—continued to be widely discussed. The decade that had begun with rabid, desperate people milling around the New York Stock Exchange—with the most desperate of them in fact throwing themselves out windows—was coming to a close with new fears. Fear of war, yes, but also distrust about the sources of information, the sources of knowledge, and the sources of belief.

Camp Relief: *S.O.S. Tidal Wave*

The War of the Worlds debacle—and especially the mass gullibility and hysteria—resonated well beyond 1938.[57] The most immediate echoes were cultural allusions in other New York disaster narratives. The following year the film *S.O.S. Tidal Wave,* set in an unnamed eastern city, made a seemingly gratuitous reference to Welles and the panic in the midst of an otherwise bland film about a fight against political corruption. Where *S.O.S. Tidal Wave* differed, however, was in its attitude toward fear. In this tale, the destruction of New York is a big gag, exploited within the story, and by the film's makers, for camp fun.

S.O.S. Tidal Wave features a popular television broadcaster, Jeff Shannon, who is being pressured by friends to get involved in the effort to defeat the corrupt but popular mayoral candidate Clifford Farrow. Shannon's uncle is murdered after uncovering evidence about Farrow's vile past, jolting Shannon out of complacency. On election day he contrives to televise the evidence that has survived.

But the corrupt politician is seemingly saved when a bigger news story

Poster for S.O.S. Tidal Wave, 1939

pushes aside the exposé. A huge storm and earthquake have hit New York, and all attention is captured by the news announcer's descriptions of an increasingly disastrous and desperate situation, one that will soon affect the entire eastern seaboard. A tidal wave created by the earthquake is rolling toward the East Coast, and panic reigns. The script calls for "a scene of New York in the throes of an earthquake and storm," including a tumbling Chrysler Building, all represented by stock footage. The source of these stock shots is clear: the script specifies "*Deluge* scenes."[58]

Just as Shannon and his comrades prepare to be engulfed by the tidal wave they cannot flee, they hear the sound of the New York teletype, bearing reassuring words about American capitalism: "Stocks held firm at the closing of the New York Exchange. Average for thirty industrials fifty-eight and a quarter—up a quarter . . ." Shannon types a message to New York: "Hasn't—tidal—wave—wrecked—New York?" A great laugh is exchanged at the New York Federated News Service Office: "Somebody's idea of a gag."[59]

Shannon bursts into the studio of KNR television, where he finds Farrow's men crowding around the "New York" announcer who has been reporting the city's destruction. Jeff grabs a metal can of film: "Here's your tidal wave! A movie!" The television station manager meekly apologizes: "We forgot to announce it was a film transcription . . ."—a direct reference to the criticism that Welles had not made a sufficiently clear announcement of the fictional nature of his dramatization. Having stopped the broadcast, Jeff Shannon takes to the airwaves and reveals the hoax, forcing Farrow to admit to his "harmless amusement." The scene shifts and we see Farrow's opponent giving a speech as the new mayor.[60]

The references to New York are laughably convoluted: in a fictional film, images of New York's destruction, which were manufactured and borrowed from a six–year-old film, are shown as real, then revealed to be fake.

Perhaps it was that Americans had already seen the footage; or perhaps by the end of the 1930s they had seen their share of New York destruction imagery. But many were blasé about the imagery, just six years after it had caused a sensation in *Deluge*. Indeed, so common had visions of New York's destruction become that amid war in Europe and Depression at home, Frank S. Nugent, a film reviewer for the *New York Times,* could simply yawn at *S.O.S. Tidal Wave* as but another in the long line of disaster films. "The shots of the Empire State Building crumbling, a liner piling up against the Subtreasury walls, Times Square melting away," he wrote, "these all have a familiar look."[61]

Nugent's casual attitude toward yet another New York disaster story may have mirrored that of audiences, but it missed the bipolar condition of most city people: dread of disaster standing alongside the hearty enjoyment, belief that the end of the city was impossible jostling with anxiety that it could happen at any moment. As war approached, the balance tipped back toward a more palpable fear.

The Man of Steel

King Kong had fallen to the new technology that H. G. Wells three decades earlier had predicted would become the dominant mode of war, the airplane. But while the movie celebrated the victory of men over the savage beast (to the point that the filmmakers themselves played the roles of the fighter pilots who get to down the creature of their own making), there remained a sense that the city was vulnerable, and that there was no protector.

The worried, apocalyptic images of Stephen Vincent Benét and O. Louis Guglielmi provided examples of how Americans nervously watched the conflicts in the rest of the world, especially the move toward war in Europe. What could possibly save New York from the endless possibilities of disaster that filmmakers and poets had imagined?

The end of the decade brought a savior in the form of Superman, the comic book hero who soon flew across the silver screen. A man of steel, able to leap tall buildings in a single bound, faster than a speeding bullet, more powerful than a locomotive. The first invader of the 1930s, King Kong, had fallen to his death from the Empire State Building, as would suicides in the coming decades, reenacting the ending of the classic film. The city—in its new form, the skyscraper—had become a threat to its own well-being. But with Superman we now had a hero who would defend the city itself from evildoers. Unlike Kong, who is a victim of gravity, Superman will fly up from the street, straight to the top of the skyscrapers.

Superman had been envisioned for a number of years. The creators, Jerry Siegel and Joe Shuster, had imagined a "super man" at the beginning of the 1930s, although their first version was a villain. By 1934 they had the basic idea of a young boy sent from the dying planet Krypton, but they spent the next four years trying to interest a publisher. Finally, in 1938, the first issue of *Action Comics,* featuring Superman, was published. More than anything before it, the *Superman* cartoon was based on the destruction of New York City. While the "man of steel" fought every manner of evil, from jewelry store thieves to Japanese spies (in one of the more racist episodes, "Japoteur"), the heart of the story was an almost daily battle to save the city from destruction. Indeed, the opening panel from *Action Comics* no. 1 is an image of a city very much like New York in 1938, except that this city, on "a distant planet," is collapsing under the force of a massive earthquake. From the roof of a flat-topped skyscraper, looking eerily like one of the World Trade Center towers, a scientist launches a rocket ship carrying his son, saving the infant from the destruction of Krypton.

Those first cartoons were simply drawn affairs, and some of the details that would anchor the story for the next fifty years—the name of the newspaper for which Clark Kent, Superman's alter ego, works, for example—were yet to be worked out. But the basic structure was in place from the start. In one of the first strips, the image of falling skyscrapers in a thinly fictionalized New York opens the scene: "For the first time in its history, the city of Metropolis is ravaged by a

Superman, by Jerry Siegel and
Joe Shuster, 1939. Skyscrapers of
Metropolis fall to an earthquake in one
of the first issues. Metropolis is just
another city in a bottle for Lex Luthor
to toy with. Another mad scientist,
another Metropolis cataclysm, 1942

terrible earthquake!" screams the caption. The evil Luthor (not named Lex until later), Superman's nemesis, arrives in another early strip, and releases a deadly bomb. Only Superman's intervention just before it hits people on the street saves the day. The first years of *Superman* were filled with every manner of destruction awaiting Metropolis at the hands of nature and evildoers. In one episode a massive creature rips the tower off of the National Bank in the financial district, grabs the money, and flees—until, of course, Superman is able to stop it. In another, a villain sends trucks rumbling through the city spraying from nozzles "not water . . . but sleeping gas!"[62]

    In 1941 Siegel and Shuster brought the cartoon to the screen, in the form of a series of shorts. Many of the stories were adapted directly from the comic book, but many were new and oriented around the theme of New York/Metropolis as the battleground of democracy against totalitarianism. The perils to the city are filtered through the politics of the day. In the face of the evil Luthor, "Superman, defender of democracy, swings into action to combat a dark menace that threatens to engulf and enslave a continent!" Superman also overcomes creatures that, like Kong, create havoc unintentionally in pursuit of something else, threatening to destroy the city as collateral damage.

War of the Worlds bred panic by imagining a Martian invasion. Superman offered a different fear—the fear of modern science and the mad scientist. Like Stephen Vincent Benét's "By the Waters of Babylon," which suggests a new scientific discovery gone bad, the Superman films are dominated by mad scientists, each with a different level of control over his invention.

The first *Superman* movie was released on September 26, 1941. The animated film's mad scientist sends a threatening note to the editor of the newspaper—"a great metropolitan newspaper," not yet the called the *Daily Planet*—saying that "total destruction will come to those who laughed at me." The destruction would begin that night. Sure enough, the first salvo of the laser-like Electrothanasia Ray hits the "famous" Tower Bridge, destroying its span. Panic in the streets ensues, and citizens are told to stay inside; the newspaper reports that the city is "in the grip of terror."

As Superman flies off to the villain's mountaintop lair, the scientist brings the newspaper building into focus on his screen and sends a ray to destroy it. The bottom of the building is targeted and begins to crumble; pieces fall; the building sways. Superman rushes back and catches the skyscraper (which looks like the Empire State Building) as it slowly sways toward an adjacent building. He pushes it back, but it threatens to fall in the other direction. He grabs it by its spire and pulls it back to true. If the newspaper building conjures Kong's Empire State, this time it is a savior, not a menace, who can reach the peak of the tallest building. King Kong had climbed an immovable object, which suggested his mountain home. But here, the tower is like rubber, bending and swaying—resilient, but in need of a steadying hand. The building righted, Superman rushes to the base to stop further attacks from the ray, which has turned the steel beams to rubble. He has a hard time pushing back the ray until he uses a good working-class tactic: he punches it backward, with a left and a right, all the way back to the mountaintop, where Lois Lane is held in captivity. Finally turning the ray back on the mad scientist, Superman ensures that the ray destroys the lab, then grabs Lois and the mad scientist and brings them back to the city, one to a prison cell, the other to a newspaper scoop. The paper's headline declares that Superman has saved the "city from destruction."[63]

Subsequent films every few weeks continued this theme. The November 28, 1941, "Mechanical Monsters" episode featured flying mechanical monsters

Superman saves a skyscraper from toppling and then beats back the powerful ray aimed at the city, from the first *Superman* movie serial, 1941

who are sent by a villain to the city to rob banks and steal from the "House of Jewels" (which looks exactly like the Tiffany's Building at 57th Street and Fifth Avenue).[64] Though they do minimal damage to the city, the sight of the flying cloud of monsters breeds terror in the city. "The Arctic Giant," first aired on February 27, 1942, refers to *King Kong* but also plays on a theme that will be at the heart of the *Godzilla* series in the 1950s: the awakening of a prehistoric creature that comes to the city to wreak havoc. In "Magnetic Telescope," a scientist up on a hill above the city has devised a machine for bringing a comet close to the earth to examine it and then send if off again, using a massive magnet. As most mad scientists do, he miscalculates, bringing the flaming comet down on the city and destroying a train station, cars, and the same bridge that was destroyed in several previous *Superman* episodes.

The *Superman* films also played into the increasingly racist view of the Japanese and Germans. "Japoteur," released on September 18, 1942, opens with a Japanese man reading about the completion of America's latest, and biggest, bomber plane. Above his desk is a photo of the Statue of Liberty. When he pushes a button, the photo turns into the Japanese flag. The man bows to it. Japanese spies manage to hijack the plane (with Lois Lane on board, in pursuit of the story) and head to Metropolis. After the hijackers are apprehended, the plane loses control and spirals down toward Metropolis's commercial crossroads (which appears something like Times Square). Superman manages to stop the plane and bring it to a perfect, soft landing in the middle of the square. The next year, in "Secret Agent," a gang of saboteurs have infiltrated Metropolis, one of them a female agent carrying in a briefcase the "plans of diabolical destruction." The ringleader looks and sounds remarkably like Hitler. "The Electric Earthquake," from July 10, 1942, merges the mad scientist and the racial monster, using Native Americans as stand-ins for the Japanese and Germans. A Native American man comes to the *Daily Planet* to declare that his people want the island of Manhattan returned. "Manhattan rightfully belongs to my people. . . . Have the island vacated immediately!" "It's fantastic! Preposterous!" declare the editors, who dismiss him as a "harmless crank." As he leaves, the petitioner issues a plain threat of what is to come. Using electrical charges attached to the bedrock of the island, the man sets off a massive earthquake that seems to shatter every skyscraper—the total devastation of *Deluge* reprised. When the man is captured by Superman and his electric earthquake network destroyed, physical matter reassembles itself with alarming alacrity. As Clark Kent and Lois Lane look over the pristine skyline, he smiles and says, "You know, Lois, the old island looks just as good as ever."

In these films, fear is largely absent, as is real tension. The only suspense

Water rushes into Herald Square in *When Worlds Collide*, 1951

lies in when Clark Kent will choose to utter the words that children in the latter half of the twentieth century came to know by heart: "This looks like a job for Superman!" Thereafter, as the score changes key, and the Superman anthem begins, we know that it is only a short time before all will be made right. Normal criminal activity—or even a bridge being knocked down, a building toppling, a small pileup of cars—these workaday mishaps don't provoke Clark Kent to undo his necktie and begin his rapid transformation into Superman.

Watching the Superman shorts from beginning to end, uninterrupted, is a de-stabilizing experience. It gives one the sense that the city is a fragile vessel, constantly under attack, crashing, breaking, bending. But it is also a resilient city—literally, rebuilt in time for the next attack. It seemed to match the earlier two decades of being buffeted, by prosperity and then crash, by Depression and then war.

But there was one other trend in the 1930s: the vision of the pristine new metropolis awaiting somewhere else. Just as Superman, in the very first 1938 edition, is seen being propelled from the collapsing Krypton capital, so too many envisioned escaping from a New York degraded by Depression and threatened by war.

In 1933 Edwin Balmer and Philip Wylie published *When Worlds Collide,* a novel of the end of earth and the creation of a modern spaceship "ark" that would take a select group to a new world. The havoc caused by the close passing of another planet sets off earthquakes and floods. Balmer noted that the story had developed "out of the belief that people are ready for some kind of change and like to dream of the possibilities."[65] In the 1951 movie version of the book, the members of this new ark arrive at a new planet, open the doors of the spaceship, and look out onto a gleaming, Technicolor nirvana.

This same dream amid Depression animated *The Wizard of Oz,* which came out in 1939, even as *S.O.S. Tidal Wave* was in theaters, and while the World's Fair, with its visions of future cities, was on display in Flushing Meadows Park in the borough of Queens. The Emerald City of Oz, portrayed in the film as a collection of green, glowing test tubes on the horizon, beckons these wayward travelers, like Benét's city in "By the Waters of Babylon." Benét's city promised more knowledge, in its libraries and museums, and thus a better world. The Emerald City promises a way home but delivers deceit, masks, and fraud, even as it ultimately delivers self-knowledge. And, of course, the Emerald City turns out to be a mirage, a farm girl's concussion-induced hallucination.

Even as these visionary dreams of a new city percolated through the cul-

Approaching the Emerald City on the Yellow Brick Road, *The Wizard of Oz*, 1939

ture—at the World's Fair, in New Deal Greenbelt programs, in Hollywood fantasies—the reality of war, and the threats to the city, had once again returned. A quarter of a century earlier, a terrorist's bomb had rocked the city. Now an accident rocked the city's psyche. On July 28, 1945, a B-25, heading toward Newark Airport from Massachusetts, hit the cloud-shrouded Empire State Building between the 78th and 79th floors, killing thirteen people. King Kong could not conquer it, or even damage it. But a simple unarmed plane, misdirected by the clouds, could rock the world's tallest building.

World War II was almost over. But new fears of attack were in the offing. The image of a great blast from the sky in Benét's "By the Waters of Babylon" would, in just two weeks, become a reality on televisions, in newspapers, and on radios, as reports of Hiroshima and Nagasaki were broadcast around the world. New Yorkers and other Americans had spent many an hour in the 1920s and 1930s watching the city destroyed by every manner of natural and man-made abuse. But what threatened now, after August 6, 1945, was a devastation that would have no warning, no drama, and no reprieve.

four

"Falls Rome, Falls the World"

Atomic Fears of the 1940s and 1950s

IN GEORGE STEWART'S 1949 POSTAPOCALYPTIC TALE OF AMERICA destroyed by the plague, *Earth Abides,* one survivor finds himself on the Palisades, like Stephen Vincent Benét's young man in "By the Waters of Babylon," overlooking New York, "strangely stirred" by the sight of the city's skyscrapers. "Now he knew, what he would not have been quite able to explain before, why he had headed for New York, even unconsciously. This, to every American, was the center of the world. According to what happened in New York, so in the long run, he could only think, it must happen elsewhere: 'Falls Rome, falls the world.'"[1]

Not only novelists but filmmakers, scientists, politicians, and policy makers all headed to New York, literally or imaginatively, to work out the meaning of the atomic bomb for American life. In the two decades after World War II, Americans obsessed over the questions posed by the existence of the atomic bomb. Thousands of books and hundreds of movies created during this period dealt in some way with life under the shadow of nuclear war. And throughout this period, it was the image of New York destroyed that fascinated everyone.[2]

To be sure, there were dozens of scenarios in government documents and Hollywood films involving the destruction of Washington, D.C., or Chicago, or Milwaukee, or, of course, Los Angeles. The home of the film industry, and rapidly becoming the nation's second city, Los Angeles was an increasingly important fictional target in the atomic bomb culture industry.[3]

And yet New York continued to dominate. As the most densely populated city, it could illustrate—as happened hundreds of times, in full color, on the pages of the nation's popular magazines and on the silver screen—the deadly effects, both immediate and lingering, of a nuclear bomb. For those urging a more robust civil defense system—the new variation on the military prepared-ness theme of the 1910s—New York under Fiorello La Guardia provided a testing ground. For those planners, architects, and government policy makers who had long urged a deconcentration of the American population, the threat of nuclear attack made the crisis more urgent, and New York provided the object lesson for new policies to encourage people and businesses to engage in "defensive dispersal." For those who saw the cold war eventually getting hotter, New York's destruction was the logical first and greatest step in the escalation of the con-flict. And for America's novelists and poets, painters and filmmakers, New York provided the best canvas on which to project their fears. Their work conveyed an attitude toward the nuclear age that was both nervous and ironic, and revealed new artistic possibilities amid the unambiguous possibility of annihilation.

Comprehending Nuclear Disaster

In 1940, just before war put most discussion of atomic research behind a cloak of secrecy, *Time* magazine reported on fears that Columbia University scien-tists experimenting with atomic fission could blow up New York. The author cheekily noted that a "gigantic explosion" had not happened "simply because of good luck. Had it happened every building in New York City and every ship at its docks—not to mention its people—would have vanished without a trace. A crater would have been blown in the earth 100 miles across, and the sea would have poured into this vast pit from southern Connecticut halfway to Philadel-phia." All this would have been caused by "some well-intentioned physicists at Columbia University who were cracking uranium atoms with neutrons as con-tentedly as small boys crack nuts."[4]

This sense of chaos bred in invisible corners of the city had a long ances-try—and a long future—in New York writing. Even as the Columbia physicists were at work, Siegel and Shuster were busy creating their *Superman* shorts, in-cluding one that would be shown on April 24, 1942, titled "The Magnetic Tele-scope." It featured another of the city's mad scientists conjuring powers beyond his control. The scientist's magnetic telescope draws a flaming comet down on the city, destroying a train station, some cars, and a bridge (the same unfortunate bridge, incidentally, destroyed in other *Superman* shorts) before fizzling in the bay. And now the magnetic telescope is out of control and threatens to draw a cataclysmic force to the city, unless Superman can stop the machine.[5]

Flip comments by journalists and light New York disaster entertainment disappeared, at least for a while, when the first reports from Hiroshima and Nagasaki filtered in. Americans, and New Yorkers in particular, were primed to imagine what would happen if they became the targets of atomic destruction. And yet it was clear from those initial reports that the disaster scenarios of the 1930s were limited in their ability to help Americans make sense of what they had heard and seen. Much of what followed—in the press, in novels, and in movies, as well as in these new comic books—was about trying to make sense of, assimilate, and then use for political purposes the nature of this new weapon. On news of the bomb, journalists, scientists, and writers of conventional and science fiction almost immediately began to evoke New York's vulnerability to this new weapon.[6] As Robert Jay Lifton and Greg Mitchell have written, "In exploding bombs over Hiroshima and Nagasaki, we frightened no one more than ourselves."[7] The morose nuclear scientist played by Fred Astaire in the 1959 film *On the Beach* expressed a reigning view of the day: who had the idiotic idea that the peace could be maintained with weapons that could destroy us? This attitude had already been articulated by the great urbanist Lewis Mumford, who had written in 1950 that total insecurity was the result of creating these horrific weapons.[8] Fear and anxiety loomed over American society, as evident in a young boy's anguished glance at a roaring jet in the western Massachusetts sky as in the deliberations of policy makers in Washington or New York.

One of the most powerful stories was that there would be no story: all would be destroyed by the bomb. In the "next war," wrote John W. Campbell, Jr., editor of *The Astounding Science Fiction Anthology,* "every major city will be wiped out in thirty minutes. Like two men having a duel with flame-throwers in a vestibule. New York will be a slag heap and any extensive form of government will be impossible."[9] Gregory Corso, in his mushroom cloud–shaped poem "Bomb," wonders, "How horrible Bombdeath is . . . I can only imagine." Picturing a city utterly destroyed, he offers the image of "The top of the Empire state / arrowed in a broccoli field in Sicily."[10] Indeed, New York gained an odd attraction to many in the decade after Hiroshima and Nagasaki, for this very reason: it was the place to go to be sure you would not have to endure the world after nuclear apocalypse. For some writers, dying instantly in a nuclear attack on New York was a "gift" that would be denied so many others. Pat Frank's 1959 novel *Alas, Babylon* is a post–nuclear attack story about a small Florida town called Fort Repose and a group of survivors of nuclear holocaust. Librarian Alice Cooksey "had small fear of death, and of man none at all, but the formlessness of what was to come overwhelmed her. She always associated Babylon with New York, and she wished, now, that she lived on Manhattan, where one could die in a bright millisecond, without suffering, without risking the indignity of panic."[11]

Scientists also quickly recognized that Hiroshima and Nagasaki could not long remain the benchmarks. The rapid development of more powerful bombs and the recognition that a new war would mean multiple bombs dropped at once made the idea of survival in New York hard to imagine. "Let's be realistic about the atom bomb," wrote F. V. Drake in 1945. "The Hiroshima bomb is already dated. . . . It is now in the power of the atom smashers to blot out New York with a single bomb, completely detonating about a spoonful of atomic charge. Such a bomb can burn up in an instant every creature, can fuse the steel buildings and smash the concrete into flying shrapnel. This dreadful forecast is a mathematical certainty."[12]

Most suspected, and scientists quickly affirmed, that as had been seen in Hiroshima, some elements of civilization would survive. Indeed, scientists argued in the press and before congressional committees about the actual impact of a bomb attack. Some passionately disagreed with the doomsday predictions.[13] But all were united in focusing on New York. They returned to New York not just with statistics about the impact of a nuclear bomb, but with stories about the effects on the city's survivors. Whether brief scenarios or longer stories, even the most mundane of scientific treatises portrayed New York's threatened end.

The *Reader's Digest* author David B. Parker in 1947 imagined a notebook of "some future historian" to emphasize the effects of radiation in the event of a nuclear attack on the city. An atomic bomb has been detonated deep in the New York harbor, awakening the "city's sleeping millions." The explosion does little to the buildings, but it sends into the air several million tons of water, which then becomes a "lethal rain" over Manhattan. Though far from the actual explosion, those on the northern part of the island are in as much danger as those in lower Manhattan. Out of a population of more than 2 million, after six weeks 389,101 are dead or missing. "Not for a whole year was New York City officially declared fit for repopulation by its survivors."[14]

The opening chapter of a widely read 1946 volume of essays, *One World or None,* is a hypothetical account by Philip Morrison, a physics professor at Cornell, about what would happen if an atomic bomb were detonated a half mile in the air above Third Avenue and East 20th Street, near Gramercy Park.[15] Other scenarios featured a bomb secretly planted in City Hall. A bomb dropped on Kent Avenue in the Bushwick section of Brooklyn. A bomb dropped from a tanker into New York harbor, onto Broadway and Center Street, over the Police Headquarters; one dropped on the Empire State Building; another dropped on the Lower East Side—American scientists and policy makers busied themselves fantasizing about New York's landmarks as targets. They chose their targets precisely because they *were* landmarks—buildings and places recognizable to a vast number of Americans. As Morrison wrote, "The street and buildings of Hirsohima are unfamiliar to Americans. Even from pictures of the damage realization is abstract and remote. A clearer and truer understanding can be gained from thinking of the bomb as falling on a city, among buildings and people, which Americans know well." In 1940, 5.6 percent of America lived in New York City. Many more lived in the greater metropolitan area, and more still had relatives living there. A larger group yet of Americans had visited New York. And everyone knew of the city's landmarks from movies, popular songs, and photographs.[16]

The nationwide familiarity not only with the city in general but with specific buildings and neighborhoods gave the descriptions greater impact—people had a visceral understanding of the size of the Woolworth Building and could imagine, however imperfectly, what it would mean for that tower to topple. When Jonathan Lear described Chinatown and all of the East Side nearly as far north as the Empire State Building destroyed, readers could grasp the size of the ruin. Many had lived there, and tourists by the millions had made the trek to "exotic" Chinatown's narrow streets.

In light of what scientists later discovered, many of these early articles and portraits underestimated the effects of a nuclear bomb on New York. R. E. Lapp's important work *Must We Hide?* (1949) was an argument against hysteria and for concrete planning for a future nuclear attack, with emphasis on the dispersal of urban populations. Lapp, who had been involved in atomic research since the early 1940s, was a leading figure for half a century in the debate over atomic weapons. While he argued for bans on nuclear testing and warned of the dangers of radiation, he was more widely known for challenging doomsday predictions and undermining what he believed were fear-mongering descriptions of the effects of a nuclear war.[17]

Lapp imagined several scenarios of a bomb dropped on Manhattan. Hypothesizing a bomb detonated in the basement of City Hall, Lapp suggests that the building, contrary to popular belief, would not be "vaporized." Similarly, a bomb dropped above Grand Central Terminal would leave people in subways "perfectly safe," although buildings in the very circle of the blast beyond "ground zero" would be hit especially hard. The effect on the Empire State Building, he suggested, would be "spectacular." But even the Empire State, like all skyscrapers an obvious target, would merely lose its masonry. The steel skeleton would survive. Much of Lapp's confidence was to disappear with the creation of the hydrogen bomb in 1952 and its ensuing development.[18]

Picturing Destruction

In Jonathan Lear's 1950 article "Hiroshima, U.S.A.," an image of a simplified New York skyline shows an area within a half-mile of the blast, with the heading "Virtually complete destruction"; in the next circle, "all but strongest buildings collapse" and fires rage over two- and three-story ruins; two miles away, the damage would be confined to broken windows. This awful picture of what might await New York would soon be almost quaint in the amount of destruction it showed. The April 1, 1954, announcement of the successful detonation of the H-bomb was accompanied by a clear map on the front page of the *New York Times.* Around an imagined center at midpoint Manhattan was a series of concentric circles. The first circle, encompassing the waterfront areas of Brooklyn, Queens, and New Jersey, as well as most of Manhattan up to Harlem, fell under the map's key as "TOTAL DESTRUCTION."[19]

    It was not enough to argue the numbers. These were incomprehensible to the average person. Those concentric rings around an imagined "ground zero" were so abstract as to be meaningless to most. Indeed, one of the problems facing both policy makers and fiction writers was the difficulty even in finding the language and the images to capture the effects of a nuclear blast. Many—in government and beyond—avoided the problem altogether. Just as the destruction seemed incomprehensible, with newsreels and photographs unequal to the task, some government reports stuck to words and tables to describe the impact of a bomb. In popular culture, films such as *On the Beach* focused on the devastation caused by radiation and thereby avoided showing the physical destruction of San Francisco and San Diego. Some hypothetical depictions were amateurish and misleading. Lapp's widely read *Must We Hide?* was accompanied by ineffective illustrations showing the effects of a nuclear bomb on lower Manhattan. On facing pages are two images: one features a contemporary view of Wall Street, looking toward Trinity Church; the facing image shows the view as it might look after a nearby atomic detonation. The "after" image obviously employs scissors and glue to create an overlay of fallen bricks and broken glass; the pictured aftermath shows far less destruction than would in fact have occurred.

    But Lapp's tepid images were not the norm. The burgeoning world of illustrations, spawned by the 1930s New Deal art projects and propelled by the

"Before" and "after" illustrations from Ralph E. Lapp, *Must We Hide?* 1949

film industry, produced spectacular renditions of the imagined destruction of New York. The merging of entertainment and edification is best seen in the work of Chesley Bonestell for various popular magazines in the late 1940s and early 1950s.

In 1950 Bonestell, a Hollywood science fiction matte and background artist, was asked by *Collier's* magazine to illustrate its issue disturbingly and provocatively entitled "Hiroshima USA: Can Anything Be Done About It?" Bonestell, who had studied architecture at Columbia University and had worked in San Francisco as a designer, had made the switch to special effects painting. He provided powerful images (many of them uncredited) for *The Hunchback of Notre Dame* (1939), *Citizen Kane* (1941), *The Fountainhead* (1949), *The War of the Worlds* (1953), as well as more docile movies such as *How Green Was My Valley* (1941) and *Rhapsody in Blue* (1945).[20]

For *Collier's* Bonestell produced a stunningly detailed portrait of Manhattan in the aftermath of an atomic bomb detonated in midtown.[21] Bonestell's cover for the "Hiroshima, USA" issue of *Collier's* is powerful: we see a mushroom cloud over lower Manhattan, around 23rd Street. Inside, the images, which dominate the first several pages of the cover story, are like a series of scene sketches for a film. Key sites by Bonestell depict the aftermath of the bomb, with a small black-and-white inset showing the actual site or building. These pictures were accompanied by a tickertape-like line at the top of each image that served almost as the voiceover from a movie: "Bulletin—Hoboken NJ—Dock Workers of the New Jersey side of the Hudson River this afternoon reported a thunderous explosion in the direction of New York. . . . They said they saw a tremendous ball of fire rising into the sky. . . . Immediate confirmations unavailable. Wire Connections with Manhattan are down. . . ."

The following year, for *Collier's* issue "World War III: Preview of the War We Do Not Want," Bonestell reprised this effort with a hydrogen bomb dropping on lower Manhattan (with effects remarkably like what many saw on television on September 11, 2001). He also portrayed what would happen if similar bombs were dropped on Moscow and Washington, D.C. Virtually every major newspaper and news magazine offered its own provocative—some might say titillating—illustrated stories about the fate of American cities in this new kind of war.

Bonestell's career as a nuclear-disaster illustrator was fueled by cold war fears made much worse by the "losses" of 1949—the "fall" of China to the Communists, the detonation by the Soviet Union of an atomic bomb—as well as the lingering horror of Hiroshima and Nagasaki. After this immediate rush of nuclear disaster "what-ifs" subsided (it was never far below the surface), Bonestell moved on to illustrating many of the most important science fiction novels, such as those of Arthur C. Clarke, and speculative books about space travel. Nuclear fears remained central to American popular culture through the 1960s. In numerous movies, apocalyptic novels, federal disaster scenarios, and planning documents, Americans were reminded that New York's destruction was an inevitable part of perhaps an unstoppable nuclear war.

Destroying New York for Political Purposes

To what end were these words and images—moving and still—employed? What appeal were the magazines and films, novels and reports making?

There was, especially among scientists and writers in the immediate postwar period, a fervent sense that if people understood the pure destructive power of these weapons—and that that power would only increase with every passing year—they would demand that the weapons be banned, or at the very least controlled by an international body.

Philip Morrison's message in the 1946 *One World or None* was clear: "If the bomb gets out of hand, if we do not learn to live together so that science will be our help and not our hurt, there is only one sure future. The cities of men on earth will perish." Parker, in his 1947 *Reader's Digest* fictional account of an atomic attack on New York, made his point at the end of the piece: "We must do everything in our power to bring about international control of atomic energy." The antinuclear movement continued to grow over the succeeding decades. But in the meanwhile, many scientists and officials insisted on a reasonable middle ground between giving up all hope and expecting a new era of sanity, led by the United Nations. They flung themselves headlong into civil defense as the only way to survive a nuclear war.[22]

Civil Defense

On October 22, 1942, fifty thousand men and women—police officers, fire-fighters, air raid wardens, medical personnel—sprang into action in response to five mock surprise bomb attacks on the city, one in each borough (in Manhattan, it was at Astor Place, and in Brooklyn on Atlantic and Fourth Avenue). "In each case," the *Times* reported, "heavy aerial bombs were supposed to have caused extensive property damage and approximately thirty casualties. The arriving protective services were supposed to find a large fire rapidly spreading, with gas and water mains broken, and the near-by streets blocked with debris." The subways were halted (though trains were allowed to discharge their passengers at the nearest stations). Buses pulled to the side of the street, wherever they were. All travel over the East River bridges and through the Lincoln and Holland tunnels was halted; ferryboats stopped their service. Mayor La Guardia declared "splendid results" for what was in fact an elaborate civil defense drill; volunteers had responded rapidly to the needs of the injured, and the vast majority of citizens reacted calmly.[23]

But La Guardia wasn't satisfied. Despite (or perhaps because of) advance warning that a drill would be conducted, many pedestrians and idle onlookers obstructed the streets and watched the commotion from office and residential windows. "'Whether it is a drill or a bombing, people must get away from the windows,' the Mayor told reporters after the all-clear had sounded. 'We will have enough to do to handle injuries and bombs without having a lot of unnecessary casualties. This is not child's play. It is a very serious business. We do not have to wait until bombs are dropped to realize that.'" During the drill, he had yelled at people on the street, watching the show. "'We are not fooling about this,' he shouted. 'We want them off [the street].'"[24]

The blasé attitude that Stephen Vincent Benét had captured in "Metropolitan Nightmare" could be seen in the actions of many citizen onlookers. Treated to a vast war pageant in their midst, many looked on as they would at one of the new Hollywood disaster movies they had become accustomed to enjoying. But in their voyeurism, these onlookers also implied that they had little faith in civil defense. For those who believed the arguments that instant annihilation was the inevitable result of nuclear war, civil defense was a perverse joke. Indeed, many anti–nuclear weapon activists engaged in civil disobedience protests during similar drills. They believed that "civil defense tests help to create the illustration that the nation can . . . shield people from war's effects: We can have no part in helping to create this illusion." Protestors flouted state law that required participation.[25]

But some artists and writers did their part to back up the civil defense initiative. Philip Wylie, in his novel *Triumph,* describes one midwestern city that survived a nuclear war between the United States and the Soviet Union. It owes its good condition to a "well-enough-organized civil defense program." And after several minutes of watching New York collapse in an earthquake-induced flood that brings every building to the ground in *King of the Rocketmen,* the leader of New York's civil defense committee proudly states his desire to rebuild the city.[26]

The Cold War

Civil defense was the mantra of policy makers, and another echo of the military preparedness debates of the pre–World War I era. But the emphasis in the 1950s was less on urging America to increase its military might than in urging citizens to become active participants in fighting invasion at home. Civil defense bled easily into national defense in the cold war.

The 1952 film *Invasion, U.S.A.* played in equal parts on the fears and the titillation of nuclear disaster. A prime example of Hollywood's manipulation of cold war fears, this commercially successful film was an overt warning about American complacency, and the susceptibility of the average American to being manipulated by evil, usually foreign, forces. At the start of the film, a cross section of Americans—a television reporter, an airline ticket agent, a window washer, an army major, and an Illinois congressman—slowly assemble in a bar near Rockefeller Center. That they gather in the middle of the day, and chat amiably but selfishly about high taxes and government interference in production, is meant to suggest a contented, lazy, and unprepared citizenry.

A mysterious man, Mr. Ohman, arrives and, as we find out at the end of

Poster for the movie serial
King of the Rocketmen, 1949

the film, hypnotizes the odd collection of barflies and shows them a picture of the future. An invasion by an unnamed nation has begun in the Pacific Northwest. Over the course of the day, the bar patrons listen to reports, and the newscaster repeatedly leaves and returns. Soon San Francisco falls and the Hoover Dam is blown up, accompanied by stock images of mushroom clouds. As the day goes on, the newscaster becomes more and more an editorialist, declaring that "this is happening because Americans didn't support a big enough military." "We have returned blow for blow," he reports, but clearly the enemy is conquering the country.

Then the main event occurs: a hydrogen bomb is dropped on midtown Manhattan. Imposing on a photograph of the city an image of the concave cup of smoke characteristic of the H-bomb, in contrast to the mushroom cloud of the

Poster for *Invasion, U.S.A.*, 1952

Scenes from *Invasion, U.S.A.*, 1952: The bomb hits midtown. World War II newsreel images are used to suggest the aftermath of the atom bomb. Manhattan in ruins

atomic bomb, *Invasion, U.S.A.* seems to draw directly from Bonestell's 1950 *Collier's* paintings. Rockefeller Center's main tower is hit and a large section falls to the ground; bricks and stones rain on the street. Though the bar and its customers survive virtually unharmed—remarkably, since it is just a block from Rockefeller Center—the scope of destruction of the city is shown using newsreel footage from London and German cities in World War II. When Washington, D.C., is invaded after New York, the reporter notes that the army is fighting back and, as the Joint Chiefs note, "we are kicking [the invaders] out of the city." Patriotic music is cued and plays in the background as we see stock film of men running to their planes and warships and shooting down enemy aircraft.

Suddenly, all the customers in the bar are awakened from their hypnotic trance. The mysterious stranger has disappeared, but they all have a new consciousness and leave with a new resolve to fight for their country and its prepara-

Civil defense information stations were set up at theaters showing *Invasion, U.S.A.*, 1952

A model of Rockefeller Center burns

Sex and skyscrapers: a publicity photo

tion for a nefarious attack. The film ends with a quotation from George Washington (as if the political message were not clear enough): "To be prepared for war is one of the most effectual means of preserving peace." Billed as "an intriguing look into the enemy's plans for conquest," *Invasion, U.S.A.* might as well have been a government-sponsored propaganda film. Indeed, civil defense advocates were pleased to advertise the film and use it as a vehicle for educating the public about civil defense efforts and the need for greater preparedness.

But the producers used far more tantalizing lures to entice viewers. Press photographs for the film featured the female stars of the film in cocktail waitress attire—short skirts and fishnet stockings—standing by the six-foot bombed-out models of Rockefeller Center and neighboring buildings featured in the film. The heart of the film is a love story that develops over the course of the day of disaster between the reporter and the young woman who accompanies the congressman. Sex and catastrophe in New York have long gone hand in hand.

The film advertised itself as a traditional thriller: "It will scare the pants off you!" was the tagline. The advertising poster featured the black-and-white image of a devastated lower Manhattan and a declaration that "they push a but-

Noel Sickles, illustration for "The Thirty-Six Hour War," *Life*, 1945

ton and vast cities vanish before your very eyes!" The cities that vanish in the film, however, are actually European cities devastated by Allied bombing in World War II. Using as stock footage documentary films with no identifying signs or landmark buildings, the filmmakers tried to give the film a greater sense of reality.

They also used special effects to create the appearance of a hydrogen bomb dropping on midtown, just east of the Empire State Building.[27] There is a disconnect, however, between the attempts at accuracy and authenticity. The film notes that thirty thousand people were killed and fifty thousand injured, and that half of the city is quarantined because of radiation. In fact, that level of destruction characterizes the smallest of atomic bombs. The explosion in the film, seen from the southeast looking northwest, covers an area of about ten square blocks—about the scope of the smallest atom bomb, the kind dropped on Hiroshima. Like the illustrations in Lapp's book, it is inexpertly done, as if an image of an H-bomb were simply cut out and applied to a view of Manhattan. Furthermore, the most detailed special effects show a conventional explosion and the top of the Rockefeller tower falling and flames shooting up. Smaller, nineteenth-century buildings, perhaps copied from Sixth Avenue brownstones, suffer only incidental damage. Though the bar is just a block from Rockefeller Center, the physical results appear rather minimal, the product of a more common bomb attack.

Invasion, U.S.A. is not significant because of its powerful acting or its compelling writing; neither is in much evidence. But the long lines outside the theater spoke to the nervous suspicion among Americans that "invasion USA" was inevitable and had best be seen and prepared for in advance.

The Beast Unleashed

A *Life* magazine reporter described a prospective conflict in which "the destruction caused by the bombs would be so swift and terrible that the war might well be decided in 36 hours." The magazine then forecast, in pictures and words, the rapid devastation caused by a nuclear war.[28] That sense of powerlessness—that once started, nuclear devastation was unstoppable—was reflected in a variety of films. The beast of the atom bomb had been unleashed, and as with the evils in Pandora's box, it would be hard to recapture the demon.

The anxiety in the earliest *Superman* comics is still there in the 1950s. In one adventure, hundreds and thousands of rocket ships are sent by the great Martler (a Martian who looks remarkably like Hitler) to destroy New York and invade Earth. Even Superman is overwhelmed: "There are so many rocket ships—a hundred thousand of them—and they're going so fast that even I cannot catch them all before they get to earth." In many of these stories, destructive forces have been unleashed and defense seems impossible, either because of the enormity of the attack, or because Americans are incompetent and unprepared.[29]

This theme was taken up in a series of films from the 1940s and 1950s. *The Beast from 20,000 Fathoms* is a 1953 precursor to *Godzilla* that features a creature from the Arctic awakened by atomic testing. The beast, driven by some unknown instinct, heads straight to New York. It pounds through lower Manhattan, crashing through buildings (in a fairly realistic new special-effects technology devised by Ray Harryhausen). The army is powerless to stop the monster.

The titular Beast can trace its lineage to King Kong, two decades earlier,

Poster for *The Beast from 20,000 Fathoms*, 1953

The beast breaks through the Manhattan grid in *The Beast from 20,000 Fathoms*, 1953

but it is also crucially different, and much closer to the beasts of the *Superman* comics of the late 1930s and early 1940s. For Kong was an unwilling visitor, taken against his will to the city. But in *Beast,* based on Ray Bradbury's short story "The Fog Horn," the enraged monster is drawn on his own power to the city. "New York is like a city besieged," a radio announcer declares after the beast rises from the East River to plow through the Fulton Fish Market. The National Guard is called out (and depicted with stock footage from civil defense readiness drills), but it can do little. "No one knows where the monster will strike next," the radio announcer tells us. "Lower Manhattan has become a no-man's land" in what is "already the worst disaster in New York's history." The newspaper—there is always an image of the front page of the daily paper in these disaster films—indicates 180 known dead. Panic, that accelerant of disaster, sends people fleeing through the streets.[30]

A sense of impotence is central to this film. The National Guard has set up barricades and tries to battle the beast. But something makes the soldiers fall asleep. Just as a nuclear weapon spreads radioactive fallout in the wake of its explosive power, the beast carries some disease that threatens to become a citywide plague. The beast not only must be captured, it must be obliterated. It finally flees into the harbor, only to surface again on Manhattan Beach in Brooklyn, where it is finally vanquished by the ingenuity of two heroes, aided by a newfangled "isotope" and the tangle of a roller coaster's tracks.[31]

The sense that, in the atomic era, New York's end might be unpreventable, at least by human intercession, gave a new opening, a new inspiration, to evangelical ministers, who offered answers beyond the earthly and human.

Building a Religious Movement: New York's End and the Rise of Evangelicalism

For evangelical religious leaders, the atomic era was proof of a coming Armageddon. Scriptural bases for predicting the "final war" were everywhere. While many of these scriptural references had been used for a century or more within the apocalyptic strain in American thought and religion, the atomic bomb seemed to have been created to justify the claims of traders in apocalyptic fear. The power and quality of its destructive impact—not only desolation but a vortex of fire—seemed to fit with biblical fantasy of the end of days. A commonly cited biblical passage was Joel 2:3: "A fire devoureth before them; and behind them a fire burneth; the land is as the garden of Eden before them, and behind them a

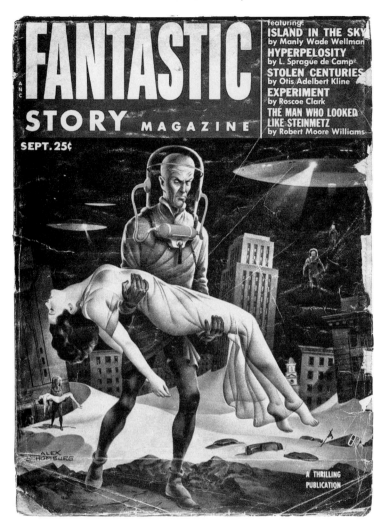

First go the buildings, then the women. Martians arriving to destroy New York and carry away the city's women. Cover of *Fantastic Story* magazine, 1953

desolate wilderness; yea, and nothing shall escape them." For W. D Herrstrom, author of *The 3rd World War and International Suicide,* the link to the present was obvious: "This sounds like the total destruction caused by atomic warfare."[32] The atom bomb was a gift to these Armageddon peddlers—its total destructive capabilities made a perfect endpoint to their sermons.

Policy makers, civil defense planners, even pacifists used New York as an example or a test case because of its size and its stature. For evangelicals, New York was central because of the apparent ability of its people to sin more aggressively than people in other cities. The Reverend Billy Graham insisted in a 1949 revival sermon delivered in Los Angeles that "a tidal wave may sweep across this city, unless we repent of our sin. Do you know the area that is marked out for the

Watching television helplessly as the "flying saucers" prepare to destroy New York in *Earth Versus the Flying Saucers,* 1956

A *Mars Attacks* trading card from the Topps Trading Card Company, 1962

enemy's first atomic bomb? New York! Secondly, Chicago; and thirdly, the city of Los Angeles! We don't know how soon, but we do know this, that right now the Grace of God can still save a poor lost sinner."[33]

Drawing on a passage from Isaiah (1:1–20) that evangelicals often cited, Graham warned that America was a "sinful nation, a people laden with iniquity, a seed of evildoers, children that are corrupters; they have forsaken the Lord, they have provoked the Holy One of Israel unto anger, they are gone away backward. . . . Your country is desolate; your cities are burned with fire: your land, strangers devour it in your presence, and it is desolate, as overthrown by strangers."[34] Graham staged his weeklong revival in New York because it was considered the sinful city of the Bible, Babylon and Nineveh combined, concentrating the catalogue of sins of the modern world: materialism, criminality, gambling, sex, delinquency, communism.

For all his venom, Graham was far less specific and colorful in his imagining of New York's destruction than were some other evangelicals. To W. D. Herrstrom, for example, New York was the new Babylon, doubtless the place referred to in descriptions of the "final war" and Armageddon in Revelation. Quoting (and modifying) Revelation 18:17–24—"That city is to be destroyed in ONE HOUR. It will sink into the earth as a millstone sinks into the sea, never to rise again"—Herrstrom cited a comment attributed to Einstein that soon there would be a new bomb "the size of a man's fist, which could blow the Empire State Building in New York fifty miles into the air."[35]

The most powerful condemnation of New York came from Asa A. Allen, in his 1954 "Vision of the Final Destruction of America." Allen, a prominent evangelist who created the first national television ministry and had hundreds of thousands of followers, developed one of the most elaborate visions of the end of New York to come from the apocalyptic wing of American religious life. Allen pictures himself atop the Empire State Building, surveying the city. He soon realizes that he has remarkable powers and can see the whole continent through the telescopes mounted there. The voice of God speaks to him and declares, "You have done foolishly. Therefore, from henceforth, you shall have wars." Allen surveys the whole country, only to return to New York, the metaphorical stand-in for the entire country, and watches as a "gigantic hand" reaches out to the Statue of Liberty and places a cup in her hand, forcing her to drink what is obviously alcohol. Lady Liberty, drunk, staggers and falls into the sea before barely managing to regain her footing.

Allen then envisions a "huge, black cloud" coming from the distant west. Out of it comes a vast skeleton, blowing cigarette-like smoke toward New York and all across the country. When the "white vapors" reach the Statue of Liberty, the drunken lady begins to takes one "gasping breath" and then coughs, the smoke searing her lungs. Staggering to one knee, the Statue finally falls, dead. Civil defense sirens scream. Soon the disaster is in full force: "I now saw millions of people falling in the streets, on the sidewalks, struggling. I heard their screams for mercy and help. I heard their horrible coughing as though their lungs had been seared with fire. I heard the moanings and groanings of the doomed and the dying."

The roots of this vision were clear even to Allen: "The only thing I have ever seen which resembled the thing I saw in my vision was the picture of the explosion of the H-bomb in the South Pacific. In my vision, it was so real I seemed to feel a searing heat from it." The newest hydrogen bomb had been tested just a few months before Allen's vision was published. But the source of the vision was also much more mundane and personal. Allen's vision is one of desolation from the ravages of alcohol and cigarettes. That drunken Statue of Liberty may have been Allen himself, who struggled with alcoholism through his adult life and died from it in 1970. The destruction of New York would be justifiable punishment for the sinfulness of the nation and each individual.

Evangelicals embraced a form of utopianism. They saw in the atomic bomb the coming of that moment of decision when individuals and society would have to choose between a life of virtue and Christianity or death and utter devastation. The atomic bomb brought hysteria and confusion to many; it made people wonder why they should plan for the future if that future could be snuffed out. It made journalists, fiction writers, and urban planners wonder whether any action matters. But for evangelists, the atomic bomb brought clarity. Concentrating their attention on New York—how the bomb might bring about the end, how the city might fare under attack—allowed evangelists to spread a compelling gospel of individual moral choice. The evangelical moment had arrived on the train of stories of New York's end.

Suburban Safety: Dispersing People from New York

If everyone from scientists to popular magazine illustrators had differing notions of how much of New York would be instantly destroyed, policy makers spoke in one chorus about one of the primary ways for Americans to prepare for a nuclear attack: get out of New York. While military preparedness advocates of the 1910s had argued for greater investment in the military as a way of defending New York, many recognized that the atomic bomb was a different kind of weapon. The notion of strengthening Fort Hamilton, or having more troops at the ready—all arguments of the military preparedness advocates of the World War I era—were utterly inadequate in the face of a silent attack from thousands of miles away, a nuclear weapon delivered by missile, arriving without warning. Civil defense had its place to aid the survivors and to prevent the chaos of the postattack city. But it was not an answer to the defense of the city.

A long-standing dream of decentralizing American cities—rooted deeply in the nation's troubled relationship with its metropolitan areas, and reflected in theories of architecture and urbanism of the 1920s and 1930s—took hold as never before. The push for dispersal can be traced to the middle of the nineteenth century, as observers of all types marveled at the rapid growth of New York and other cities. Frederick Law Olmsted's view was that cities were essential and should be beautified and improved, but he also saw the suburb as an essential complement to the city, one that would prevent the city from overgrowing its own natural place. *Decongestion* and *dispersal* became keywords in the worlds of architecture and urban planning by the Progressive era.

Dispersal was, therefore, hardly new as a planning idea in the aftermath of World War II. But it gained new urgency in the atomic age. It also gained a patriotic, civil defense element that it hadn't had before. For dispersal had begun already in earnest, with the creation of military factories and new towns outside major cities during the war.[36]

Arguments about dispersal in the press and scientific journals intensified immediately after the end of the war. William Fielding Ogburn, in a 1946 article in the *American Journal of Sociology,* made a simple and powerful case, using New York as his example: "If all the buildings and people on Manhattan Island could be destroyed with two or three bombs, then such destruction could be avoided if the peoples and the buildings were removed and placed elsewhere." "In the atomic age," he wrote, "the very concentration of this urban population becomes a weakness." Acknowledging that the challenges in undoing centuries of growing urban concentration were great, he pointed out that history is filled with examples of civilizations that radically transformed themselves to survive. Some urban policy makers suggested a slow evolution of the city and its industries. But others argued for radically accelerating the transformation of cities: instead of moving a few key facilities and encouraging growth in new places, they urged an aggressive plan of decentralization.[37]

The Soviet Union's acquisition of the bomb, as well as successful tests of the first and second generation of hydrogen bombs, made the dispersal argument more persuasive. Moving industry to New Jersey would be scant defense against the power of the new H-bombs. Dispersal would mean shifting industry and military plans far out of the orbit of the metropolis. Admiral Lewis L. Strauss, chairman of the United States Atomic Energy Commission, made a startling announcement about the detonation of a far more powerful H-bomb: "The United States can now build a hydrogen bomb big enough to destroy any city." He was asked to clarify: "New York?" He answered without hesitation: "The metropolitan area, yes."[38]

Certainly, dispersal threatened the character of the oldest cities. Could cultural institutions survive in those cities if industry and wealth left? Could culture flourish in the new communities? Didn't the economy depend on density of people and businesses? Weren't cities the "nerve centers of our national economy," as Paul Windels, president of the Regional Plan Association of New York, had said?[39] But Ogburn, echoing the decades-old arguments of Mumford and others who had suggested that the advantages of cities were soon lost when they got too big, asked: "Do the desirable products of city life come only from big cities? . . . Might they not be had from cities of fifty thousand population?"[40] Scientists and military planners looked at New York as the "model" of urbanism that needed to be changed.

Ralph E. Lapp's *Must We Hide?* illustrates this thinking. Billed as a straightforward "guide" to what Americans faced in the atomic age, the book had a clear point of view: we can survive a nuclear war, but to do so we must transform our cities. In 1962 Lapp wrote that "the missing link in civil defense is confidence that survival is possible." He was especially insistent that the core of a nuclear war survival plan would be to decentralize American cities and disperse the population. A popular view that underground shelters could serve as protection was hardly an answer to Lapp and other commentators. Not only would shelters be ineffective, but retreating underground would be an admission of defeat: "To seek shelter as a nation would be to admit a helplessness."[41]

Neatly tying together the utopian dreams of regional planners who viewed decentralization as an improvement to the quality of American life with the civic demands of the nuclear era, Lapp reminded readers that "our cities today are excellent targets for an aggressor. Ten years from now they will be even better targets unless we do something about them very soon. . . . We must make our targets as unattractive and as invulnerable as possible. At the same time we will be molding our cities into places better adapted for living and better suited to modern means of local transportation." With nearly one in twenty American people living in New York City, the city and its surrounding region constituted the "vulnerable heart of the United States." "Dispersion is protection against a disaster we hope will never come." New York was Lapp's prime example, as it had been in describing the aftereffects of a nuclear bomb.[42]

The goal was simple: by decentralizing business and industry and dispersing the population, "we may reduce the attractiveness of our cities to a point where they are not worthy of an atomic bomb." The United States needed to require that cities "devastated by incendiary attacks"—which he noted were "an awesome sight from the air"—rebuild in less dense layouts. Cities like New York, where "such a high value is placed on a small area of ground in the business district that the city has been given a vertical structure," were a glaring weak point. They represented, Lapp declared, "special targets for atomic attack." Not only did skyscrapers concentrate people and business, but the emphasis on glass made skyscraper cities susceptible to radiation from the bomb. "The Achilles' heel of New York" was the acres of windows that would be "no barrier to the primary radiation from the bomb." Lapp explored three different options: the Rod City (a long, thin urban settlement, somewhat akin to Le Corbusier's linear city notions of the 1930s), the satellite system, and the one that most accurately captured the form metropolitan areas would assume over the coming two decades, with rings of highways and suburbs, and abandoned central areas: the "Donut City." Whatever the choice, the future was clear: "The bomb is forcing a social revolution comparable in scope to the industrial revolution."[43]

The passion with which policy makers urged dispersal make it seem as if the outbound bridges and tunnels would be crammed with people and industry fleeing as fast as possible. The exodus was not so rapid, but the essential story of New York's inhabitants leaving for the suburbs of Long Island and New Jersey was profound: New York City had 7.9 million inhabitants in 1940 but did not reach 8 million for sixty years, while the metropolitan region exploded to well over 20 million in the same time period. Immediately after the war, newspapers regularly reported that New Yorkers were fleeing New York, either to the suburbs or to rural retreats, in large measure because of their fear of nuclear war. A classified ad in the *Wall Street Journal* touted an upstate estate as having "good bomb immunity." The fear that New York would be the key target for a nuclear attack, paired with anxiety about a more racially diverse city, spurred the centrifugal movement to the suburbs.[44]

The Dangers of Urban Chaos

In many scenarios of a nuclear attack on New York, one of the most menacing prospective effects is urban chaos. Feeding into cold war fears of a population lulled into complacency by the prosperity of the 1950s, yet always prone to mob action, writers projected a riotous wake to a nuclear attack.

Ralph E. Lapp, the scientist who sought rational preparation for a likely nuclear war, argued that one of the greatest dangers of the era was social disintegration. The evidence was the panic resulting from the October 30, 1938, Orson Welles broadcast of *War of the Worlds.* According to Lapp, the chaos brought about by Welles's convincing fiction showed that Americans were not "mentally or socially prepared for an atomic attack." Furthermore, a new fascination for unidentified flying objects was "a great credit to the public imagination," Lapp wrote, "but not to its stability."[45] The *War of the Worlds* fiasco persisted as a cultural landmark as policy makers and journalists spun off more and more elaborate hypothetical examples of the kind of frenzy the show had inspired. If that radio show, in the pre–atomic bomb days, could set off such a panic, what would a real attack, perhaps perpetrated by treasonous citizens in our midst, do?

Fiction writers—poets, novelists, and filmmakers—also found this a powerful theme: that the second casualty of war (the first being the hundreds of thousands instantly killed) would be the unspoken social forces that kept society together. Gregory Corso's "Bomb" pictured not only shattered skyscrapers but a shattered social community:

> Yet no other death I know has so laughable a preview I scope
> A city New York City streaming starkeyed subway shelter
> Scores and scores A fumble of humanity High heels bend
> Hats whelming away Youth forgetting their combs
> Ladies not knowing what to do with their shopping bags.

David B. Parker, in his account of a hypothetical attack for *Reader's Digest* in 1947, noted the crazed and doomed citizens rushing everywhere in panic. No one in the story is prepared "for the chain reaction of hysteria which seized the inhabitants of New York as they tried to get off their narrow island. It was the worst panic known in all human history." Thousands are crushed in subway stations, on bridges, and in the tunnels that lead out of the city. Panic clogs every means of getting off the island.[46]

In Richard Foster's *The Rest Must Die* (1959), seven nuclear bombs are dropped within a couple of miles, but not directly onto Manhattan. The conceit of bombs dropped on Long Island allows for the devastation of much of the city's skyline while preserving the underground world of subway tunnels, as well as the people. The novel is about a group of people—amid several thousand—who survive underground for a month before finding their way out to safety. As with

The cover of the 1980 Watermill edition of *War of the Worlds* features flying saucers above New York City

serious works of speculative fiction in popular magazines such as *Collier's* and *Life,* Foster's novel is intended to be scientifically accurate. In an author's note Foster notes, "This is a story about something that has never taken place—although it could happen tomorrow, next year, five years hence, or a hundred years from now—and as such it is almost entirely drawn from imagination. The few facts, however, which relate to radiation, fallout and the more direct results of the dropping of several multimegaton bombs are as accurate as the author could make them." As with so many movies of the period, the character of the scientist is central, to make the disaster more realistic and to offer a solution, a way out.[47]

Told by the scientist that radiation levels are too high, the survivors venture up only once to see the physical effects of the bomb. "It was almost too

In the ruined subway tunnels weaving below the dead city the survivors fought each other like savage animals

35¢

GOLD MEDAL BOOK

s853

THE REST MUST DIE

RICHARD FOSTER

Cover of Richard Foster, *The Rest Must Die*, 1959

much. Bob's first sight was of the sky. It looked as it had always looked. . . . Then his gaze came down to the ground level and it was like some realistic movie." The city is now indecipherable. "To those who had lived in New York," Foster writes, "the city represented a certain picture, mostly painted in outlines placed against the horizon. Now there were no more outlines. There was only a strange, silent flatness with here and there in the distance a charred skeleton to emphasize the buildings that were no more." The survivors look, desperately, for clues that would help them find their city: "Bob looked in every direction for the sight of something he could recognize. New York City had been full of landmarks; now there were none. Nothing but little hills and valleys of rubbish, clumps of broken concrete and brick and twisted steel, looking as though it had been flung there by an angry god." The survivors return to their new home, the cavernous subway tunnels. (There is further irony here: much of the action of the novel takes place beneath Pennsylvania Station. Just a few years later, in 1963, Pennsylvania Station would begin to come down, razed not by an attack from the outside but by development pressures.)[48]

Despite this dramatic moment, the physical disaster is a small part of the novel. The bulk focuses on the chaos and warfare among the survivors below the streets of the devastated city. This approach leaves Foster time to explore more titillating aspects of a world literally turned upside down. A woman who has gone stir crazy in the underground world stands on a desk, takes off all her clothes, and asks, "Are there any real men here?" As in Du Bois's "Comet," the destruction of New York means a loosening of postnuclear boundaries of behavior. A pulp novel to be sure, *The Rest Must Die* nonetheless engages serious themes of the breakdown of human society in the wake of disaster. The bonds that had held people together, and the social rules that had kept the city in some sort of balance, collapse into chaos.

The group is found by a pilot doing reconnaissance from Hoboken. It turns out that the bombs were not the beginning of a war but the end—it lasted just a few hours. "They destroyed New York City and Washington. We destroyed Moscow and Leningrad. Then peace was declared," says the pilot. In an unintentionally comic understatement, he continues, "I guess it scared everybody. Anyway, all fission and fusion weapons are being turned over to U.N. control now."[49] This scenario echoes the films *Captive Women* (1952), *The World, the Flesh, and the Devil* (1959), and *The Day the Earth Caught Fire* (1962): through catastrophe, humans will learn that abolition of atomic weapons under the authority of the United Nations is the only answer.

In *The Rest Must Die,* two of the group, Bob and Nancy, decide to stick together. But the disaster has spurred them to change. Johnny, another survivor, declares, "If my past was destroyed, so was yours. . . . What are you going to do if we get out of here. . . . Are you going to forget what you learned the minute you get up into the sunlight again?" Bob decides that he wants to do some good in the world (his advertising career is not worthy enough): "I don't want to go back into advertising. . . . I'd like to do something that would have some meaning in the world, but I don't know what it can be. I think I'd like to work for something like the U.N. but I don't have the qualifications." Bob and Nancy head off to Chicago, hand in hand.[50]

But there was an opposing viewpoint to the fear of chaos and panic, the breakdown of social mores. The extraordinary fantasies of human chaos portrayed in the city in the wake of nuclear disaster highlighted, by sheer excess and contrast to the life of the real city, the essential glory of the still-extant New York: its capacity to hold, in relative peace, so many people, in such dense numbers, and from so many varied races and classes.

The films that showed an empty city illustrated this principle best.

Empty City

Fear was everywhere. The problem for emergency planners was that the city was too dense with people, too concentrated with industry and commerce crucial to the nation, and too unstable to sanely handle a nuclear attack. Equal to the fear that New York would become the ultimate atomic target in the cold war was the opposite: that the city would be emptied of its people. Filmmakers and fiction writers dwelt uncomfortably on the specter of New York's abandonment. In these narratives, the buildings remained, but the people were gone. While popular magazines overflowed with the descriptions of the destruction of nuclear war, novels and filmmakers found equal inspiration in imagining the city deserted.

The theme of emptiness is not new. We have seen throughout the history of New York destruction fantasies the theme of the city drained of its people. Indeed it is one of the most common representations of postapocalyptic New York. J. A. Mitchell's *The Last American,* W. E. B. Du Bois's "The Comet," Upton Sinclair's *Millennium,* George Allan England's *Darkness and Dawn*—these and many more began with the conceit that the city has been destroyed and the people have been killed or have disappeared, leaving no trace, no remains. Silence is the essence of these apocalyptic stories.

But there was a new nervousness to expositions of this theme in the 1950s. It was actually imaginable that radiation could be the greater killer, the invisible killer, leaving a city relatively unscathed physically, but utterly devoid of living people. In Frederik Pohl's "Knights of Arthur," the protagonist says simply: "Anyway, there wasn't much damage, except of course that everybody was dead. All the surface vessels lost their crews. All the population of the cities were gone."[51]

The Twilight Zone, Rod Serling's enormously popular and influential television series that premiered in 1959 on CBS, returned a number of times in its six-year run to the theme of nuclear disaster, with the emptiness and loneliness of the survivors at the heart of several episodes. One of the most famous of all Twilight Zone episodes came in the series' first season. "Time Enough at Last" features a hapless bank teller, Henry Bemis, who craves only to be left alone to read. Taking his lunch break to read in the bank vault (a headline in his newspaper declares, "H-Bomb Capable of Total Destruction"), he survives a nuclear explosion that hits the city. He comes to the surface to find a scene of total desolation, himself the lone survivor. He prepares to commit suicide until he looks up and sees that he is sitting next to the remains of the public library. Books are scattered everywhere. Although the bank has a small-town feel to it, the huge steps and columned entrance of the library suggest the grand entrance to the New York Public Library, which appears regularly in nuclear disaster scenarios.

"One More Pallbearer" (1962) takes place in an underground bomb shelter in the middle of New York City. Paul Radin, a millionaire, has decided to stage an elaborate nuclear attack hoax to get three people who have wronged him over the course of his life to beg his forgiveness in exchange for a place of safety. He lures them to his shelter—three hundred feet below street level—and then shows them a manufactured video of a nuclear attack on New York. (The workmen who install the television and sound system are impressed: "I don't know where you got your sound effects. But you'd swear a bomb was exploding, a big bomb. . . . You'd swear the whole world was getting blasted!") His guests refuse his offer of a place in his shelter in exchange for groveling apologies. Radin ultimately goes insane, hallucinating that a nuclear war has in fact occurred. He exits his bomb shelter (onto a set that looks suspiciously like that from "Time Enough at Last") and believes he sees the world devastated. As the show ends, he is cowering not in rubble but on a sidewalk of Park Avenue, as passersby avoid the obviously troubled man. The voiceover—that of the show's writer and producer Rod Serling—is merciless: "Mr. Paul Radin, a dealer in fantasy, who sits in the rubble of his own making and imagines that he's the last man on Earth, doomed to a perdition of unutterable loneliness because a practical joke has turned into a nightmare. . . . He is a pallbearer at a funeral he manufactured himself."

Finally, in another disturbing episode, "Midnight Sun" from 1961, Serling again sets the disaster in Manhattan. "This is New York City and it is the eve of the end," Serling intones, "because even at midnight it's high noon, the hottest day in history, and you're about to spend it in the Twilight Zone." The orbit of the earth has shifted and suddenly the city is drawing closer and closer to the sun, with the temperature rising every hour. Though the source of the threat is an environmental disaster of unknown cause, the sense of impending doom resonates with a fear like that usually reserved for nuclear disaster. It is a telling coincidence that "Midnight Sun" was first shown on television on November 17, 1961, the day the United States successfully launched its first Minuteman missile from an underground silo.[52]

Burgess Meredith sits amid the ruins of the city in the *Twilight Zone* episode "Time Enough at Last," 1959

The episode takes place in the apartment of a young painter named Norma who is capturing the hot sun on canvas. She, like her neighbor Mrs. Bronson, has chosen not to flee the city. The radio continues to offer updates on the temperature and to warn remaining citizens to lock their doors and look out for "cranks and thieves." A crazed man with a gun does break in and steals the last of Norma's water, all the while yelling that she should stop painting the sun. Finally, Mrs. Bronson succumbs to the heat, after demanding: "Paint something cool. . . . Don't paint the sun anymore!" Norma is now alone. Her oils melt and begin to run off the canvas. The thermometer explodes, and Norma screams and faints.

But that is not the end. Norma awakens to find it dark and cold out-

A manufactured scene of New York being destroyed by a nuclear bomb, and the hallucinations of a millionaire in *The Twilight Zone*, "One More Pallbearer," 1962

The Twilight Zone, **"Midnight Sun," 1961**

side. She is thrilled to find that it has all been a horrible hallucination. She tells Mrs. Bronson how relieved she is by the cold. But Mrs. Bronson and a doctor called to revive Norma know the truth: the midnight sun was a delusion, and not the coming apocalypse. In fact, the earth is moving farther from the sun, getting darker and colder by the minute. Saved from her horrifying dream, she wakes to an equally horrifying reality.

Out of the Ashes of the 1950s Apocalyptic Imagination: A New Appreciation of Urbanism

Prosperity had returned to America in the late 1940s and the 1950s, but the pictures and stories presented in the images in disaster films were unrelentingly pessimistic.

Many films did offer hopeful endings to horrific scenes of disaster. In *Invasion, U.S.A.,* viewers are led to believe that the "dream" of the barflies will transform them and their fellow citizens into active, patriotic participants in the defense of America. In *The Rest Must Die,* the survivors literally and figuratively escape from the destruction of New York in order to build new lives. But the power of the imagery of the hydrogen bomb—well known from newspaper and television and other films—was much more powerful than the vain attempts to harness patriotic civil defense activism. Philip Wylie's *Triumph* includes a didactic set piece—a radio program that is being aired in South America (the whole Northern Hemisphere having been destroyed) that describes, city by city, how America was destroyed, with lavish, gruesome detail about New York's end.[53]

And yet something else is going on here. Percolating through these endless and often aesthetically striking fantasies of New York's end was something quite different from fear: a new appreciation of the city itself.

Dispersal, for example, also taught its opposite: an appreciation of the city and a denigration of the suburbs. While the proliferation of suburbs was real and profound, the standard historical narrative of the flight from New York vastly overstates what happened. New York remained the most important American city, not only economically but also symbolically. Indeed, many in the press and in popular culture questioned the increasingly common wisdom of fleeing to the suburbs or beyond. Judith Meril shows, in *Shadow on the Hearth* (1950), that the comforts of suburbia would be no real protection if the bombs were to drop on the city. The story concerns a Westchester County mother and two daughters stranded at home after a nuclear attack on New York City. Much of the city is destroyed; several bombs also have landed in the outer boroughs. The radio reports that "Manhattan itself is almost completely destroyed from the Battery up as far as Ninety-Sixth Street, with only a narrow strip of land west of Ninth Avenue apparently intact." The heart of the novel is a domestic melodrama, however, as Gladys Mitchell waits for her husband to return home and tries to deal with her daughters' possible radiation sickness. She harbors two suspected subversives, her maid Veda and Dr. Levy, the older daughter's science teacher. But the novel is an effective portrait of the dream of suburban detachment, and how an urban disaster would give the lie to that dream.[54]

The same year, a *Commonweal* editorialist mused about whether New Yorkers should abandon their city. It was clear to almost anyone that New York was the "first target," even before Washington, D.C. The author recognizes that as he writes this editorial in his mid-Manhattan office, he is effectively "sitting on a powder-keg." Knowing this, why wouldn't everyone flee if they possibly could—"Why do people stick around?" Is some "dim Freudian bent toward self-destruction" behind this? A "mixed-up, confused and almost instinctual" desire to bring about one's end? No, the writer concludes, it is something different:

A man knows that he is a part of it—these buildings, these streets, these subway crowds, these commuter queues—and that if one day they are blasted into nothingness, then he should be there at his desk, his bench or on his back porch when it comes. It is only fitting. A New Yorker (or a Chicagoan or Detroiter) would be downright embarrassed to be caught hiding in the hills of Arkansas on the day that St. Patrick's Cathedral (or the Wrigley Building or Willow Run) became a heap of rubble. One stays where one is, hopes for the best and plans to do his part should the worst come.[55]

Many disaster novels and short stories simply assumed that in "World War III" New York, as the obvious target, would be instantly destroyed. Stories of how people survive in New York "after" were obviously central to the culture of the period. But what is striking about many imaginings of New York's actual destruction or its postapocalyptic appearance and social life is that the city remains a compelling magnet. While some journalists quietly asked the question, "Don't you think Manhattan is expendable?" most rejected this attitude outright. The survivors of worldwide catastrophe still need to get to the city. New York, leveled and irradiated, is the place where the most important events are happening.[56]

In the many postapocalyptic stories and films, a stop in New York is required. We have already seen in Stephen Vincent Benét's "By the Waters of Babylon"—a precursor to and influence on postapocalyptic literature of the 1950s—that the young man is pulled to the city; his father's order to stay away propels him to find out the secrets of the Place of the Gods. The Godzilla-like character in *The Beast from 20,000 Fathoms* is drawn to New York. And in *The World, the Flesh and the Devil,* Harry Belafonte's character makes his way from Pennsylvania to New York after a mysterious event that has killed virtually everyone.

Indeed, this was the attitude not just of individuals but of New York's city builders. As Tom Vanderbilt has argued, in the years after New Yorkers learned of the effects of the atomic bomb, and then the hydrogen bomb, they began an era of building some of the most impressive modernist skyscrapers the world had yet seen. Lever House, the Seagram Building, the United Nations Secretariat Tower—all were built during the high point of the fear of nuclear attack, the most intensive civil defense debates, the bomb shelter craze, and the push to decentralize American business and homes. Furthermore, it is not as if these buildings were built "bomb proof," as is occurring in construction since 9/11—for example, the bunker-like Freedom Tower at Ground Zero. Indeed, quite the opposite. While R. E. Lapp insisted that the "Achilles' heel" of New York was its emphasis on building glass-encased buildings that would allow radiation in,

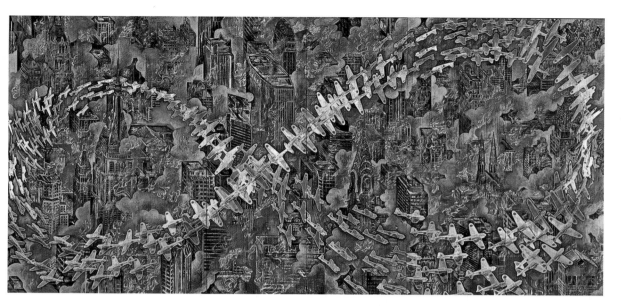

Plate 1. Makoto Aidi, *Picture of an Air Raid (War Picture Returns)*, 1996. Exhibited, to great controversy, at the American Effect exhibition at the Whitney Museum of American Art in 2003

Plate 2. Nicolino Calyo, *Burning of the Merchants' Exchange, as seen from the Bank of America, corner of Wall and William Streets, N.Y., December 16th and 17th, 1835*. Colored aquatint, Museum of the City of New York, bequest in memory of Mr. and Mrs. J. Insley Blair

Plate 3. Joseph Pennell, Liberty Bond poster, 1917

Plate 4. R. W. Boeche, cover illustration for H. G. Wells, *The War in the Air*, 2002

Plate 5. Frank R. Paul, cover illustration for *Amazing Stories*, 1929

Plate 6. José Clemente Orozco,
The Collapse, 1931

Plate 7. O. Louis Guglielmi, *Mental
Geography*, 1938

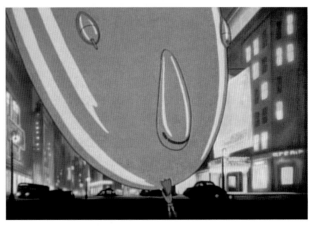

Plates 8–10. *Superman* film serials, "Arctic Giant," "Electric Earthquake," and "Japoteurs," 1942

Plate 11. George Tooker, *The Subway*, 1950. Egg tempera on composition board. Sight: 18¹/₈ × 36¹/₈ in. (46.04 × 91.76 cm). Whitney Museum of American Art, New York; purchase, with funds from the Juliana Force Purchase Award 50.23. Photograph by Sheldan C. Collins

Plate 12. Chesley Bonestell, cover illustration of a nuclear attack on New York, for *Collier's*, 1950

Chesley Bonestell

Plate 13. Chesley Bonestell, illustration for John Lear's "Hiroshima U.S.A." in *Collier's*, 1950

Plate 14. Poster for *Deep Impact*, 1998

Plate 15. Earthquake hits the headquarters of DC Comics at 1700 Broadway, Gotham City, in *Batman: Cataclysm*, 1999

Plate 16. The World Trade Center towers standing but in flames in *X-Force: Sabotage, Part 1*, 1991

Plate 17. Album cover for Busta Rhymes's *E.L.E. (Extinction Level Event): The Final World Front*, 1998

Plate 18. The original poster for *Spider-Man*, 2002, with the World Trade Center towers reflected in Spider-Man's eyepiece. The towers were removed after 9/11.

Plate 19. A scene, used in advertisements for *Spider-Man* and deleted from the final cut

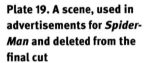

Plate 20. *Spider-Man: Coming Home,* 2002

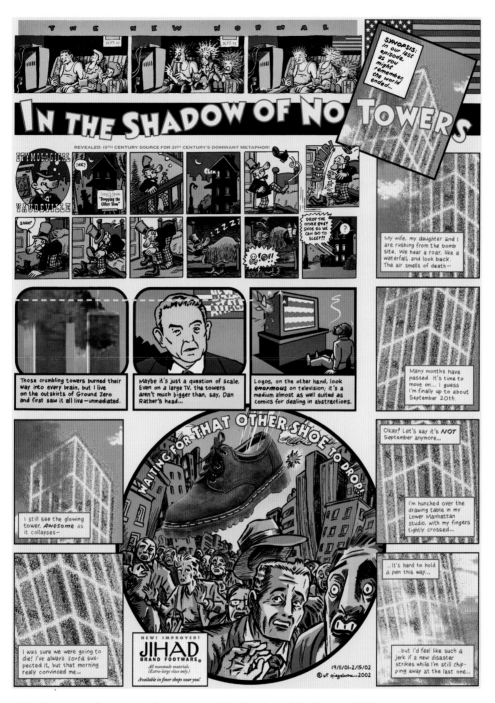

Plate 21. A page from Art Spiegelman, *In the Shadow of No Towers*, 2004

Plate 22. Poster for *The Day After Tomorrow*, 2004

Plate 23. Alexis Rockman, *Manifest Destiny*, 2004

Plate 24. Atta Kim, *Fifth Avenue and 57th Street*, 2006

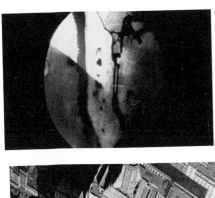

The final minute of *Fail-Safe*, 1964: a scope on the bomber reveals the target to be Manhattan. The lively street life of a New York stoop. The top of the Empire State Building. The fluttering of pigeons on Times Square, just before the bomb hits

debate what should be done. Professor Groeteschele believes that nuclear war is survivable and requires calm action, as in any war. He accepts that New York must be destroyed, as "compensation." But he insists that government and corporate documents be secured first to facilitate the rebuilding process after the devastation of the bomb. "Our economy depends on it," he says.

Much of the power of the film comes from the depiction of the president, wrestling with his decision in a windowless room, with only a telephone and an interpreter (who translates his conversations with the Soviet premier) to keep him company. "We let our machines get out of hand," he declares. "Two great cities may be destroyed. . . . What do we say? 'Accidents may happen'?" The film is cool and detached in an intentionally harrowing way. The inspiration for the director, Sidney Lumet, was a quotation from Ralph Waldo Emerson, that "things are in the saddle and ride mankind." Most of the film focuses on people in power sitting, or standing, or staring—doing, it seems, nothing, because the "things"— nuclear bombs and malfunctioning computers—are in the saddle.

Amid the terror, and the waiting, some of the characters admit to thinking what is inutterable: that an atom bomb explosion can be beautiful. A young woman who meets Groeteschele after a party declares: "That's the beauty of it

New York's architects and their clients went right on building them. cade following Lapp's manifesto, New York built the most glazed world. It was as if, in the face of Hiroshima, in the face of all warni face of the disaster scenarios in the movie houses, on television, an zines, New Yorkers and their builders consciously chose to treat the p popular culture as thrills and fears for entertainment. They most certi not to be treated as lessons that would lead to radically redesigning architecture or abandoning city life.[57]

Paradoxically, then, the imagining of New York's destruction bomb was a way to reassert the importance not only of the city but of more generally. While planners considered the threat of the atomic bor portunity to press for decentralization and dispersal, others were resis for change. They were seeing, either for the first time, or in a new light, t of urbanism. Out of the crucible of the atomic bomb came a renewed d the idea of the city.

This about-face from the grim spectacles of the early 1950s em 1964 in one of the most powerful films of the atomic age: *Fail-Safe*.

Fail-Safe

Based on a 1962 novel by Eugene Burdick and Harvey Wheeler and set *Fail-Safe* is about an accidental nuclear attack on the USSR by a Strate Command (SAC) bomber group. The error is technological, compoun human fallibility and fealty to technology. The U.S. president—a Kennec figure played by Henry Fonda in the film version—finds himself compe order SAC to blow up New York to compensate for the American mis destroying Moscow. The hope is that the destruction of New York and M will result in disarmament and peace between cold war antagonists. Pub in the wake of the Cuban missile crisis, *Fail-Safe* reflects the sense of dre inevitability of nuclear war, or at least nuclear accident.

The film version opens with the words: "New York City 5:30 A.M film will begin and end in New York. However, it quickly shifts to a nightm a bullfight being experienced by General Warren Black. After awakening, eral Black flies to Washington, D.C., looking over the New York skyline a plane takes off from La Guardia and heads south. He will return later in the to this very view with a different mission.

When news of the mistaken bombing of Moscow hits, military lea

[nuclear war] . . . there won't be any survivors." Groeteschele responds: "I've heard nuclear war called many things, but never beautiful." "They won't say it, but that's what they feel." This confession is followed later, in the Omaha war room, when a man looks up at the graphic board of the warplanes flying in formation toward their final destination and whispers, "Beautiful."[58]

After being cloistered for much of the film with the president in his tiny, windowless safe room, or in the control room with dour faces and television screens showing abstract movement of the bombers, viewers are suddenly released into the city. As the plane, with General Black on board, approaches Manhattan, ready to drop the bomb, brief scenes of New York street life flash on the screen: pigeons, children playing, people dancing on a stoop, cabbies arguing over an accident, the Playland amusement center in Times Square. All the abstract talk about destroying Moscow and New York, about saving documents for future generations, all of it disappears with the sight of New York—real, street-level, messy New York. Lumet seems to be surveying the joys of the city, emphasizing that what will be lost is not only individual lives, but the whole world of the city, what Mumford called the greatest of human creations. As the bomb drops, the screen flashes even faster, speeding through the images the viewer has just seen, with a grating sound effect. We see a small boy, and then a black screen. The film is over, save for a note from Columbia Pictures that this scenario is highly unlikely to happen.

Lumet has said that he wrestled with how to mark the ending, the moment when the bombs hit New York, but decided, "I just felt we couldn't go out on a mushroom cloud." He wanted, instead, to bring the individual, human aspect to the fore. The nightmare of General Black is a way to bring the threat and reality of nuclear devastation back to the individual. The final images of city life were designed to focus on what was destroyed of greatest importance: "the human elements . . . that's what has been cut out." So in the final moments, as the map of Manhattan is centered in the plane's onboard radar, Lumet switches from the abstract to the real and the human and shows "ten little pieces of life" in New York that would end when the bombs hit.

Lumet's argument was not simply against nuclear proliferation but *for* the city, for the great, dense city that had received, a couple of years before *Fail-Safe,* its most eloquent defense with the 1961 publication of Jane Jacobs's *Death and Life of Great American Cities.* A new appreciation of traditional urbanism— in fact, a ringing manifesto—appeared amid the nuclear fears.[59]

Here Is New York

E. B. White's essays for the *New Yorker* constitute perhaps the finest defense of American cities offered by any writer. In "Here Is New York"—originally published in *Holiday* magazine—White offers one of the most quoted defenses of the city. White begins this seemingly breezy essay on New York by surveying the types of people who inhabit the city—the lifelong New Yorker, the commuter, and then "the greatest of them all . . . the person who was born somewhere else and came to New York in quest of something." It is this group "that accounts for New York's high strung disposition, its poetical deportment, its dedication to the arts, and its incomparable achievements. Commuters give the city its tidal restlessness, natives give it solidity and continuity, but the settlers give it passion. . . . New York is not a capital city—it is not a national capital or a state capital. But it is by way of becoming the capital of the world."[60]

The joyous chaos that White loved, and which he so adoringly describes, is muted at the end of the piece, as White admits to an anxiety from living in the city at the dawn of the nuclear age, a fear which he shared with many Americans. In the wake of the attacks of September 11, 2001, this part of White's essay was widely distributed, as an almost uncanny prediction of that day:

> The subtlest change in New York is something people don't speak much about but that is in everyone's mind. The city, for the first time in its long history, is destructible. A single flight of planes no bigger than a wedge of geese can quickly end this island fantasy, burn the towers, crumble the bridges, turn the underground passages into lethal chambers, cremate the millions. The intimation of mortality is part of New York now: in the sound of jets overhead, in the black headlines of the latest edition.

> All dwellers in cities must live with the stubborn fact of annihilation; in New York the fact is somewhat more concentrated because of the concentration of the city itself, and because, of all targets, New York has a certain clear priority. In the mind of whatever perverted dreamer who might loose the lightning, New York must hold a steady, irresistible charm.[61]

In this passage, White throws a cold shadow on an otherwise uplifting piece for a vacation magazine. He projects several key ways of thinking about the end of New York in the atomic age. First, White captures the sense that New York's end would be public, printed in the "black headlines of the latest edition." The story within the story is that newspapers, the radio, and television are central actors in the drama of a New York destroyed. The destruction of the city will be made final when the "latest edition" of the paper reflects it.

White also succinctly captures the reality of the time: New York had become vulnerable in a way it had never been before. A generation of crime and violence, fires, terrorism, brutal poverty, and physical degradation had not been able to push New York off its trajectory as the "capital of capitalism" and the cultural capital of the world. But the bomb changed everything: the indestructible city was now mortal, as vulnerable as any other. Indeed, because of its density, its tall buildings, its importance, New York had become the most vulnerable of cities: the most attractive target, yielding the greatest physical and human damage and causing the greatest psychological pain. It suddenly seemed possible, for the first time, as E. B. White observed, that the city could be wiped away in a second. This reality gave the fantasies of the city's end greater impact: you have to look hard at what you might really lose. Certainly there were powerful political purposes to the many disaster scenarios of the 1940s and 1950s, but a powerful undertone was the question of the value of the city: what would we lose if New York were to be no more?

It was not a nuclear bomb that brought down New York, physically or otherwise, but rather a series of structural shifts that left the city in decay and virtual bankruptcy by 1975. White wrote his essay when New York was at the pinnacle of its importance as both a real and symbolic center of economic and cultural might, even though historians would later see the seeds of New York's decline before 1945. One can imagine Alfred Eisenstaedt's photograph of the couple kissing on VJ Day in Times Square as the opening illustration for White's essay: the photograph captures the sense of relief, joy, sexual thrill, and feeling of community that could happen only at New York's crossroads. The last illustration, however, would not be fighter jets headed our way—"no bigger than a wedge of geese"— but the burned-out tenements on Charlotte Street in the Bronx.

five

Escape from New York

Fictions of a City's Decline and Rebirth

IN WOODY ALLEN'S HIT FILM OF 1973, *SLEEPER,* THE HEALTH FOOD store owner Miles Monroe (played by Allen himself, of course) is awakened from a two-centuries-long sleep, in the year 2173. It turns out that his world was destroyed "when a man named Albert Shanker got hold of a nuclear device." The joke is increasingly dated, but in 1973 it prompted instant recognition.

Shanker was president of the American Federation of Teachers and one of the most militant unionists of his day. His advocacy on behalf of teachers and civil rights earned him widespread loyalty, but his confrontation with New York City in the 1968 Ocean Hill–Brownsville teacher strike has been identified in hindsight by some historians as one of the symbols of New York's decline through the 1960s and into the 1970s. The strike, which left students out of school for months and seemed to set black parents and students against Jewish teachers, was a reflection of the racial tensions that beset the city, as well as a spark for further conflict. Many have accused Shanker of helping to bring the city down.

With his deft one-liner, Allen neatly encapsulated the shift, over the decade since *Fail-Safe,* in the imagination of New York's end. A bomb dropping on New York—this was now standard fare, and easily digested with a joke. But what really got under New Yorkers' skins, what really evoked rage and resentment, was the immigrant from the Lower East Side who led the American Federation of Teachers in a series of militant strikes in the late 1960s. The nuclear bomb had become the devil we knew, who lived quietly, if menacingly, on the mountain. But down in the city, the real danger was in the form of this angry unionist, fomenting racial and ethnic strife in a nearly bankrupt city. The nuclear shadow still loomed, but New Yorkers had gotten used to it. They could joke about it. What enraged and depressed them were threats much closer to street level and to their daily world: loss of jobs, crime, racial strife, an aggressive teachers' union, failing subways, the South Bronx. The urban crisis had supplanted the bomb as the central motif of the New York destruction genre.

The scenarios of nuclear disaster never came true, but New York's economic and physical decline in the 1960s and 1970s, which created what many called "war zones," proved to be fertile ground for American popular-culture makers. Artists imagined the end of American civilization by portraying New York's future as a huge prison or a crime-infested jungle in such movies as *Fort Apache the Bronx* and *Escape from New York.* Articles in local and national newspapers and magazines highlighted images of the burning Bronx and of looting during the 1977 blackout, among other images of urban crisis. In ways not portrayed with such directness since the racial "invasion" stories of the early twentieth century, popular culture of the 1960s and 1970s linked New York's imagined destruction with the growing concentration of minorities in the impoverished city. After quotas were abolished in 1965 and New York experienced a renewed influx of immigrants, from the American South, Mexico, Puerto Rico, and Asia, visions of the city's end once again centered around the threat of racial and ethnic violence. The signature image of this era's postapocalyptic scenarios remains the 1968 film *Planet of the Apes,* which couched fears of nuclear holocaust in thinly veiled terms of race war. The film's last image—of a nearly buried Statue of Liberty—is deeply etched in popular consciousness as a symbol of New York's descent, while the national bicentennial year, 1976, has served as a convenient landmark of New York's lowest point, when the city seemed ready to go into bankruptcy and a *New York Daily News* headline put into the mouth of President Gerald Ford the infamous kiss-off "Drop Dead." That year *King Kong* returned, in the worst rendition of the beast in New York film history, this time to stomp on the World Trade Center towers. The sorry remake was an apt representation of the city's rapid fall from grace. It was a very different city from thirty years earlier when, on VJ Day, New Yorkers and all of America celebrated in Times Square—in the capital of the American Century.

New York may have eased its way out of urban crisis in the 1980s and 1990s, but urban crisis never disappeared from the imagined city. The most powerful images of that crisis—the crime, drugs, urban decay—persisted well

The final scene from _Planet of the Apes_, 1968

Beneath the Planet of the Apes, 1970

into the "rebirth" era of the 1980s and 1990s. Indeed, the irony is that during the city's era of greatest prosperity, including the 1980s, we see some of the most powerful depictions of New York's end. The disconnect between reality and perception has to do with other cultural trends, to be sure. As the millennium approached, American culture became fascinated with violence and disaster scenarios of all types, from police-chase television programs to animal-attack exposés to nuclear apocalypse movies. New York was a convenient venue for this cultural development.

Many portrayals of the city's end are born of love for the city, not disgust. While visions of Armageddon focused on New York were certainly powerful, especially as evangelical Christianity expanded in the 1950s and onward, the bulk of novels and Hollywood films were produced and created by those who cherished the city. They may have lamented its state, especially during the 1960s and 1970s, but they did not reject the city. Rarely is the city destroyed in films of this era. The central theme seems to be not emptiness, as we saw earlier, especially in 1950s, but something very different: a devastated city in which, nonetheless, people can live. This was for many the sense of New York in the 1970s and early 1980s: a dying place filled with ruins and with people who had nowhere else to go, or nowhere else they would choose to go.

But while New York didn't disappear, optimism about the city was in short supply. In fact, the era from the middle of the 1960s through the end of the millennium was characterized by the lack of any utopian visions of a postapocalyptic world. There are no manifestoes such as Du Bois's "Comet" or Sinclair's *Millennium.* The film *The World, the Flesh, and the Devil* suggests that racial unity and a rejection of nuclear weapons might evolve in the wake of the apocalypse, but such optimism is rare in the urban crisis era. Only from some religious evangelicals, who grew in political and cultural importance through the last quarter of the twentieth century, do we see a positive spin on the disasters of the present, as having the potential to bring the Rapture and a new world. Optimism in the codas of novels and films takes the form of a vague hope for a calmer, somewhat more peaceful world. Resilience is the watchword—the city might survive but there will be no revolutionary shift in a better direction. Following Robert Venturi's modest dictum for architecture in the wake of modernism's dreams, New York disaster fantasies suggested, at best, that New York would be "almost all right." If the city survives, the best we can hope for is a utopia of the normal.[1]

Persistence of the Nuclear Threat

The fear of nuclear attack persisted, waxing and waning in importance in the political and cultural life of the city. It diminished as a central cultural preoccupation in the 1970s, only to resurface during the Reagan years, when the cold war threatened anew to turn hot. Under renewed fears of nuclear war, and the warnings of a powerful anti–nuclear energy and weapon movement, writers and filmmakers revisited the theme of the effects of a bomb dropped on New York.

The most influential popular study was Jonathan Schell's 1982 *Fate of the Earth,* which became the bible of the anti–nuclear weapon movement. Offering an update on the narratives from the 1950s of the outcomes of nuclear bombs dropped on New York, Schell describes the effect of "typical" bombs in 1982. His example is, of course, New York. He imagines for his readers two different types of bombs—a one-megaton bomb, about eighty times the power of the Hiroshima bomb, and a twenty-megaton bomb—dropped either above the Empire State Building or at its base.[2] The "smaller" bomb, exploded about a mile and

a half above, would "gut or flatten almost every building between Battery Park
and 125th Street," an eight-mile stretch. "The physical collapse of the city," he
writes, "would certainly kill millions of people. The streets of New York are narrow ravines running between the high walls of the city's buildings. In a nuclear
attack, the walls would fall and the ravines would fill up. The people in the buildings would fall to the street with the debris of the buildings, and the people in
the street would be crushed by this avalanche of people and buildings. Winds
would blow up to four hundred miles an hour. And that is the small bomb. The
larger, twenty-megaton bomb would have 1,600 times the power of the Hiroshima bomb." The zone of destruction (which Chesley Bonestell had portrayed
as perhaps a half-mile), would have a radius of twelve miles and an area of more
than four hundred square miles, "reaching from the middle of Staten Island to
the northern edge of the Bronx, the eastern edge of Queens, and well into New
Jersey."[3]

Novels continued to mine the fear of nuclear attacks. In Robert Buchard's
Thirty Seconds over New York (1969), an attack on New York comes by way of
a crazed American colonel of Chinese descent. Even a children's book such as
James and the Giant Peach played on the fear of something falling from the sky to
destroy the city. As the great peach floats toward New York, terror hits the streets.
The peach lands on the spire of the Empire State Building—where Bonestell and
dozens of others had focused their apocalyptic images—and becomes the talk of
town.[4]

But by the time New York had sunk into bankruptcy in 1976, the theme
of nuclear apocalypse in New York had lost its dominance. One reason is that
popular culture embraced what those people on the street, mockingly watching Fiorello La Guardia stage a civil defense exercise, had recognized: that civil
defense would never work. Tom Wicker, in a 1983 essay in the *New York Times,*
wrote of the "hardest truth." Criticizing the Federal Emergency Management
Agency (FEMA), which was holding fast to the decadeslong belief that 80 percent of the American population could survive a nuclear war, Wicker declared
this view simply "ridiculous." Civil defense, he wrote, "cannot make nuclear war
generally—or probably even marginally—survivable."[5] An increasingly common
view, which built on the protests of the 1940s and 1950s against civil defense,
was that these civil defense scenarios were built upon wildly optimistic assumptions—about how much warning the city would have; about the continued operation of subways, buses, and cars; about the orderliness of evacuations. In direct
contrast to the ark motif that had been common across the twentieth century—in

Second Deluge and *When Worlds Collide*—Physicians for Social Responsibility offered a study critical of FEMA's survival forecasts, which the group titled *The Counterfeit Ark.*[6]

While FEMA moved steadily forward with elaborate scenarios of how to evacuate those New Yorkers who chose to leave, many city and federal officials, along with many New Yorkers themselves, scoffed. To the notion that New Yorkers would smoothly exit the city on subways, buses, trains, and the Staten Island Ferry, a former head of the New York Office of Civil Preparedness responded typically: "Christ Almighty! It took me twenty-five minutes to get through the Brooklyn-Battery Tunnel this morning because there was a little snow." A Brooklyn state senator wondered why so much confidence was being placed in the efficient movement of the trains during an attack when "the Transit Authority can't keep the trains rolling during an average rush hour." And to FEMA's recommendation that people rush into a bomb shelter in a crisis, New Yorkers offered another Bronx cheer. FEMA's own studies showed that a collapsing twenty-two-story building—not particularly tall by New York standards—would leave a thirty-three-foot pile of debris on top of an underground bomb shelter. New York's civil defense officials urged that the city's nuclear warning sirens be turned off. New York's City Council reflected this growing skepticism of civil defense by voting not to participate in crisis relocation planning.[7]

Some of the most biting critiques came in popular culture. *Dr. Strangelove; or, How I Learned to Stop Worrying and Love the Bomb* (1964) is a savagely comic evisceration of the idea that rational planning could save us from nuclear war, or from the aftermath. *Fail-Safe* as well reminds us of the devil's choices that the nuclear era might present us with. There would, of course, be no "civil defense" and early warning against the "friendly fire" the movie portrays. *The World, the Flesh, and the Devil* attacks civil defense in the most direct terms. Early in the film, as Ralph (played by Harry Belafonte) makes his way to New York, he passes by the pathetic remnants of the elaborate civil defense infrastructure. He grabs a gun and bullets from a now empty civil defense office in his rural Pennsylvania town center. As he gets closer to New York and sees the wreckage and emptiness along the way, civil defense signs are seen in the background, bearing the mantra "alert today, alive tomorrow." And on the George Washington Bridge and at the entrances to the Lincoln Tunnel, Ralph sees a scenario far more likely than any civil defense authority predictions of an orderly and speedy exit. Ralph passes the thousands of cars jamming the entrances, their owners gone. A permanent traffic jam is the lasting memorial to New York's end.

Harry Belafonte, as Ralph Burton, in a deserted Times Square in *The World, the Flesh, and the Devil,* 1959

Finally, in the 1970 novel *Thirty Seconds over New York,* which also has powerful cold war overtones, Robert Buchard suggests how difficult it would be to stop a terrorist hijacking a warplane with a nuclear weapon on board. As the novel nears its end, it becomes clear that nothing can be done to stop Fang Sen, part of a Chinese conspiracy to attack America, from dropping the bomb and destroying this "proud and rotting city that ruled over the whole world." The military, watching it all on screen, can do nothing: "The fantastic American war machine was at a standstill because no procedure had been devised to prevent this kind of incident. The men crowded into the three war rooms were naked, disarmed, alone in the face of this absurd and incredible thing: the 'bomb under the doormat,' the anonymous bomb, origin unknown, making no strategic sense—one lone bomb, gratuitously dropped with the sole purpose of razing a city, not to start or win a war." In the next second the report from the Omaha command center:

"New York no longer exists." Buchard, a soldier and later a French army reporter and television news reporter, asks at the end: "Was that the way it began?"[8]

The arms race continued and the nuclear threat was very real, but nuclear apocalypse was no longer the central theme in the imagination of New York's end. Just as city officials had proposed disconnecting the civil defense warning system, so too New Yorkers and Americans seemed less obsessed with the nuclear disaster theme. They were less invested in civil defense and therefore more resigned to complete annihilation in the event of a nuclear war. New Yorkers had also changed in other ways: many were no longer New Yorkers but suburbanites. With the growth of suburbs and the decline of the city in the 1960s and 1970s—the direct result of the 1950s dispersal policies and a host of other policies favoring suburbs over cities—many more people lived beyond the smallest concentric rings of target New York. Dispersal advocates may not have come close to reducing the allure of New York as a target, but nonetheless, by the 1960s they had achieved a significant decentralizing of New York.

Incomprehensible and utterly terrifying in the 1950s, nuclear war had by the 1970s become, ironically, a manageable fear. Nuclear war was, in terms of culture, passé. It was no longer the central problem—culturally and psychologically—of the time, and it was no longer the focus of works of fiction and film but rather, ironically, just a vehicle to explore other themes. Nuclear war didn't disappear; it just receded into the background. It was the scene-setting fact—"a nuclear war has led to New York becoming an irradiated danger zone"—but not the primary subject.

In 1976, at the nadir of New York's economic crisis, the singer-songwriter Billy Joel issued his *Turnstiles* album. One song on the album, "Miami 2017 (Seen the Lights Go Out on Broadway)," portrays New York's fiery end and a future world where everyone has fled southward to Florida. He suggests that the destruction looks little different from what New Yorkers already knew: blackouts, ruins in the middle of midtown, arson. "They burned the churches up in Harlem," he writes, "but no one really cared." The extinction in his apocalyptic vision of Broadway's lights—the bright symbol of the city said in another song never to sleep—is all but imperceptible to a jaded audience. And when the nameless invaders torch Harlem, it seems like just another day in nearly bankrupt New York. This is, in fact, the true poignancy in Joel's elegy for the city—not the physical destruction to these landmarks but the fact that none of it would leave much of an imprint because New Yorkers "see it all the time," in Harlem and the Bronx, and even at the crossroads of the world, Times Square, once the center of both popular and elite culture. Nuclear war was disastrous. But it wasn't so different from what New York was doing to itself.[9]

The Urban Crisis: Reality and Interpretation

New York's urban decline in the 1960s and 1970s was not the steepest, nor the longest lasting, nor the most all-encompassing. Detroit or St. Louis could easily claim a more tragic decline with no countervailing "rebirth." St. Louis literally dismantled itself and became, after Chicago, the largest exporter of bricks—all taken from the neat row houses that had once made up a booming city whose leaders hoped it would be the next Chicago or even New York.[10] But just as New York had symbolized American might and celebration on that VJ Day in 1945, so too it came to symbolize the depths of American economic depression and urban blight. The image of the kiss in Times Square on August 15, 1945, had been supplanted by the image of Charlotte Street in the Bronx, a ruin of a neighborhood that not even the president of the United States—three of them in a row—seemed able to improve.

The scope of New York's decline has been well documented, and is stunning, though it can now be spoken of as history (unlike Detroit, where the crisis is ongoing). Even in the glory days of New York's economic might, problems had loomed. As in most other older cities, manufacturing jobs fell rapidly: in New York the number of manufacturing jobs had been decreasing since the Great Depression and continued to do so through the 1970s. The decline—due to plant closings and relocation to the South and West, overseas, and to the suburbs—accelerated from the mid-1950s onward, bringing a massive loss of manufacturing jobs, a decline in the city's tax base, and a consequently rapid rise in its debt. By 1966 a majority of the region's manufacturing jobs were located outside the city proper. All this happened just as huge numbers of black and Puerto Rican people flowed into the city after World War II, pushed off the land because of the mechanization of farmwork and pulled by the opportunities of the city (including those that were fast disappearing), as well as freedom from the southern backlash to civil rights demands. Tensions grew between an increasingly poor minority community—the "last of the immigrants"—and older ethnic enclaves from Italy and eastern Europe. Discord between white union leaders and black communities came to a head—and came to symbolize all of the tensions between whites and minorities—in the 1968 Ocean Hill–Brownsville school controversy.

To many contemporary scholars, conservatives and liberals alike, New

York's decline began at the end of the 1960s, or, more precisely, at 5 A.M. on January 1, 1966, when city transit workers went on strike. John Lindsay's eventual acceptance of a strong contract for the transit workers signaled the beginning of the fiscal crisis. With ever higher demands from various municipal unions, and resultant tax increases and growing debt, the city was on a collision course with bankruptcy. The fiscal crisis of the city in 1975 was, according to this narrative, the result of overly generous contracts to the city's unions, especially the municipal unions, despite the absolute necessity of more stringent budgets. This now-dominant view holds that liberal policies toward crime, welfare, and union contracts created a "dependent individualism" built on a "riot ideology" that led to "free-handed" public spending and a flight from the rigorous moral code of the New Deal era. This narrative can now be found in virtually every survey of New York history.[11]

In fact, New York's decline was as much assassination as it was suicide. Those huge municipal debts were mounted not primarily by expensive social programs but in the massive effort to remake lower Manhattan as an office and financial center. The city government subsidized huge building projects such as the World Trade Center while at the same time destroying manufacturing enterprises. Indeed, one of the great historical ironies is that on the site of the World Trade Center was a bustling district of thirty thousand jobs, centered on the emerging radio and television industries. Radio Row it was called, and it might have become Silicon Alley. It was all leveled. Manufacturing in New York, and the world of those middle-class jobs, was destroyed not by the free hand of the market. It was destroyed in large measure by public policy. By the end of the millennium, manufacturing workers made up less than 10 percent of New York's workforce. Los Angeles had 13 percent.[12]

By 1975 the result of these structural and public policy choices was a city of widespread poverty, unemployment, racial segregation, and fury, combined with a physical landscape of ruin, the result of disinvestment, urban renewal, and arson. It was a film set waiting for the director's call for "Action!"

In *The Day the Earth Caught Fire,* the brief view of Manhattan's skyline is celebratory. It is the view of a glorious city, although we know that it is soon to be destroyed. In *The World, the Flesh, and the Devil,* the city is a cool, elegant sculpture garden of skyscrapers. It is haunting and beautiful in its emptiness. But in the fantasies of urban destruction amid the real urban crisis of the 1970s and early 1980s, New York is never clean, never beautiful, never cool, and never empty. These fantasies present a city of excess—too many people (especially black and brown ones), too much trash, too much violence. Susan Sontag's description of the science fiction movies of the 1950s is perhaps even better applied to the urban apocalypse movies of this era: "Science fiction film . . . is concerned with the aesthetics of destruction, with the peculiar beauties to be found in wreaking havoc, making a mess."[13]

But who is responsible for the mess? A powerful theme of the atomic bomb–inspired narratives of the 1950s was that if New York was to be destroyed, it would be because of mankind's self-destructive instinct. As Einstein said, the atomic bomb changed everything, except the way people think. Many of the 1950s disaster films, such as *Invasion, U.S.A.* and *Captive Women,* posit overt critiques of American society for its lack of preparedness and lack of vigilance. Nonetheless, responsibility for the actual destruction of the city usually lay far from New York. In other words, when the city is destroyed, the city itself is still victim, even if the people of the city (in their political inaction) and the country (in its belligerent or merely incompetent actions) may be culpable.

But in the fantasies of the urban-crisis era, New York's destruction is not caused by a Martian invader or a split-second event like a twenty-megaton bomb dropped a thousand feet above the city by the Soviet Union. The mess is the effect of years of social disintegration, and the responsibility lies with the people themselves. This view paralleled the popular narrative: that the city's excessive spending, coddling of criminals and welfare recipients, and acceptance of social disorder had led to its downfall. Eventually, studies of the structural roots of a widespread urban crisis would suggest that New York was victim to the same larger forces that had undermined most major cities of the Northeast and Midwest. But that view was slow to gain wide acceptance, and never overcame the competing blame-the-victim narrative.

Popular writing contributed to the juxtaposition of nuclear fear and fear of urban crisis. Journalists took the apocalyptic language of nuclear disaster and applied it to the city's dramatic decline. "Broken Apple," "S.O.S. New York," "The Destruction of Lower Manhattan," "Necropolis," "The Last Days of New York"—these are some of the journalistic and literary characterizations of New York's urban crisis. The semantic substitution had begun long before the era we usually associate with the urban crisis, with such accounts as a *U.S. News and World Report* story from 1955, "New York in Trouble." Lewis Mumford, who had warned in 1950 about the insecurity created by the atomic bomb, complained in *The City in History* (1961) of a different kind of urban disaster: "The arena, the tall tenement, the mass contests and exhibitions, the football matches, the international beauty contests, the strip tease made ubiquitous by advertisement, the constant titillation of the senses by sex, liquor and violence—all in true Roman style. . . . These are symptoms of the end: Magnifications of demoralized power; minifications of life. When these signs multiply, Necropolis is near, though not a stone has yet crumbled. For the barbarian has already captured the city from within. Come, hangman! Come, vulture!"[14] The journalist Midge Decter woke up after the night of looting during the New York blackout of 1977 and described the feeling of having "been given a sudden glimpse into the foundations of one's house and seen, with horror, that it was utterly infested and rotting away."[15] At the nadir of New York's crisis, Bishop Paul Moore gave a powerful sermon at the Cathedral of St. John the Divine on Easter Sunday. He lambasted the government for abandoning the city like "rats leaving a sinking ship." "Look over your city and weep, for your city is dying," he intoned from the pulpit, invoking Jeremiah, long a favorite of evangelicals. "In sections of the Bronx, Brooklyn and Harlem, great hulks of buildings stand abandoned and burned." He concluded, with some of the leaders of the city and the nation in his audience: "Cut through the fog of statistics and see the moral decisions behind them. Be part of the rising, not the dying!"[16] Jason Epstein, editor of the *New York Review of Books,* wrote a long essay about the problems in New York, focusing especially on the destructive impact of the Lower Manhattan Expressway and the World Trade Center. After a survey of the city's obstacles, he offered a rather grim bit of optimism: "Who knows? We may survive. It's hard to imagine how, but it's hard to imagine that we won't."[17]

Richard J. Whalen's 1964 article in *Fortune* was followed by a 1965 book that summarized the city's coming urban crisis as well as any. Entitled *A City Destroying Itself: An Angry View of New York,* it was a merciless summary of the city's failings. The downward spiral was, for Whalen, in large measure caused by structural shifts affecting urban centers across the country: the decline of the middle class, the flight to the suburbs, and the physical decline of the old urban centers. "New York is destroying itself under the impact of forces that are being felt in every city. New York represents the fullest expression—for good or ill—of our urban culture. It is the macrocosm of every city's problems and aspirations. It matters, therefore, to Americans everywhere what New York is—and what it is not."[18]

But the crisis was also a destruction of the spirit. "How fares the human spirit in this great metropolis?" Not well, according to Whelan. The "apathy and venality" of politicians was matched by the "cold unconcern of the city's builders," the "remoteness and indifference of the city's business and financial leaders," and the selfishness of virtually everyone else. "If people are driven and their senses dulled, if they are alienated and dehumanized, the city is on the way to destroying itself." New York had always been on the "edge of madness," but with a riot in Harlem in 1964, Whelan argued, New York had become the "most nervous city in America." "The city," he declared, "is not safe." There were not simply crime waves but a "relentless rise of flood waters" of crime. Floods had been put to many metaphoric uses in the course of New York's history. Here, crime was not merely a threat that hurt individuals but a flood that would drown the city.[19]

The focus of these accounts returned repeatedly to one place: the South Bronx. Indeed, it was often one street—Charlotte Street—that bore the weight of the entire urban crisis. Stewart Alsop, who had written a frightening description of the effects of a nuclear war in "Your Flesh Should Creep" for the *Saturday Evening Post* in 1946, found himself, by 1972, writing about a different form of urban disaster: the modern urban ruin of the South Bronx. It was not simply that the neighborhood exhibited the new pathologies of big cities, but rather that those pathologies were leading to the abandonment of the city. The South Bronx, he wrote, is "visibly dying." The area came to be the symbol not only of New York's despair but of the decline in America's cities more generally.[20]

The urban crisis as projected on screen and written on the page explored and exploited new themes. Four themes in particular were pervasive in the films, novels, and journalism of this era: a devastated and dangerous New York walled off from the rest of the world; a city of infertility, where no children will be born; a city bent, through urban renewal and the removal of "blight," on destroying itself; and a city ruining itself through environmental degradation.

The image of New York as walled off, physically segregated from the rest of the country, has an old lineage, dating back to the barricade that protected the seventeenth-century settlement of New Amsterdam and gave the name to the city's most famous street. Indeed, one of New York's central clichés is that it is on the edge of the nation and continent—culturally and socially, as well as physically. But the notion of a wall to keep people from leaving or entering New York is a shocking rhetorical move, as it is New York's magnetic draw—its ability to pull in immigrants from foreign lands, artists, writers, people with money, and the youth of the heartland—that has largely defined the city. Still, this motif of containment fits with the reality of the latter decades of the twentieth century: for a hundred years, New York had been expanding, by tens and hundreds of thousands of people a year. But beginning in 1945 the metropolitan area began to balloon while the city itself declined in population. Many fled the city and, when they got to their suburbs, sought to prevent what they had left—violence, drugs, physical decay, minorities—from coming over the bridges and through the tunnels to their new, across-the-river paradise.[21] The farther people fled from the city, and the longer they stayed away, the more dangerous the city came to seem in their minds. Filmmakers and novelists took the real conditions of the city to their logical conclusion. New York could become a place where no one wants to enter, but everyone wants to exit.

One of the best examples of fortress New York comes in *Escape from New York,* one of several important New York disaster films of the early 1980s, when the city was already in urban despair. The film begins where *Fail-Safe* ends: with a radar view of Manhattan Island. This was a central fear of the nuclear age: that the city would become just a few diode lights on a radar screen, extinguished almost as easily as turning a switch. But in *Escape from New York,* we quickly see that this is not the radar of an attacking fighter jet but rather the federal government's own monitoring equipment, surveying the federal prison called Manhattan in the year 1997. The entire island has been turned into a maximum security prison, but a prison with no guards inside. The bridges and tunnels have been destroyed, making Manhattan truly an island once again. The president's plane has crashed into the city, and the government needs someone to fly in and rescue him. Snake Plissken (played by Kurt Russell), a convict and ex-soldier, is offered his freedom in exchange for the safe return of the president. Just to be sure he doesn't flee, he is wired with an explosive device that will be disarmed only when he returns with the president. Plissken floats a glider into the city, circling the mayhem and landing on top of the World Trade Center, solid as ever amid the destruction. The film takes him through the horrible streets of Manhattan, where complete anarchy, physical and social, reigns.

For the *New York Times* film critic Vincent Canby, this portrait of Manhattan—"There are no services, no government, no work. The place is a random trash heap"—could have been "the nightmare of someone who decided to stay in town last weekend." The film, he argued, "works so effectively as a warped vision of ordinary urban blight that it seems to be some kind of hallucinatory editorial."[22] For *Time*'s Richard Corliss, the film had the opposite effect.

> It makes more sense to see *Escape from New York* as a ferocious parody of popular notions about Manhattan today—the mugger's playground and pervert's paradise made notorious in comedy monologues and movies like *Death Wish* and *Taxi Driver.* In *Escape,* parking meters are spiked with gaping corpse heads, bridges are mined to kill, the New York Public Library houses an evil

Poster for *Escape from New York*, 1981. Manhattan Island Prison

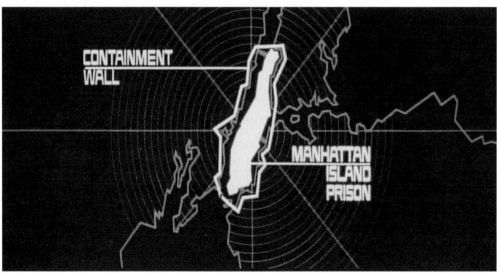

genius named Brain, and Penn Station is littered with train carcasses out of a Brobdingnagian toy chest. John Carpenter is offering this summer's moviegoers a rare opportunity: to escape from the air-conditioned torpor of ordinary entertainment into the hothouse humidity of their own paranoia.[23]

The motif of the walled city operated in a variety of ways. In *Escape from New York,* the federal government has chosen to isolate the Manhattan Island Prison with a huge "containment wall" that allows no one in or out. A similar notion plays out in the film *After the Fall of New York,* although in a slightly different way. New York is a war zone, controlled by the Euracs, who seek the remaining healthy humans for experiments, while exterminating the rest. One character declares: "Getting into Manhattan is easy; it's getting out that's impossible." A film that hit the theaters in 1982, *1990: Bronx Warriors*, featured the Bronx patrolled by helicopter while its citizens—organized into vicious gangs—are prohibited from leaving. The pilot of a police helicopter watching the border expresses an extreme view of a popular disdain for the inhabitants of the most devastated borough: "If it were up to me, I'd clean the whole goddamn borough with napalm. Just sizzle 'em out of existence. . . . Just be thankful we never have to go down there . . . scum of the earth. . . . Lousy cockroaches think they own the whole fucking borough."

But in some films and novels, the wall that separates the postapocalyptic city from the rest of the world is invisible. In *The World, the Flesh, and the Devil,* Ralph hints at this when he wonders why no else has surfaced or returned. "I keep expecting everyone to come back." Charlton Heston's Detective Thorn, in *Soylent Green,* scoffs at the idea of leaving Manhattan: it is illegal to go to the country, and every other city is just like New York. In Paul Auster's *In the Country of Last Things,* New York is an overcrowded, impoverished, and desperate city; no one can leave, though many seek a dangerous exit across harsh territory. And finally, in Madeleine E. Robins's *Stone War* we find a city that is left to defeat its demons after a great disaster, without aid from anyone outside the city. No aid comes, no one returns, the city rests in a liminal space, a victim of disaster, left to fend for itself. Only when an internal battle has taken place, and a great wrong confronted, can people return to rebuild.

The city as a dangerous, degraded, and diseased place needing a protective wall fit neatly with another prevalent theme: the death of the city through infertility. Catastrophe and romance, we have seen, seem indelibly linked. Indeed, in many New York disaster scenarios, it is in the crucible of disaster that romance is born and sexual relations consummated. But the apocalyptic visions

Apocalypse now: abandoned buildings from the 1970s stand in for a future New York in *1990: Bronx Warriors*, 1982

The Brooklyn Bridge lies in ruins in *Captive Women*, 1952

After the Fall of New York, **1983**

of the urban crisis era point specifically to a new theme: the problem of reproduction in the fantasies of New York's end.

Captive Women, on a par with *King of the Rocketmen* in the cheap-
ness of its special effects, nonetheless holds interest for its prurient subplot.
The "Mutates" are a band of survivors whose ancestors' genes were mutated by
nuclear radiation. They dream of producing a people devoid of physical scars.
To that end, they allow only couples of a certain fitness to marry and reproduce.
But even these couples continue to reproduce children with deformities, albeit
milder ones. The only way a mutated man can be genetically "cleansed" of this
thousand-year-old curse is to reproduce with a "norm" woman and produce a
"clean" baby, thereby starting the long process of purifying the race. (There is
no suggestion that a norm man could marry a mutated woman and produce a
healthy child.) The film's hopeful ending comes when a norm woman falls in
love with the hero (who is, of course, very modestly scarred), the chief of the
mutates.

The interest in sterility as a central issue in the New York destruction genre flowed from the growing understanding of the effects of radiation, which causes sterility as well as physical and mental retardation of babies who were in utero at the time of the exposure. Many of those effects became clearer with time, in second-generation victims of Hiroshima and Nagasaki, though those living near testing sites also developed symptoms. But the issue blossomed as a subject in popular culture only in the 1970s and 1980s, in the ordeal of the urban crisis. Indeed, the notion of a city that could no longer reproduce seemed analogous to the economic sterility of the city. The language and issues of nuclear disaster fears were transposed into the rhetoric of urban apocalypse.

The Italian-made *After the Fall of New York* (1983) opens with an African-American man playing a trumpet and a destroyed New York skyline in the background. "See?" he declares. "They baked the big apple." The city has been decimated and is now a huge pile of waste and rubble under the control of the Eurac—half-man, half-ape—military force, which years earlier had come from "across the ocean" to foment nuclear war and contaminate the entire city. Gangs (such as the "Harlem Hunters") are everywhere and the streets are battlegrounds. There are few recognizable landmarks, save for the Statue of Liberty, which again stands as the symbol of lost glory. The Euracs are bent on exterminating the few remaining survivors of the local population. Among native New Yorkers is only one fertile woman; there hasn't been a human child born in fifteen years since the nuclear holocaust. If the Euracs can find the nameless woman and destroy her five hundred eggs, the resistance will die. The Pan American Confederation sends a small team, headed by the warrior Parsifal, to find her and help renew the human race. The goal is not to save New York but to take her and the few remaining other people to the galaxy Alpha Centauri and start a new human race. Parsifal and his team head through old PATH train tunnels (the bridges and other tunnels were destroyed and never rebuilt) to find this last fertile woman.

The theme of the sterile city had a long life, persisting into the new millennium, in such novels as Auster's *In the Country of Last Things* and in the 2001 film *A.I.: Artificial Intelligence*. But in the 1970s a new set of environmental fears took hold. Earthquakes, destructive creatures, catastrophic weather—these were the long-standing themes of nature's exceptional wrath and persisted in the late-twentieth-century New York destruction genre. But destruction of the environment—soiling our own nest—took greater hold on the imaginations of writers and filmmakers.

Nature as New York's destroyer is one of the most persistent of themes. Nature's wrath could be the tool of an angry God or simply the random result

The Day the Earth Caught Fire, **1962**

of the incomprehensible movement of the galaxy's celestial objects. Response to natural disaster is varied, from efforts to stop an impending disaster to the creation of a literal or figurative ark. But beginning around midcentury, we see a growing emphasis on mankind's role, not only in destroying himself and his cities but in transforming the natural forces of the planet. Natural catastrophe has become the earth's angry response to man's hubristic manipulation of the basic building blocks of the universe.

We have already seen how mad scientists appearing in the *Superman* comics of the late 1930s and early 1940s figured out ways to direct comets toward cities or otherwise misuse nature. And we have seen how nuclear testing—the dress rehearsals for the war no one wants—awakens beasts that terrorize New York and other cities in such films as *The Beast from 10,000 Fathoms* and the *Godzilla* series. In the British film *The Day the Earth Caught Fire* (1962), dual tests by the United States and the Soviet Union, at opposite poles of the earth, push the earth's axis out of kilter, sending the earth closer and closer to the sun.[24]

But real-life tests effected even more fundamental shifts in the imagination of disaster. The atomic revolution meant not only that cities could be destroyed in an instant, and perhaps all the people eliminated by radiation death, but that the world itself could be made uninhabitable. The urban crisis of the 1960s added a new layer of environmental fear. We could ourselves, through normal procreation and our instinct toward crowding, violence, and political corruption, create cities of environmental ruin. The environmental movement of the 1960s had awakened Americans to the silent killers they had used and imbibed on a daily basis.

Some of the best and most didactic urban crisis–era critiques of the environmental degradation of New York came from comic books. In a 1962 issue of *The Fantastic Four* the undersea monarch Namor, the Sub-Mariner, launches an attack on New York City in retaliation for the dumping of radioactive materials into the ocean by the "surface men." An amphibious monster named Giganto is sent by Namor to assault the city, cutting an enormous swath of destruction.[25] The battles between Marvel Comics' Namor the Sub-Mariner and the surface men are in part about the pollution of the waters where Namor and his people of Atlantis live. In a 1973 issue of *Sub-Mariner,* "Invasion of New York," Namor brings an army to the surface not to destroy the city but to recapture Tamara, a mermaid held in captivity by the United Nations. Namor complains, on his way up, about the "befouled" river waters."[26] Perhaps the best example of comic-book environmental awareness is *Kamandi: The Last Boy on Earth,* in which the protagonist paddles a raft through a New York City reclaimed by the sea.[27] Only the tops of buildings are visible, with such recognizable landmarks as the Empire State Building and the State of Liberty clearly identifying the region. *Kamandi* is set hundreds of years after a "great cataclysm" has altered the world.[28]

Humans fouled not just the water, but also food. Revelations about the dangers of DDT and other pesticides found their way into futuristic fantasies about the manipulation of our diet. Following up on his role in the two *Planet of the Apes* films, Charlton Heston starred in a radically different New York disaster film. While *Planet of the Apes* built to the revelation that the earth had been destroyed by nuclear war, *Soylent Green* pictured a New York in the grip of another very human problem. The film is set in 2022 in a New York of forty million people, the entire city looking a bit like Orchard Street in the city's Lower East Side, circa 1910: crowds of people dressed in dirty old clothes, living in cramped quarters, or even sleeping, one atop another, on staircases. Everyone squabbles

Soylent Green, 1973

over the modest scraps of food available. Most just eat what is becoming the primary source of food: Soylent Green.

Heston plays Thorn, a police detective, charged with investigating the death of the head of the manufacturing company that makes the Soylent Green wafers. Thorn gradually uncovers a massive conspiracy, and the revelation is revolting: the primary ingredient of Soylent Green is processed human remains. The impoverished masses, who live strictly segregated from the wealthy, are lured to a euthanasia center, where they are treated to fantasies of their choosing, perhaps still available beyond the city's limits but strictly forbidden to them, as they slowly fall asleep forever.

The nightmare is not a post–nuclear war apocalyptic tale. In fact, its allusions refer more to the Holocaust. Toward the end of the film, Thorn's friend Sol (played by Edward G. Robinson) takes the evidence of Soylent Green's composition to a secret council hidden in the public library. They want to bring the evidence to the Council of Nations. "Good God," Sol declares, when he recognizes the difficulty, if not the impossibility, of bringing the Soylent Green conspirators to justice. "What God?" an old woman with a thick eastern European accent asks. "Where will we find him?" It is after this that Sol decides to end his life. At the end of the film, Thorn, mortally wounded, urges the people sleeping on the floor of a church to fight against the conspiracy. "Soylent Green is people!" he yells as he is taken away on a stretcher. "We've gotta stop 'em somehow!" But, it is too late for a hero to save this degraded world. The film ends not with the conspiracy revealed but with a scene of tulips swaying in a field, perhaps from Thorn's final wish at the euthanasia center.

The most powerful New York disaster scenarios involving environmental changes are those of climate change that utterly destroy the city. For example, in J. G. Ballard's disturbing novel *Hello America* travelers from Europe have returned to the abandoned continent after environmental disasters of the 1980s and 1990s and the disappearance of fossil fuels. Europe's effort to open greater areas, such as the Arctic, to settlement leads to melting of northern ice floes, upsetting the natural balance of the Gulf Stream. As a result the Mississippi River dries up, and all of America becomes a desert. New York is a now a southwestern landscape of sand dunes and cacti. The Hudson is dry. Sand has drifted up to the second story of most buildings. In the center of Times Square stands a giant saguaro cactus, thirty feet tall; in Rockefeller Plaza, salt grass chokes the "sand-filled concourse." Inevitably, Ballard also pays homage to the Statue of Liberty, victim of so many attacks over the past two centuries. The "drowned mermaid" had sunk after a failed attempt to rescue her during the evacuation of America at the time of the great ecological crisis, sometime in the twenty-first century. She was "left to break up in the cold waters of the next century," somewhere beyond the shore now littered with "dozens of rusty hulks . . . relics of the panic a century earlier when America had finally abandoned itself." Following a route common in disaster fantasies, the travelers head down the New Jersey turnpike to Washington, D.C., where they find Abraham Lincoln up to his knees in sand. One would have to go to Las Vegas to find vegetation: the desert gambling mecca has become a tropical landscape.[29]

The image of dystopian New York—even as environmental degradation was occurring in the present—was set in the future. But as popular culture imagined an apocalyptic future for the city, others imagined the apocalypse much closer to home, in the city's own destruction of itself through urban renewal and "blight" removal.

The sense that New York had little respect for its physical past has a long legacy, going back at least to Philip Hone's succinct summary in 1845 of the New York attitude toward the past: "Overturn! Overturn! Overturn!"[30] But in the 1960s and 1970s the combination of economic crisis and the shredding of the city by urban renewal projects gave literary depictions of the city's physical transformation an apocalyptic overtone. Though Walker Evans had romanticized the work of demolition experts and their "loving destruction of a building" in an article for *Fortune* in 1951, after a decade of urban renewal projects few were still willing to follow him in celebrating the work of the urban planner.[31] The photojournalist Danny Lyons titled his portrait of the transformation of lower Manhattan to make a clear point. *The Destruction of Lower Manhattan* showed the wholesale demolition of hundreds of eighteenth- and nineteenth-century buildings to make way for the skyscrapers of the new economy. In the process, an older colonial and Dutch city was irretrievably lost. These losses were decried by a diverse range of writers, including Louis Auchincloss, A. J. Liebling, Gay Talese, and Arthur Miller, as well as artists such as Claes Oldenburg, who made art of detritus recovered from urban renewal projects.[32]

One of the most poignant essays of this genre was Gay Talese's "Panic in Brooklyn."[33] The panics of World War II had been about the threat of German attack. In 1964, when Talese wrote the story, the panic was caused by the city's own destroyer, the urban planning guru Robert Moses. Talese describes the sense of resignation and pain felt by a community in the shadow of the Verrazano Narrows Bridge project. The loss is total—the community has been destroyed at the hands of the planners. Residents stand powerless in the face of the "inevitability of development" and the nervous worry that they will be the last ones to leave. Protest is impossible, as Robert Moses seems beyond reach. There are angry confrontations in city council, but ultimately it seems that protest can only fail. Even the planners working for Moses are not immune—in Talese's story, one of those planners realizes that construction of the bridge will require the demolition of his mother-in-law's house.

The focus on the destructive tendencies of urban redevelopment brings us full circle, back to the Bronx in the mysterious 1981 film *Wolfen. Wolfen* seems, on its face, a typical example of the urban-crisis genre. The city is terrorized by the wolfen, beasts that appear out of nowhere, ghost-like, to rip their prey to shreds. Seeking a pattern in the wolfen attacks, the police detective Dewey Wilson (played by Albert Finney) finds his way to the South Bronx, specifically Charlotte Street. The South Bronx as breeding ground for a pack of vicious wolves that terrify Manhattan—this has the feeling of another *1990: Bronx Warriors*.[34]

But *Wolfen* rises beyond the crude with its interest in who the wolfen are and what they are after. The movie becomes a mystical rumination on the city's own process of tearing itself down, and thus an especially powerful exploration of the urban-crisis theme. Native Americans assembling in a bar near Charlotte Street know the secret of the wolfen, and slowly reveal it to Wilson. The wolfen are "life that will prey on us just as we prey on this earth." The wolfen,

Albert Finney as Dewey Wilson in the Bronx in *Wolfen,* **1981. The final image of the film**

increasingly denied their habitat in the sprawling, polluting urban society, have retreated "to the ghetto, the slum areas of your cities . . . the graveyards of your fuckin' species," as one man puts it. "In their eyes, you are the savages." The Native Americans who deliver this message, unlike the dominant white culture, are portrayed as being in tune with and protective of nature and natural forces.

The South Bronx, ground zero for urban depravity in the city that symbolizes urban depravity, is the site of new investment in the form of the Vanderveer Towers, an apartment complex planned by one of New York's biggest developers to rise from the devastated streets. The home of the wolfen—an abandoned church amid the mass of rubble—is on the blighted site scheduled for the future towers. The wolfen, it appears, have lashed out in order to stop the final desecration of the neighborhood by rapacious eminent domain. "They kill to protect" their home, proto antigentrification activists of the sort that would populate the musical *Rent!* in the 1990s. The wave of killing is finally stopped by detective Wilson, who, surrounded by wolfen, destroys the model of Vanderveer Towers, signaling to the beasts that the urban-renewal scheme will not go forward. The last image of the film is of the Native American men standing atop one of the diagonal cables of the Brooklyn Bridge, making echoing calls—perhaps as signal to the wolfen, perhaps as admonition to the city to regain its connection to nature and to resist the destructive tendencies of its builders. The way out of the urban crisis was at hand, but not through profiteering and disrespect for nature.

Urban Rebirth

In 1984, on the heels of countless movies portraying a physically and morally crumbling city of the present and future, came a new hit disaster film. In this film a band of unlikely saviors seeks the cause of the demons who are wreaking havoc on the city. But for those who know *Ghostbusters,* that description utterly misses the central humor of the film: it is a camp takeoff on a disaster movie, playing on the tropes of urban crisis and New Yorkers' emotional need for heroes. The "ghostbusters," a bumbling trio of geeky "parapsychology" professors (played by Bill Murray, Dan Aykroyd, and Harold Ramis) who have been dismissed from Columbia University, are called on to catch petulant green demons bent on causing mayhem in the city's finest hotels and apartments. Soon they realize they have tapped into something much more dangerous: the city is threatened by an ancient Sumerian God named Gozer the Gozerian, who has found a home in a Central Park West apartment tower. After defeating Gozer, who has managed to

Ghosts are released into the city in *Ghostbusters*, 1984. A failed attempt to control the problem ends up creating a King Kong–sized Stay Puft Marshmallow Man

occupy the sultry body of Dana Barrett (Sigourney Weaver), and sending Barrett, gauzily clothed, to the roof of the apartment tower, the trio manages one last bumbling act: they inadvertently unleash a new creature, following in King Kong's path, to terrorize Manhattan's streets: a gigantized advertising symbol, the Stay Puft Marshmallow Man. Like all good creatures who invade New York, it pounds its way down the avenue, only to meet its end—in this case, melting into a sticky pile of marshmallow goo.

Set in a newly prosperous New York, the film makes clear it is not exploring the decrepit ruins of a declining New York. *Ghostbusters* celebrates the slimy green monsters as annoyances rather than true dangers to people and the city. The film lampoons the history of creatures attacking New York, as well as the OK Corral–like image of heroes marching down the street together to face their nemesis (in this case by crossing the streams of their weapons in a sly reference to male urination humor). Clearly, the fortunes of New York had shifted, and consequently, so had the tone of its disaster movies. From dark portraits of urban crisis in the not-so-distant future, American culture began offering in the 1980s and 1990s a new generation of disaster narratives, dedicated more to humor and entertainment than to warning.

By the early 1980s, when some of the classics of the urban-crisis genre hit the screens, the city had survived the worst and was about to enter two decades of robust economic development and resurgent wealth. One might have expected, then, a fairly dramatic shift in the nature of New York disaster scenarios, a sloughing off of the urban-crisis motifs of *Escape from New York* and other such films. We might even have anticipated a decline in the desire to imaginatively destroy New York, and a move to places more surely dystopic than this newly scrubbed, crime-free city. Los Angeles, the second city of disaster, does come into its own in this era, serving as setting for an increasing number of disaster films and novels. But what is striking is the persistence of disaster narratives in films and novels set in a New York City that seems increasingly safe from economic or even military disaster. Indeed, even as the millennium approached, and New York was arguably in the midst of its greatest, and latest, economic boom, American culture's fascination with violence and disaster scenarios of all types—from police-chase television programs to animal-attack exposés to nuclear apocalypse movies—continued to grow, and New York remained a favorite venue. The obsession with destroying New York still pervaded every aspect of our culture. The ever growing number of New York disaster films and novels, as well as software programs, album covers, comic books, and greeting cards, give the lie to the theory that destruction fantasies are simply a way for American society to "let off steam" by projecting a particular era's fears onto screen, paper, and canvas. The imagined destruction of New York was also—and especially in the last decades of the twentieth century—an homage to the city that, phoenix-like, once again renewed and reasserted itself as the capital of capitalism.

America celebrated the "return" of New York in the way it knew best: with entertaining and even humorous images of the city's destruction. The city's resurgence was welcomed in two ways. First, the city's newly cleaned-up sites—

new skyscrapers, a clean and safe Central Park, buffed historic landmarks—found their way into a series of disaster films with traditional themes. There was a spate of assaults by invading creatures (Quetzalcoatl and the old standbys Godzilla and King Kong), as well as natural disasters (meteors and earthquakes), all of which came to happy endings (despite conveniently forgotten destruction that takes place during the course of each movie). Second, although the images of New York as a crime-ridden city persisted long after its crime rate had fallen well below average among America cities, a new humor and campy engagement with urban disaster characterized the films of the 1980s and 1990s. Whether in the films *Mars Attacks, Independence Day,* and *Ghostbusters* and its sequel or on the television show *Futurama,* the destruction of New York came to be meant for laughs. Right up to September 11, 2001, humorous images of New York's fictional destruction pervaded American culture.[35]

But just as that urban rebirth was skin deep—poverty and physical degradation continued to pervade many parts of the city, especially beyond Manhattan—so too the campy disaster film was only the surface of American culture's engagement with New York. As the city approached the millennium, a new darkness in some New York disaster narratives shared screen time with the ebullient humor of others. Indeed, there was a new depth to the bleak vision of New York's end in some films, fiction, and graphic novels. Moving beyond violent urban-disaster movies or science fiction films with happy conclusions, a set of works in the 1980s and 1990s seemed bent on breaking through the shield of escapist entertainment and invoking a new sense of fear and dread about the future of the city.

This is the stew that American culture was cooking as New York headed toward the new century, and September 11, 2001.

Unruly Nature

Traditional displays of nature's wrath—the flood, the meteor, the comet, the earthquake, the storm—persisted in late-twentieth-century works and were rendered in increasingly dramatic and realistic form. Even before the most horrific of the urban-crisis movies hit the screens, a resurgent New York was featured in a classic nature-versus-man film. *Meteor,* which opened in 1979, featured some of big film stars of the day—Sean Connery, Natalie Wood, Henry Fonda—and proved to have a lasting influence on filmmakers. A comet collides with an asteroid in space and a five-mile-wide meteor hurtles fatally toward the earth. Sean

Poster for *Meteor,* 1979

Connery, playing the responsible but renegade scientist Paul Bradley, proposes the radical notion of blowing the rock up with a weapon he has developed in anticipation of just such a threat. Connery's invention, though, has been taken from him and put to illegal cold war purposes by the military: it secretly aims nuclear weapons at the Soviet Union. As it turns out, the Soviet Union has its own secret weapon. And so goes the parable: in the face of Mother Nature's violence, the United States and the USSR need each other if they are to survive.

A sliver of the meteor hits Hong Kong, giving a sense of the devastation ahead: huge waves rise and crash down on the city. But the main event is still to come: another chunk of the meteor is heading toward the eastern seaboard. As New York awakens to a new day, viewers are taken on a brief aerial tour of the city in all its glory, with the knowledge that disaster is on its way. Though it is an aerial view of the skyline, the effect is vaguely reminiscent of *Fail-Safe:* a last look at what is about to be lost. The meteor rips through Manhattan's skyscrapers and continues its path through the center of the island, carving a smoldering, half-mile-wide swath through Central Park.

For the time, the effects were stunning. The final image of the meteor's trench burning through the island looks like an updated version of a Chesley Bonestell illustration: taken from an oblique angle, highly detailed, richly colored. But there is an odd disconnect between this devastation and the movie's hopeful, last-minute victory. As the scientists, deep within their bunker, listen to radio reports about the successful destruction of the large meteor in space, they cheer and celebrate. No one heads to the surface to see the disaster caused by the smaller piece hitting the city. In contrast with the on-the-ground experience of the rubble in the urban-jungle disaster movies, the wreckage in *Meteor* is lovingly anesthetized.[36]

Meteor was the inspiration for other natural disaster films of the next two decades, including *Armageddon* and *Deep Impact,* both from 1998, which brought new technology to bear on these old themes. In *Armageddon,* a Texas-sized asteroid is headed for the earth. As it approaches, smaller pieces pepper the earth. While reference is made to cities around the world, the film delights in showing the missile-like effect of thousands of meteorites hitting New York's buildings and streets. Taxis and buses explode; the Chrysler Building's signature spire is sheared off (as in *Godzilla* of the same year). And as the dust settles on this first meteor shower, a panoramic shot of the city shows the two World Trade Center towers standing, but barely: one has taken a direct hit to the top floors, the other has had the bulk of its middle taken out and seems about to topple.

The Chrysler Building is sheared by a meteorite in *Armageddon*, 1998

Aftershock: Earthquake in New York, 1999

Deep Impact, which offered equally dramatic images of New York's destruction, also tells the story of an immense asteroid that hits the earth; this one creates a tidal wave that envelops the city. Director Mimi Leder pays homage to the long cinematic history of destroying the Statue of Liberty, offering a uniquely horrifying—and entertaining—vantage point. From underwater, she captures Lady

Cover of *Batman: Cataclysm*, 1999

Liberty standing tall, but with the tidal wave towering far above, about to engulf the statue. This is followed by a panoramic view of the waves cresting over the skyscrapers, as Manhattan Island is enveloped. The allusion is to *Deluge,* with its impressive early special effects. But the realism of the imagery evoked gasps of horror and delight in viewers. Later in the sequence, the Statue of Liberty's head floats underwater down an avenue among tumbling people and cars.[37]

The disasters need not come from outer space. Ever since 1906, earthquakes, though relatively rare among natural disasters, have been a favorite fear and fantasy of urban destruction. Two 1999 works showed the continued fascination with how the noble skyline, built on that supposedly unmovable bedrock, would fare in the face of a shifting and cracking fault line. *Aftershock,* a television movie, featured powerfully detailed and realistic images of the city in the wake of a massive earthquake. As always, the Statue of Liberty suffers a dramatic collapse, as do the Brooklyn Bridge and the Manhattan Bridge, the Stock Exchange, the Guggenheim Museum, Times Square, and countless skyscrapers. As with many physical disaster narratives, the human disaster—riots and looting that break out in the wake of the earthquake—is as terrifying as the natural event. The bulk of this film, however, is focused on rescue and rebuilding, and not the destruction itself. The film ends with scaffolding around a reconstructed Statue of Liberty, the city and its ideals restored.[38]

Godzilla, 1998: the lizard tramples a New Yorker, and leaves a hole in the MetLife Building

A far darker, but ultimately equally redemptive, tale is told in the graphic novel *Batman Cataclysm,* based on *Batman* comic books. The book dwells in the possibilities of a massive earthquake hitting New York stand-in Gotham City; a remarkable series of full-page images of Gotham's destruction in the wake of the earthquake makes up the core of the book. The images are especially striking when viewed from a post-9/11 perspective: buildings collapse in on themselves, pancaking floor by floor down to the ground; smoke billows through the city. But the storyline also allows the writers and illustrators to present the full range of urban destruction scenarios. The earthquake is just the beginning. The tremor unleashes looting and rioting reminiscent of the 1977 blackout. The urban crisis simmers just beneath the surface, needing only this natural disaster to release it. Prisoners escape from the jail on Blackwell's Island. Tidal waves and fires follow the earthquake. And into the void of chaos flows a terrorist cabal, whose leaders proclaim that Gotham has finally met its end. Batman and his superhero colleagues who help save the city realize, in the midst of its devastation, how much they love it. "I hardly recognize the skyline," says Robin. "That's because there's not much of it left," responds Batman. "Gotham's going to be a long time getting back on its feet." "If it ever does," says Robin. "At least it's over," declares Batman. "For now."[39]

Each type of destructive event in New York's history has provided an opportunity for the city's imaginers—its writers and journalists, painters, and filmmakers—to offer narratives of the city's future. While at times—during the violent class tensions of the late nineteenth century, for example, or in the depths of the city's economic despair of the 1970s—the stories New Yorkers told about themselves emphasized the apocalyptic, an equally powerful narrative has been one of renewal, destruction followed by robust growth and rebuilding. This was especially in evidence at the end of the twentieth century, when disaster fantasies usually ended with a coda of renewal. Many of the most dramatic films of New York's destruction in this era, for example, end with the city saved from utter destruction. In the 1998 *Godzilla,* the Chrysler Building crashes to the ground, hit by a stray missile aimed at stopping the monster's march through the city. Godzilla, in fact, does relatively little damage to the city; most of the de-struction is self-inflicted (much to the chagrin of some fans of the "classic" Japa-nese *Godzilla* films). *Deep Impact* ends with the clear sense that New York (and Washington) will be rebuilt by a new generation. Fantasies and premonitions of New York's destruction at the end of the century ended with an expectation that the "city resilient" would return.[40]

All these are earnest films: some are loaded with clear messages, but most offer sheer entertainment spectacle set in a city that people slowly were beginning again to enjoy and not fear. The films of late twentieth century used increasingly powerful computer technology to celebrate the city through entertaining fright. But another mode grew in importance in the last twenty years of the century: an ironic, campy spin on the New York disaster genre.

Winking at Catastrophe

Ghostbusters II, released in 1989, nearly a decade into New York's resurgence, played even more lovingly on the urban-crisis motifs and the New York disaster genre than its predecessor. Instead of portraying real threats from the urban-crisis era—armed gangs and postapocalyptic nightmares—the film shows a city threatened by its own bad attitude. Crime is down, prosperity up, but New Yorkers, as always, are angry people. This is praise and self-congratulation masquerading as criticism. New York has returned to greatness but has a few rough edges (which citizens are secretly proud of). The conceit of the film is that beneath the city flows a river of ectoplasm that has remained invisible to the people above. But New Yorkers' rising anger has caused the river to boil up, releasing ghosts and gremlins into the city to wreak havoc. (Despite their destructiveness, there is no fright in these monsters. They are actually cute, in a horrible way, and they are designed to be appealing and funny.) New Yorkers will have to curb their anger if the demons are to be stopped. Though the mayor proclaims, "Being miserable and treating other people like dirt is every New Yorker's God-given right!" the Ghostbusters press their appeal to the whole city. They urge the city to band together and rise above the city's faults and divisions in order to defeat the demons. "I can't believe that things have gotten so bad in this city that there's no way back," says Ray Stantz, played by Dan Aykroyd. "I mean, sure it's dirty, it's crowded, it's polluted, it's noisy and there's people all around who would just as soon step on your face as look atchya. But come on! There's gotta be a few sparks of sweet humanity left in this burnt-out burg!" The imagery of the urban crisis is still current, but now it is an object of fun. The history of violence, poverty, and unemployment is subsumed under the tongue-in-cheek critique of New York that the people aren't friendly enough. That is the extent of urban crisis in the late 1980s. And the day is saved by a benevolent creature. Upending the expectation of a destructive Godzilla or King Kong—or even the Stay Puft Man—we see an unshackled hero: the Statue of Liberty as she shuffles down Broadway. Awak-

Poster for *Independence Day*,
1996. An invading spaceship
settling over Central Park

Centuries—and cycles of New York's destruction and rebuilding—speed by as Phillip Fry lies cryogenically frozen in the opening sequence of *Futurama*, 1999. Visiting "old New York" a thousand years in the future

ened by the pleas of New York's citizens, Lady Liberty heads to an art museum in the Custom House, where a portrait of a sixteenth-century tyrant, Vigo Von Homburg Deutschendorf, has come to life and is uniting the demons in order to tear apart the city.[41]

Often in this period the classic disaster film and the campy comedy of New York disaster merge. *Independence Day* (1996) combines a fervent dedication to the disaster movie genre with a slant toward the campy and silly. The first half of the film builds to an explosive peak when invading, unstoppable Martian spaceships decimate the cities of the world. The two key images in the film—the money shots of disaster porn—are the attacks on the White House and the Empire State Building, which are obliterated by the vast spaceship that hovers over each city before blasting these landmarks into fiery nothingness.[42] It is only the day after the cities are destroyed—Independence Day—that the heroes regroup in Area 51 to devise a desperate plan to defeat the Martians. The film alternates between terrifying imagery and hokey winks at science fiction films of the past. Captain Steven Hiller (played by Will Smith), the hero who will save the day, also manages to get into a fistfight with one of the invading creatures (which may or may not actually have fists). And Jeff Goldblum as David Levinson offers some fine scenes of mad scientist humor as the crew struggles to get the alien craft working.

The camp celebrations of New York in the 1980s and 1990s explored all the past themes, not just imagined outer space invasions or creatures raised from somnolence. The critiques of urban renewal and demolition of historic New York that were common in the urban-crisis narratives are now turned into fodder for humor. Matt Groening's *Futurama* television series, which began airing in 1999, finds much to enjoy in the rapid destruction of the city, and in the remnants of "old" (circa 1999) New York. The opening of each show recaps how Fry, a bike messenger in 1999, ends up in a deep freeze until he wakes up in the year 3000. As the years spin by, New York is destroyed by laser-firing Martian spaceships, returns to nature, is rebuilt as a medieval castle city, is destroyed by Martians again, and finally turns into a futuristic city. With his two new friends, Bender and the one-eyed Leela, Fry goes down a ladder to see the exhibition of "old New York," on top of which the new city has been built. The Chrysler Building tower lies toppled; sharks swim in the Rockefeller Center ice skating rink. The "roof"—really the floor of the contemporary city—is visible on top of the demolished skyscrapers. The Empire State Building still stands, though only the top half is visible in the new city (the tube mass transit system has a stop halfway up the building). Bender tries to be helpful: "Hey, it's the ruins of everything you knew and loved. That ought to cheer you up." But Fry is devastated. "It's all gone. Yesterday it was here. Now it's gone. Even the urine smell is gone. It's like some horrible nightmare!" But of course the viewer is laughing as Fry cries. There is no "horrible nightmare." Both urban crisis and atomic disaster are, for the moment, distant from New Yorkers' imaginations.[43]

For the moment. Because alongside the freewheeling farces and camp celebrations were far darker visions of New York's end.

A New Darkness: Premillennial Anxieties in Fiction

There was nothing mysterious about nuclear apocalypse—the only question was who might cause it, and how people would survive afterward. The urban crisis, for all the complexities of the underlying causes that had led to physical, economic, and human ruin, was still straightforward in its effects: violence was the currency, and rubble and decay the background. But in the world of the novelists J. G. Ballard, Paul Auster, or Madeleine Robins, or of films such as *Wolfen,* we find forces at work well beyond human control—ambiguous causes of disaster, mysterious forces that are never revealed, depravity that seems to know no bounds and no end. These works move beyond both the nuclear fear and urban crisis, even as they use both as narrative background. Gone is the escape of many science fiction movies of the 1950s and 1960s and their function of inoculating us, as Susan Sontag argued, against real fears of the world's end through filmic displays of graphic destruction. It is almost as if filmmakers and novelists recognized that science fiction disaster films of the 1950s and 1960s were, as Sontag wrote, "the emblem of an *inadequate response.*"[44] They sought instead, as the millennium approached, more troublesome images of the destruction of the city, to get beyond mere escapism. Amid the city's growing prosperity, the fear of powerlessness, of a city utterly beyond human power to shape, seems pervasive. In these works, there are no "lessons" to be learned, no argument for civil defense or against nuclear weapons, and no urge to "love thy neighbor." There is only destruction and despair.

The most harrowing vision of the future is from a lesser-known book by Paul Auster, whose previous work (such as *The New York Trilogy*) had established him as one of the best storytellers of the city.[45] *In the Country of Last Things* takes the form of a letter from Anna Blume, who has ventured into an unnamed city to find her journalist brother, who had secreted himself in order to report to the rest of the country the horrors taking place there.

This is not a postapocalyptic story in the traditional sense. There are vague references to climate change and epidemics that have led to the ruinous state of the city, and to its authoritarian and utterly unstable governmental system. But what Blume finds is not a city in the midst of rebuilding after a horrible disaster, or a complete ruin where people live in primitive ways. It is something far worse: it is a city that is in inexorable physical and social decline, en route to its end. "Slowly and steadily, the city seems to be consuming itself, even as it remains." The book describes Blume's unsuccessful quest to find her brother, and her efforts to survive in this living hell. That hell is in part defined by overwhelming, near-universal poverty, rampant crime, collapsing infrastructure. Whole areas have been decimated by disease, rubble is everywhere, the homeless are the majority, and it is dangerous to go out at any time, especially with something valuable like a shopping cart (used to carry scavenged bits of the ruined city). The huge Sea Wall Project has made it impossible to leave. Much of the description sounds like an exaggerated—though scarcely hyperbolic—version of the South Bronx, as portrayed in any number of urban crisis novels and films. This city is not unlike the New York in *Escape from New York* or *1990: Bronx Warriors.*[46]

But in this city, poverty, crime, and general depravity are just the beginning. The basic principles of life have been overturned. No children are conceived any more. People exercise in order to run themselves to death. People go to high buildings not for the view but to leap off, to the thrill of people below. Explosions are heard, but neither the blasts nor their results are ever seen. Weather is utterly unpredictable. Feces is harnessed for energy, and all corpses "are required to be taken to one of the Transformation Centers" and turned into fuel. Whole sections of the city are leveled. "These are the last things," Anna writes. "A house is there one day, and the next day it is gone. A street you walked down yesterday is no longer there today." The city, she says, "robs you of certainty." It also robs you of memory: "It's not just that things vanish—but once they vanish, the memory of them vanishes as well."[47]

Anna fails to find her brother and is trapped in the city. She scavenges her way through the weeks and months and lives with a couple, Isabel and Ferdinand, who have managed to piece together a modest existence in a decaying tenement. Anna eventually makes her way to Woburn House, a settlement house where she helps provide for the poor, until even it collapses under the weight of the need. Amid all of the chaos she finds the most unlikely thing in this hell—love—when she meets Samuel Farr. Calling on a motif so common in apocalyptic works—*The Twilight Zone*'s "Time Enough at Last" episode; *The World, the*

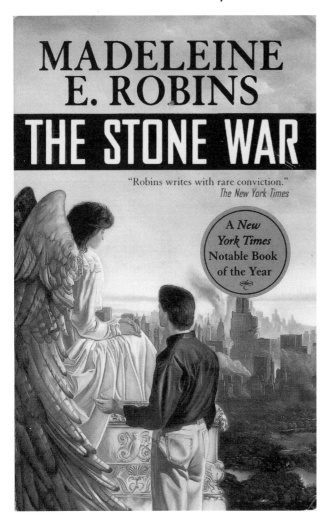

Cover of Madeleine E. Robins,
***The Stone War,* 1999**

Flesh, and the Devil; and *The Stone War* and *The Day After Tomorrow*—she ends
up with Farr in the city's main library. He has decided to write a history of what
happened to the city, and she assists him. But like the boys in Graham Greene's
short story "The Destroyers," Blume and Farr survive by dismantling their home
step by step: they must burn books to keep warm in the horrible winter. The
couple is separated and then reunited at Woburn House. There they make their
plans for an escape, via Fiddler's Rampart. The letter, and the book, end with
Anna promising to write more when they are free.

The epigraph for the book comes from Hawthorne's 1843 tale "The Celestial Railroad": "Not a great while ago, passing through the gate of dreams, I visited
that region of the earth in which lies the famous City of Destruction." That story's

narrator is deluded into believing himself en route to the Celestial City. *In the Country of Last Things,* however, offers not even a vision of heaven in its hellish city.

There is something equally affecting about Robins's novel *The Stone War,* which follows a deeply unsettling path before reaching a much more hopeful place than Auster's work. In many ways it is a pulp fiction story of a mysterious disaster that hits New York. John Tietjen returns to find his family and to battle the evil monsters—portrayed as something out of an L. Frank Baum story: straw men with pumpkin heads, wracked people with no faces—that are terrorizing the city. There is a little magical realism, with gargoyles and lions from the New York Public Library coming alive. Some good people are turned into angels. The novel feels forced.[48] One reviewer praised the "striking imagery, especially for readers familiar with Manhattan," but brushed the whole aside as "not much more than a poorly motivated, unconvincingly dramatized obsession."[49] But it was cited by the *New York Times Book Review* in its year-end listing of "notable books." Gerald Jonas, who reviewed the novel for the *Times Book Review,* called *The Stone War* "hard to read, hard to love, and hard to forget." The story is compelling because, "just when you begin to realize exactly what has happened to New York, you also begin to understand that what you are reading is not a proper disaster story at all but a love story—about love lost and found, and the price to be paid when people ignore the human disasters in their midst."[50]

The book opens in the disturbed present: the city is already under siege, a place of violence and crime, where the rich stay in guarded communities and thousand of homeless live in shanties. No one goes into Central Park; it is risky to travel too far off the beaten track. The novel has the feel of a 1970s movie about the city under siege. Armed guards stand in the lobbies of every apartment building. Curiously, and tellingly, no one sees the disaster as divine retribution for the sins of a twentieth-century Gomorrah, and no one wastes time calling upon God to put things right. Self-reliance is the theme throughout.

But there is a mystery from the start. The reader never finds out what caused the disaster, what shape it took at first, why it has been nearly impossible to get into or out of the city during the six or eight months of the siege. We know there was an earthquake, but there is clearly more to the story than that. Tietjen makes his way back to the city to find his children and ex-wife. Along the way he speaks to a variety of people and pesters them to reveal what happened. But no one seems to know for certain; the accounts are confused and contradictory. Everyone tells "conflicting stories, as if what had happened to the city was so huge that no one touched by it could know the whole story. Fire, gas explosions, quake, bombs, flooding, riots, disaster. As bad as his dream." Tietjen soon drops the question, concentrating instead on finding his children and creating a safe haven. Inevitably, though, "sooner or later, the conversation always came back to the same question: *What happened?* 'cataclysmic breakdown in communication'? 'You know: all those agencies that were holding New York together just went on strike at the same time'?" Before long he is answering the way everyone else does: "What happened?" someone asks him. "I don't know," Tietjen responds. "Someone told me on my way back here that *everything* had happened."[51] The reader is discomfited by *The Stone War*'s violation of the most basic conventions of the disaster genre: there is no explanation of the cause of the present situation and there is no climactic explanation of what happened.

The book is instead about anthropomorphizing the city. It is the city itself that draws John Tietjen back, to save itself. It is the city that is "sick" and is aching to be renewed. At the center is Tietjen and the other survivors' love for the city, and their new love for each other. An unlikely romance blooms, though it is never consummated, between the thirty-seven-year-old Tietjen and sixty-year-old Barbara McGrath. Tietjen discovers McGrath in the Metropolitan Museum of Art, held hostage by a brainwashed curator who captures survivors on behalf of the leader of the "monsters," John Gable.

The Stone War has little time for fight sequences. The author is far more interested in the workings of The Store, the apartment building at 72nd Street and Fifth Avenue that serves as the home of thirty-odd people spared by the disaster, who have gradually found one another. In the climactic battle with Gable, who has holed up in Grand Central Terminal, it is not the ragtag group of citizens who win the day. When all looks lost, the deus ex machina comes in the form of the two stone lions that have for a hundred years stood in front of the New York City Public Library. Named Patience and Fortitude, they come alive and rush to save the day against the monsters. "Something is on our side," Tietjen says. "It is the city itself rising up to help us," he thought, "but he did not tell them that."[52]

This victory makes Tietjen realize that only they, the city's own survivors, can bring New York back. The federal government is handcuffed, because something is preventing any help from coming in. "Now it begins," he thinks, "Sweep the city clean, make it thrive. When they come, the outside, when they finally come back, they'll find us rebuilding, keeping the city going. Now we can build. We can make it better, we've got good people here. And maybe, when they come . . . maybe then we'll find out what struck the city down and created Gable and

Poster for *King Kong*, 1976

those things. That's what we need to purge from the city. When we find it we can make it pay. Destroy it."

    The Stone War ends without solving the central mystery. Jit, a lost boy in Central Park with telepathic powers and the ability to shape events, is both the unknowing source of the calamity, and the confused savior of the city. When the curse has been lifted it is almost as if the world has been righted, somehow: "It was time for the World to come back. Time to go home. They started back across the Park, empty of shadows."[53]

A.I.: Artificial Intelligence, 2001. A similar image in *Armageddon,* 1998

The Steel Colossus: The World Trade Center as Target

In the months before September 11 the World Trade Center was eerily present, as if from a post-9/11 vantage point, in a number of disaster scenarios. In the disaster-filled rush to the millennium, those two towers, unloved by most architects and most city dwellers, largely replaced the Empire State Building as the venue for monsters, bombs, and comic book heroes.[54] From the moment the first person jumped from the Empire State a month before the building opened to the public, the tallest New York skyscraper became a target of American culture. In *King Kong, Deluge,* and the *Superman* movies in the 1930s, in *Fail-Safe* in the 1960s, in *Futurama* and *Independence Day* in the 1990s, in *The Day After Tomorrow* in the new millennium, the Empire State Building has had a lead role in portrayals of New York's end. Yet while every era has found a use for the Empire State in apocalyptic fiction, there has been a curious delicacy about depicting harm to the building: the structure is an obvious target in a disaster movie, but no one seems to want it destroyed violently. *Independence Day* presents one of the few detailed, graphic images of the building being destroyed.

Truly spectacular destruction scenes have been reserved instead for other buildings: the Chrysler Building is summarily beheaded in *Godzilla* and *Armageddon* (both in 1998), for example, and Rockefeller Center is decimated in *Invasion, U.S.A.* (1952). But in its short life, the World Trade Center had been subject to more than its share of realistic disaster fantasies. Even as it was being built, opponents, still hoping to change the design, offered up disaster scenarios. In 1968 a group calling itself the Committee for a Reasonable World Trade Center desperately tried to lessen the height of the buildings as they were under construction. A particular fear of the group was that the enormous difference between the height of the Trade Center towers and other skyscrapers created a risk of an accidental airplane crash. Immediately after the completion of the complex, King Kong made his return to the new tallest building in New York. Though intended as a serious remake of the 1933 classic, the 1976 *King Kong* was quickly branded an unintentionally humorous version. The film begins aboard an oil-exploration vessel off Indonesia. This time around, Kong is exhibited in a stadium and, in the film's climactic scene, climbs the twin towers of the World Trade Center. After jumping from one tower to another, he stands atop the flat surface of one of the identical towers as armed helicopters fire upon him. Mortally wounded, Kong falls and lands in the huge plaza below. Had the film been more compelling—frightening in its destruction or simply sad in its denouement—it might have become a symbol of the urban crisis. But it became nothing but forgotten.[55]

In the varied portrayals of the World Trade Center under attack or as victim of natural disaster, it is presented alternately as the first and most vulnerable target, almost waiting to topple over onto the rest of the city, or as the most solid of New York landmarks. It is surprising, in fact, how often the towers remain standing amid devastation, the monoliths among the ruins. In *King Kong*

The twin towers are attacked in *Challenge of the Superfriends*, 1978

The World Trade Center towers serve to measure the size of the waves in *Deep Impact*, 1998

the Trade Center is simply a stage set for Kong's final ascent and tragic descent; the towers themselves are as solid as Kong's Pacific island mountain. The Trade Center Towers in the film are as everyone assumed them to be—indestructible— even as Kong jumps from one to the other. In *Escape from New York,* the rest of New York is a wreck, but the World Trade Center is a clean landing place for

Snake's glider. In *Aftershock: Earthquake in New York,* New Yorkers gain solace from seeing, amid the toppled skyline, that the towers are still standing. And in Spielberg's *A.I.* the only buildings that manage to stand, not only through the flooding, but through the centuries of the following ice age, are the twin towers.

Far more common have been dramatic destruction scenarios featuring the towers. The climax of *Meteor,* made just five years after the World Trade Center was completed, is the collision of a meteor fragment with the towers. A massive ball of fire comes flying through the sky, directly toward the World Trade Center. The towers explode in a blinding light and, with the cameras trained upward from the plaza below, they disintegrate. In a 1991 comic book uniting the X-Force team with Spider-Man, the superheroes are battling Black Tom Cassidy near the top of one of the Trade Center towers when a bomb goes off, ripping the top twenty floors from one of the towers. X-Force is trapped on the floors just below. But the buildings appear in no threat of falling, until the Juggernaut, a massive red Hulk-like creature, slams into the base of one of the towers in rage and it topples over, leaving the superheroes amid the rubble.[56] In *Batman Cataclysm,* a graphic novel from 1999, the World Trade Center, under the pseudonym of the Davenport Center, is among the skyscrapers that "topple like dominoes" when an earthquake hits Gotham City. As "five million tons of concrete, steel, and glass fall. The wind created by the center's collapse drowns out even the screams of those inside."[57]

In *Deep Impact* (1998), the Trade Center towers help to measure the disaster of the oncoming tsunami. The Statue of Liberty is submerged, just before the most dramatic image of the movie: the wave cresting to the height of the World Trade Center. In a final image at the end of that long scene showing the impact of the tidal wave, we see the tops of the twin towers, all but covered now by water. A similar image became the signature image of *Independence Day*—the Statue of Liberty face down in the bay, and the Trade Center towers still standing, but decapitated and crumbling.

In 1998, just three years before September 11, 2001, the hip-hop artist Busta Rhymes released an album entitled *E.L.E (Extinction Level Event): The Final World Front,* with a cover featuring a fireball exploding over lower Manhattan, reminiscent of Bonestell's 1950 *Collier's* cover. Another hip-hop act, the Coup, produced art for the cover of its album *Party Music* in June 2001 featuring the two band members standing beneath the twin towers, explosions bursting out of the upper portion of the buildings. DJ Pam the Funkstress is holding batons, as if she is conducting the scene in the background. "Boots" Riley holds an elec-

"Old New York City," the opening scene in Times Square from *Final Fantasy: The Spirits Within,* 2001. Barrier City, a safe haven in lower Manhattan

Fallen skyscrapers in the forbidden zone of "Man-Hattan" in *A.I.: Artificial Intelligence,* 2001. The Chrysler Building uncovered by aliens a thousand years in the future

tronic guitar tuner, but he appears to be pushing it like a detonator. Riley later explained, "It was originally supposed to be more of a metaphor for destroying capitalism—where the music is making capitalist towers blow up. The politics of the Coup have more to do with the people organizing each other." Fans argued that because there is nothing else in the sky, no reference to other buildings in New York, the Trade Center towers were "intended to depict the destruction of a generic 'tall building.'"[58]

But they had chosen those towers, just as I had chosen them while experimenting with Flight Simulator. They were irresistible, as everyone knew. Even their designers imagined that at some point a plane—perhaps intentionally—would fly into those towers. Though they were derided by architectural critics, the towers quickly captivated the imaginations of dreamers, Hollywood, and bohemian types alike. Just as they were going up in 1968, a young Frenchman, Philip Petit, flipped through a magazine while waiting for a dentist appointment and saw an architectural rendering of the completed World Trade Center. A vision of walking between the towers came into his mind. Six years, later, on August 7, 1974, just as the towers were being completed, and just before the American political system underwent a massive convulsion caused by Richard Nixon's resignation as president on August 9, Philip Petit walked out onto a tightrope between the towers. "They called me," was how he explained his act. "I didn't choose them. Anything that is giant and manmade strikes me in an awesome way and calls me. I could secretly . . . put my wire . . . between the highest towers in the world. It was something that had to be done, and I couldn't explain it."[59]

In the summer of 2001 the thrilling spectacles, the slapstick spoofs, and the dark premonitions of New York's destruction all vied for attention. As a president who had been elected by a minority of the voters settled in and planned his fall domestic agenda from his ranch in Texas, and as terrorists quietly made final preparations, scenes of New York's end flickered on movie screens across the country. The spring had already brought a hurricane to New York, via the children's television show *Sesame Street*. Big Bird was devastated to see his nest destroyed: "My home! My nest! My everything!" he cried. But the Bird and the show were resilient. Gordon declared: "You're right, Big Bird. It's not all right. But it *will* be all right."[60] And in the summer months, American imagemakers portrayed disasters that were remarkably similar to what was to happen in September. Up to the very moment of the attacks on 9/11, these fantasies seemed irresistible to writers and filmmakers.

The Japanese animation movie *Final Fantasy: The Spirits Within*—the first attempt to make a dramatic film with realistically animated human characters—opened with a scene of a devastated, abandoned Manhattan. The year is 2065, and phantomlike aliens are preparing a final assault on the earth. Dr. Aki Ross, a young scientist, lives in Barrier City, a Buckminster Fuller–inspired enclosure over much of what was once lower Manhattan, designed to protect the inhabitants from the phantoms. The rest of the city lies destroyed and uninhabited. In an opening scene Aki ventures out into "old New York" to Times Square, where she seeks the remaining life forms, in hopes that they might help in the battle against the aliens.

A bigger, and more successful, summer film event was the release of a two-decades-long project of Stanley Kubrick and Steven Spielberg, *A.I.: Artificial Intelligence.* David, a mecha—a robot indistinguishable from a human being—has replaced a couple's comatose, apparently terminally ill son. But after the real child miraculously awakens from his cryogenic freeze, restored to health, David is abandoned. He desperately searches for his human "mother," taking a *Wizard of Oz*–like journey through the world and its snares. He makes his way, a child searching for home and mother, back to a forbidden zone, overflowing with water, called "Man-Hattan": the city of his manufacture. But the Oz of 1939—a glowing, Emerald City of futuristic skyscrapers—is gone. In New York, circa 2001, he floats past the flame of that ever-present disaster movie icon, the submerged Statue of Liberty, past the lonely World Trade Center towers peeking out above the water, and back to the laboratory where he was "born." David eventually floats to a submerged Coney Island, where he finds what he thinks is his mother—a statue of the angelic Blue Fairy from a *Pinocchio*-themed amusement-park ride. The film fast-forwards two thousand years, when aliens visit the city, which is now encased in ice. Only the World Trade Center towers peek above the flat desert of ice. The aliens have carved out avenues as if they are undertaking an archeological dig. They have uncovered skyscrapers, like the Chrysler Building, which stand like Egyptian statues carved into the clay walls along the Nile, symbols of the lost city. David is discovered frozen, with his hand reaching out to the winged angel.[61]

One film that was in production when the jets hit the World Trade Center towers and was released just a few months later featured something altogether different and perhaps more powerful than any of the explosive visions of the city's end that proliferated in the last decade of the century. In *Vanilla Sky,* David Aames (played by Tom Cruise), a spoiled rich kid, dreams of waking one morning to find that the city is empty. He makes his way down a deserted Central Park

West, then takes Broadway to a Times Square ghost town. This is too much for him: he gets out of the car to look around this perpetually crowded, loud, traffic-choked intersection. The lights and signs are on, but no one is around.[62] He begins to jog, then sprint through the square, terrified and crazed. He finally stops and screams to the vanilla sky. Here is the most terrifying nightmare of all—the people all gone and a city that is nothing without its people standing silently, meaninglessly, awaiting, against hope, a return of life. The billowing smoke that encompassed all of lower Manhattan on that clear Tuesday morning in September 2001 made us all consider that the city might be robbed of its people. We wondered for a brief moment whether the "island fantasy," as E. B. White called it, had finally come to an end.

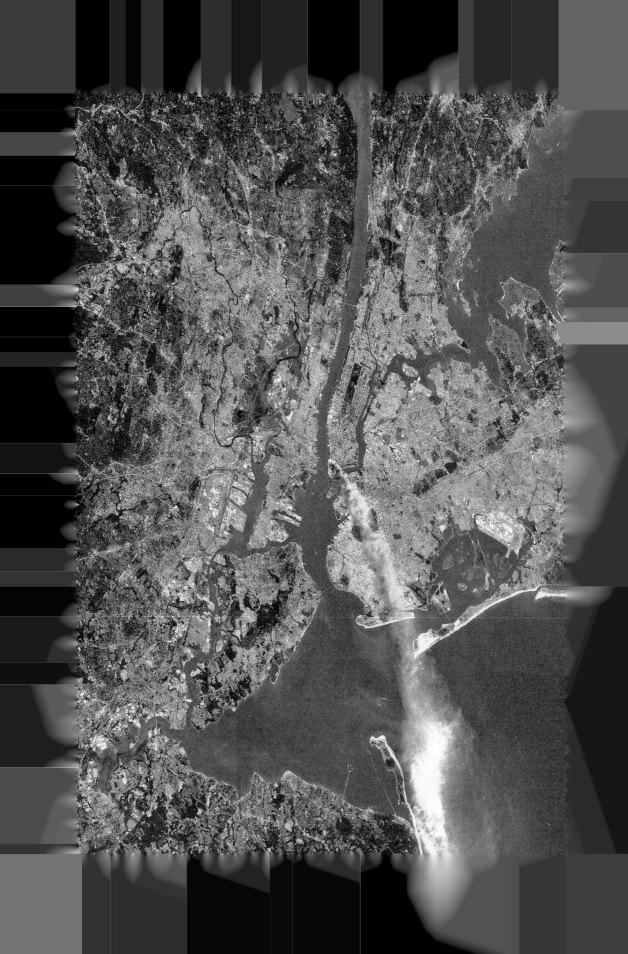

six

The Future of the City's End

New York and Its Fantasies After 9/11

AFTER SEPTEMBER 11, 2001, THE "CITY THAT NEVER SLEEPS" WAS awake for a different reason: fear.[1]

Fear of death borne in the air: a jet, an anthrax microbe. In lower Manhattan, the dust from the collapse of the World Trade Center towers was rapidly scrubbed away. Night and day trucks rumbled off with more rubble.[2] But the fear persisted: there were letters to open, cross-country trips to take. Fear became a psychic anthrax, an almost invisible powder creeping under the windowsills of thought, sifting into the corners of minds.

It was the most perfect and horrific demolition job: two quarter-mile-tall towers exploding, then imploding, one-acre floors falling each through the next, two hundred times over. Survivors, blanketed in the gray mist of urban disaster, headed north and east bearing their stories, their fear, throughout the city.

Fear and this city, as we have seen, were no strangers. New York has burned and been occupied by soldiers. It has been besieged by epidemics and riots. Our popular culture has been in dress rehearsal for the city's destruction for decades: in books, at the movies, in computer games. Still, no amount of history, no rehearsals, could prepare New Yorkers for September 11 and the days, months, and, for some, years of grief and worry that followed.

Usually, the rest of the country has feared New York, rather than New Yorkers fearing their city. New York, ascending to dominance by the early nineteenth century, became the most feared city of all. In New York, Ameri-

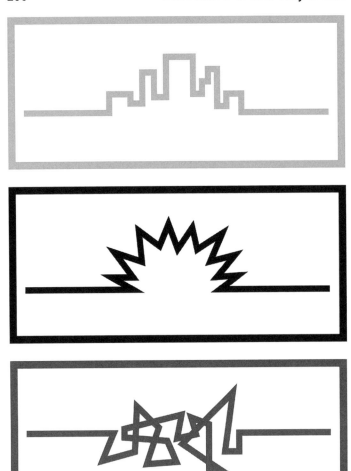

Paul Sahre graphic for the
Week in Review section of
the *New York Times,* July
10, 2005

cans saw the poor, immigrants, and people of all races. In New York, crowding, crime, disease, and radicalism were not only found but nurtured and propagated.

Within the city, fear has always been present. To nineteenth-century New Yorkers, who may have been told stories of the city's burning during the seven-year British occupation in the Revolutionary War, who lost friends and family members to the cholera epidemics of the 1830s, who perhaps watched the burning of much of lower Manhattan in 1835 or who later saw rioting mobs rage through the city in 1863, the notion that the city was forever was absurd. And in the twentieth century, the city at the height of its power was hardly immune to fears of sudden catastrophe, the distinct possibility of nuclear attack. September

**NASA satellite image of
Manhattan immediately after
the attack of 9/11. Image no.
scf4320-054/Science Faction/
Getty Images**

11 bombed the city back to the atomic age, when a roar in the sky could instantly
evict daydreams from New Yorkers' minds and substitute apocalyptic visions.

Virginia Woolf wrote in *A Room of One's Own* that after World War I it
was not possible to hum poetry. On the surface, lively lunches at Oxbridge pro-
ceeded as before. But the "humming noise, not articulate, but musical, exciting,"
was gone. The war had "destroyed illusion and put truth in its place."[3]

Many suggested confidently that such was the case with 9/11: the world
had changed. A controlled fear—a constant hum of worry, rather than of poetry—
seemed part of this new world, this new New York. But after the initial silence,
then the muted tones, the city somehow went back to humming. Perhaps September 11 did not create a new city, but in many respects it ferried the city back

to an older, more visceral New York, where it was understood that the city was at risk. While the rest of the country remained on edge, New York was even more so. New Yorkers understood again that their city was a target. But New Yorkers went rapidly back to their business, the business of living in their city.

In many ways American culture returned very rapidly after 9/11 to "normal," which is defined in part by a return to the popular fun of New York disaster movies. New York has seen a doubling in the number of corporate headquarters and subsidiaries since 1990—when everyone predicted that there would continue to be an outflow of people from the city—suggesting that fear has not overpowered the pursuit of profit. Despite 9/11 and despite the daily threats in the papers—real or for political benefit—corporations and tourists alike keep returning.[4]

That "normalcy," however, hides a powerful sense of unease that pervaded American culture immediately after 9/11. In works that confronted 9/11 directly, or those that tackled issues of technology and the global economy or environmental degradation, there was a sense that the enemy was invisible and elusive and its attacks inevitable. Around the world, acts of terror multiplied in the years after 9/11 and the American invasion of Afghanistan and Iraq, leading to a feeling that terrorism could happen anywhere—London, Mumbai, Indonesia. Similarly, the global economy seemed utterly incomprehensible, and its workings beyond control by traditional regulatory means. The collapse of Enron—built on image and accounting gimmicks—left people disgusted but also confused. The largest transnational corporations seemed unstable, built of smoke and mirrors. Finally, warnings of global warming and the degradation of the earth's environment threatened worldwide catastrophe, not a thousand years from now but in decades, and maybe sooner. American unease in the wake of 9/11 was not simply about an attack from an Islamic enemy; it was an awareness that any act could provoke disaster: the melting of a glacier or the turn to terrorism of a law student in Egypt. The tipping point suddenly seemed very close at hand.

Quelling Destructive Fantasies in the Aftermath of 9/11

September 11 was its own form of New York disaster movie, played out live on every screen in the world. And in the days afterward, Americans voluntarily submitted themselves to watching the horror of the destruction of the twin towers, of people jumping to their deaths, of a great pile of collapsed skyscrapers burning, smoking, filling the air with toxic clouds and paper. This was the ultimate, all-encompassing disaster movie, which Americans watched for days on their television and computer screens.

Even as America and the world immersed itself in the picture of New York under attack, we rebelled against fictional accounts of the same scenes. The reality was so awful that it was simply no longer enjoyable to imagine it. My heart-pounding flights on Microsoft's Flight Simulator became unimaginable. My proposal for an exhibition at the New-York Historical Society entitled Destroying New York, which I was proofreading and was ready to mail out on the morning of September 11, and which I had pitched successfully as a "fun" exhibition, was now unseemly and insensitive. What had been not only acceptable but enjoyable and profitable on September 10—thinking of new ways to set the heart palpitating by watching New Yorkers die—a day later was offensive and unpatriotic. Even selling pictures of the Trade Center as it was before 9/11 was deemed profiteering, although many were selling mementos honoring the towers and the people who worked in them. Profiting from real and imagined disaster—one of the engines fueling the New York destruction genre for two centuries—immediately became an outrage.

Suddenly, everyone loved New York. The near-universal view was that New York was a blameless victim. This generated a sense of sympathy and compassion that New York had rarely if ever seen. At least briefly, the ongoing trope of New York as a city of murder and mayhem (the reality of which had been declining steadily in the late 1980s and 1990s, even if the fiction persisted in "urban crisis" films and novels) was washed away. What José Martí had suggested during the blizzard of 1888 about the common experience of all New Yorkers, high and low, now seemed to apply to all Americans: "a sudden rush of kindness, as though the dread hand had touched the shoulders of all men."[5]

The ground had been prepared with the city's economic and cultural resurgence in the 1980s and 1990s. Although 40 percent of its citizens remained below the poverty line, crime had declined sharply, and successive mayoral administrations had made attracting tourists and multinational businesses to the city a primary goal of public policy. By 2001 Times Square had been colonized by Disney, Virgin Records, Condé Nast, and Reuters, as a center of mainstream entertainment and communications. City leaders had made much of Manhattan safe and clean for tourists. A nation far more willing to be sympathetic to New York was fully on the city's side after 9/11. Pity after the disaster blossomed into a surge of love for New York.

As the shockwaves of 9/11 rippled through American society, the culture of violence came under scrutiny. Because so much of that culture had centered on New York, the chorus for changing films and television shows was all the more powerful: to modify a violent film centered on New York now was a patriotic act, a necessary salve on the wounds of Americans in the name of a united front against terror.

Within days of 9/11, popular-culture producers of all types instituted an unofficial self-censorship to protect consumers from reminders of the attacks.[6] Video game producers altered content (including scenarios of terrorist attacks on New York and Washington) in order "to avoid stirring emotions unnecessarily and unwillingly offending the public," as one executive said. On September 14, 2001, Microsoft announced that it would delete the World Trade Center from its 2002 edition of Flight Simulator.[7] The attacks of September 11 brought out of the woodwork many devotees of Flight Simulator and their guilty secret: the lure of flying into the World Trade Center was a central appeal of the program. Months later, when Kabul fell, journalists found a reference to Microsoft's Flight Simulator in an Al Qaeda member's home.[8]

The Marxist hip-hoppers Coup, who had sought to highlight their critique of capitalism by imagining the destruction of the Trade Center, quickly backpedaled, insisting that the image was "not supposed to be realistic in its depiction. The Coup advocates change, but change through peaceful means, never through violence."[9] The CD liner image, completed in July, was quickly altered for a November release. The new cover had a less offensive image of a martini glass filled with flaming gasoline.

Movies filmed in New York but not yet released before 9/11 faced a dilemma: move forward with the World Trade Center as part of the skyline, or digitally edit out the towers. The poster for *Spider-Man* was edited to remove the reflection of the twin towers from Spider-Man's eyes, and a scene was removed (though seen by millions in promotional trailers before 9/11) in which a web hanging between the twin towers catches a helicopter. Filmmakers adopted similar editing strategies in films including *Zoolander, Serendipity, Men in Black II, People I Know,* and *The Time Machine.* They claimed that they were simply trying to avoid offending and disturbing audiences unnecessarily. It seems equally likely that filmmakers worried that the sight of the towers would detract from the narrative and undermine the escapist pleasure that is the essence of big Hollywood films.[10]

Commentators across the political spectrum predicted that the attacks of September 11 would finally be the straw that broke the back of a culture of violence. For years, the rising tide of "disaster porn" had provoked worried efforts

Cover and inside flap of video game box, *Command and Conquer: Red Alert 2,* 2001. The original version of the cover showed the World Trade Center towers in flames; the revised cover, top, excised the towers but still suggests the city under attack; opening the cover flap of the software box reveals an explosion at the base of the World Trade Center towers

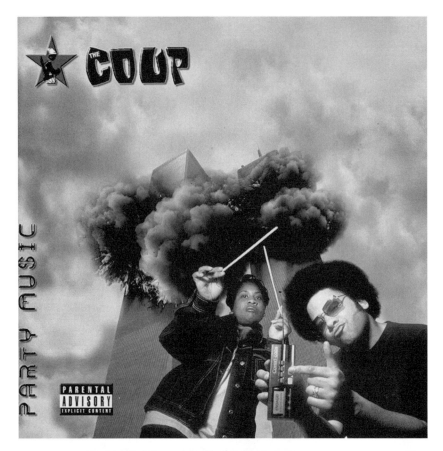

The cover for the Coup's CD *Party Music*, as issued before 9/11, and as reissued

After 9/11 the impending collision of the moon and New York City was cut from *The Time Machine*, 2002

from reformers, from both the left and the right. Studies seemed to back up what many feared: that the violence of movies and video games could provoke violent behavior among the nation's youth.[11] The prevalence of video cameras made it easier to capture images of crimes and natural disasters as they were happening. The corporatization of news meant that sensational reports and footage of disasters of all types made the top of evening newscasts.

In the wake of 9/11, journalists and theorists, news commentators and politicians realized that the language of the disaster movie had shaped the initial, unscripted response to 9/11, and they were appalled. "This is not a movie," argued Anthony Lane, a film critic for the *New Yorker,* in an impassioned essay just two weeks after 9/11.[12] "What happened on the morning of September 11th," Lane argued, "was that imaginations that had been schooled in the comedy of apocalypse were forced to reconsider the same evidence as tragic." Perhaps, he suggested, "the disaster movie is indeed to be shamed by disaster." Lane expressed what many intellectuals and commentators feared in the wake of 9/11: that our culture had immersed itself in violent movies over the past generation, effectively dulling our ability to comprehend real disaster. September 11, he argued, might represent "not only an official rebuke to that license but the fiery end of the ride."

Leon Wieseltier, the literary editor of the *New Republic,* underscored Lane's critique with a blistering attack on those who would seek, after 9/11, a "balm in culture."[13] According to Wieseltier, analogies between Ground Zero and the work of Frank Gehry, or Piranesi, or other architects of the "fragment" were not simply in bad taste but an inevitable product of a society that preferred to flee from a confrontation with evil and find solace in pat sentiment. A year later, nearing the first anniversary of September 11, Wieseltier was appalled by how thoroughly the actual date and horrors perpetrated on that date had been supplanted by "September 11," a media phenomenon that quickly moved the reality of the tragedy into a realm of sentiment and emotion. "The media," he wrote a year later, "is greedy for tears." September 11 "was the deadening of September 11. It was deadened, like all images and ideas that are hallowed, by repetition, and also by sentiment, which is what our popular culture uses to drive away lasting significance. The American heart is the bouncer at the door of the American mind."[14] You can almost hear him pounding the table and insisting that popular culture had no business trying to portray 9/11. It would only sentimentalize and sterilize the tragedy.

The critic Slavoj Žižek had little time for these debates over whether 9/11 had been or would be made "just another media spectacle . . . a catastrophe version of the snuff porno movies." Instead, he wondered, "Where have we already seen the same thing over and over again?" The disaster movies were, in Žižek's thinking, the unconscious reflection of our repressed knowledge that "we live in an insulated artificial universe . . . [that] generates the notion that some ominous agent is threatening us all the time with total destruction." Just as people who live behind the walls of gated communities are sure that crime is on the rise "out there," so too does our own isolation—from the world but also from classes and races within the United States—breed a profound fear of what might be threatening us. Our very well-being in a world of inequality and violence paradoxically haunts us with "nightmarish visions of catastrophes." "America got what it fantasized about, and that was the biggest surprise."[15]

All this debate and rapid response by film studios and record companies might seem to indicate that the ship of American culture had taken a sharp turn away from the disaster spectacles of the previous decade. But it was a short-lived detour. *Collateral Damage*—a typically violent Arnold Schwarzenegger vehicle—had been scheduled to open in October 2001; it was delayed, but only until March 2002. On the other hand, Sony Pictures Entertainment accelerated the release of *Black Hawk Down,* an extremely violent film about a failed rescue effort in Somalia in 1993, from March 2002 to December 2001, in a bid to exploit the jingoistic sentiment aroused by the invasion of Afghanistan.[16]

Audiences responded as they always had, proving film studios and directors wrong in their calculations. Film critics attacked as dishonest and even

cowardly moviemakers who used postproduction editing to eliminate poten-
tially disturbing images. As one fan wrote, "We're giving up our culture to protect ourselves from pain."[17] Some audiences felt duped by retouched skylines.
Directors who chose to leave in the twin towers—such as Sam Raimi, director of
three *Spider-Man* films (the first of which was released in 2002), and Cameron
Crowe, director of *Vanilla Sky*—were praised. Martin Scorsese, in *Gangs of New
York,* chose to leave the World Trade Center in the final scene of the movie, in
which the characters view Manhattan from Brooklyn and see the city of 1863
transforming before their eyes into the city of 2002.[18]

Within months, violence and disasters made their way back onto screens.
Not many moviemakers were willing to show New York's destruction explicitly
on screen immediately after 9/11, however. If the desire for—and the profit in—
violent movies and videos could not be quelled, at least the location of the disaster could be changed. Hollywood could avoid criticism while feeding audiences
the disaster imagery they craved, by shifting the destruction to other cities. Los
Angeles has competed with New York in the disaster genre for several decades,
and now it found new life, or death. The hit television series *24* subjected the
city to an atomic bomb and bioterrorism. Baltimore was destroyed in *The Sum
of All Fears* in 2002. San Francisco fell to the *Hulk* in 2003, and again in *X-Men:
The Last Stand* (2006). In *Category 6* (2004), a made-for-television film, three
storms converged over the Midwest and headed northward to decimate Chicago
(after doing a fair bit of damage in Las Vegas and leveling the St. Louis Arch). And
"because people love scary wind," the film brought in 16.68 million viewers. It
almost bested another kind of disaster show, the ABC series *Lost,* about a group
of badly behaved people stranded on an island after a plane crash.[19] Another
made-for-television disaster movie, *10.5* (2004), is centered on the West Coast.
In an opening scene the Space Needle in Seattle tips over and crashes after the
city is hit with a 7.9 magnitude earthquake. But the worst is yet to come, as after-
shocks of 8.4 and higher head south. The Golden Gate Bridge is destroyed, and
Los Angeles's towers tumble down as the "big one" rumbles through southern
California and finally does what many have joked about for years: turns the coast
of California into an island.

As disaster porn survived 9/11 and thrived, writers began to doubt the critiques of Wieseltier and others. They questioned the argument that culture could
not respond adequately to the disaster, that it could only make Wonder Bread out
of a tragic event or, worse, turn it into heart-pounding entertainment. The novel-
ist W. G. Sebald's views were expressed posthumously in *The Natural History of
Destruction,* published in 2003. He urged fiction writers to pay more attention to

The Sum of All Fears, 2002

The Golden Gate Bridge collapses in the TV movie *10.5*, 2004

The TV movie *Category 6: Day of Destruction*, 2004

destruction. Focusing particularly on the failure of German writers after World War II to write of the destruction of German cities by Allied bombers, he wondered why there was no "literature of the ruins," no adequate account of the 131 German towns and cities attacked, the six hundred thousand killed, the millions of homes destroyed. What Wieseltier might applaud—that culture makers of all types were cowed into avoiding the subject—Sebald decried. Indeed, he worried that "to this day, any concern with the real scenes of horror during the catastrophe still has an aura of the forbidden about it, even of voyeurism." The problem is not too much writing about the disaster, or too many images, he insisted, but too little and too few.[20]

Susan Sontag once argued, in her classic 1977 work *On Photography,* that "photographs shrivel sympathy." She wrote that "flooded with images of the sort that once used to shock and arouse indignation, we are losing our capacity to react." But in her 2003 book *Regarding the Pain of Others,* she stepped back from that view. She rejected the notion that ours has become a "society of spectacle," in which reality disappears before a train of images. Echoing Žižek, she called this view, which suggests that violence and horrors are mere images, "a breath-taking provincialism" that "suggests that everyone is a spectator . . . and no one is a victim." She wondered still whether "images of slaughter lead to pacifism . . . or to greater militancy" but was prepared by 2003 to err on the side of optimism.[21]

Sontag defended those who found beauty in Ground Zero against those who jealously sought to defend the site's tragic purity, like cats marking their territory. "That a gory battlescape could be beautiful," she reminded us,

> in the sublime or awesome or tragic register of the beautiful—is a commonplace about images of war made by artists. . . . To find beauty in war photographs seems heartless. But the landscape of devastation is still a landscape. There is beauty in ruins. To acknowledge the beauty of photographs of the World Trade Center ruins in the months following the attack seemed frivolous, sacrilegious. The most people dared say was that the photographs were "surreal," a hectic euphemism behind which the disgraced notion of beauty cowered. But they *were* beautiful, many of them.[22]

The tide had turned. Now it was acceptable to speak about what people had felt even on that morning—that the sight of the World Trade Center towers collapsing was horrifyingly beautiful. Within less than a year, in the world of art and culture, New York was no longer safe, despite the changes to album covers and films and software, and despite a trend toward picturing other cities in disaster movies. The early prediction that American culture would stay away from imagining New York's destruction (and from violence in general) was quickly proved wrong. How long ago those solemn declarations seem. After a brief lull, projecting New York's end was back in style.

"Disaster Is My Muse": Art Spiegelman and 9/11

But first of all, how would American culture deal with 9/11 itself?

Literature was far slower than movies to approach the theme of 9/11 and especially of New York's destruction. Just as Sebald argued that German literature had failed to engage with the destruction of German cities in World War II, so too the destruction of 9/11 was left to journalists to describe. Too frightened by the weight of criticism, too fearful that they would be described as melodramatic or kitschy, or simply too close to the event (since many writers and publishers are based in New York), few writers of fiction confronted the actual horrors at Ground Zero. Journalists, meanwhile, in a spate of books published in the year or two after 9/11, detailed every minute of the disaster.[23] Novelists began to broach the subject in oblique terms only a few years later. When they did, a mood of unease, tempered by a new appreciation of the city, pervaded the novels that touched on 9/11 and its aftermath.

Don DeLillo's *Cosmopolis,* a novel concerned with globalization and its discontents, appeared early in 2003, evoking not the specific event but the disquiet of a world whose sharp divisions had been so violently laid bare on 9/11. In December 2001, DeLillo had written an impassioned essay in the *Guardian* about the real object of the terrorist attacks:

> In the past decade the surge of capital markets has dominated discourse and shaped global consciousness. Multinational corporations have come to seem more vital and influential than governments. The dramatic climb of the Dow and the speed of the internet summoned us all to live permanently in the future, in the utopian glow of cyber-capital, because there is no memory there and this is where markets are uncontrolled and investment potential has no limit.
>
> All this changed on September 11. Today, again, the world narrative belongs to terrorists. But the primary target of the men who attacked the Pentagon and the World Trade Centre was not the global economy. It was America that drew their fury. It was the high gloss of our modernity. It was the thrust of our technology. It was our perceived godlessness. It was the blunt force of our foreign policy. It was the power of American culture to penetrate every wall, home, life and mind.[24]

New York's "high gloss of modernity," where so much of the invisible global economy becomes visible, where millions and billions of dollars are traded across computer screens in the blink of an eye, is the subject of *Cosmopolis.* The thin story follows billionaire Eric Packer on a daylong limousine ride from one end of 57th Street to the other for a nostalgic haircut at his father's barber shop. Disruptions on the street prolong the trip; it will take him much of the day to go five blocks. As Packer passes north of Times Square, he glances out to see the physical struggles over the global economy, which he helps fuel with his Internet purchases of Japanese yen. Packer watches a protest against a visit by the president evolve into an anarchist riot. Some of the protestors have managed to take over one of the electronic billboards in Times Square and have changed the message. It now reads: "A specter is haunting the world—the specter of capitalism." Masked protestors jump on Packer's limousine and begin to spray-paint it; a bomb goes off and protestors rush in to occupy an investment bank building. Packer—literally in a bubble—reflects on the events around him as he speaks on the phone with his wife. "And if they kill you," she says, "it's only because you permit it, in your sweet sufferance, as a way to re-emphasize the idea we all live under."

"What idea?" . . .

"Destruction," she said . . .

"The urge to destroy is a creative urge."

"This is also the hallmark of capitalist thought. Enforced destruction. Old industries have to be harshly eliminated. New markets have to be forcibly claimed. Old markets have to be re-exploited. Destroy the past, make the future."[25]

The riot, and the sense that he was blessed to be part of the immolation of the city, is "exhilarating" for Packer. There is an oblique reference to the World Trade Center towers—"the last tall things made empty, designed to hasten the future"—but little more to make this a "9/11 novel." Rather, the book is a disturbing, hyperbolic look at the tyrannical powers of financial markets, the stark contrast between the virtual worlds of effortless communication and wealth, and the real world of traffic jams and riots on global cities' streets.[26]

In Michael Cunningham's *Specimen Days,* which, like his earlier novel *The Hours,* threads together three historical time periods with literature, the New York City of 2003 is on edge as a boy blows himself up right next to Ground Zero. It soon becomes clear, with another suicide bombing in New York and then one in Chicago, that a larger apocalyptic movement is taking hold in the wake of 9/11. In the third chapter, which takes place a century later, the "Child's Crusade," as it has come to be called, turns out to be the beginning of a destructive century, which leaves much of the United States a desolate wasteland. New York has become "Old New York," an entertainment destination, complete with androids who will terrorize tourists in Central Park for a price.[27]

Ian McEwan's *Saturday* follows the thoughts and dramatic events of the British Dr. Henry Perowne, a couple of years after 9/11 but before the London bombings of 2005. The background is an anti–Iraq war march through London, which leads him into a confrontation that threatens his family. Along the way, he worries about the potential disasters facing him and his city in the wake of 9/11 and during the Iraq war. There is an undercurrent of dread and a sense of the world spiraling out of control, but ultimately Perowne regains peace and satisfaction in his family.[28]

Into the void of conventional literature, Art Spiegelman launched the first and still the most significant literary work on the meaning of 9/11. He played out his own personal experience after 9/11 in the pages of his "comix" book *In the Shadow of No Towers.* At the heart of the book is Spiegelman's effort to

I still see the glowing tower, *Awesome* as it collapses—

Cover of Art Spiegelman, *In the Shadow of No Towers,* 2004, and details. © 2004 by Art Spiegelman, reprinted with permission of the Wylie Agency, Inc., and Pantheon Books, a division of Random House, Inc.

They passed some guy on Canal Street painting the towers. Glancing south, they could only see the billowing toxic smoke... the damned model had moved.

wrestle with the imagery of destruction and its impact on himself and his country. He began drawing immediately after 9/11 (his black twin towers were on the cover of the first post-9/11 issue of the *New Yorker*) and continued through the invasions of Afghanistan and Iraq. He uses the comix to examine the uses of imagery of 9/11. The book opens with three panels: a family sleeping in front of the television on September 10, the family staring shocked and bug-eyed at the television the next day, and the family asleep again on September 12, with one change: a flag up behind them. They sleep—journalists and politicians as well as average citizens—patriotic but unthinking.[29] Spiegelman rages that in 2004 "New York is transformed into a stage set for the Republican Presidential Convention, and Tragedy is transformed into Travesty."[30]

But he also recognizes the powerful personal impact the attacks of 9/11 had on his own psyche and his view of the world. He jests nervously about "wait-ing for that other shoe to drop," with an image of a Doc Martens shoe falling on a crowded New York street. For all his distrust of the jingoism of the days and months that followed, the fear he felt was real and powerful—he lived blocks from the World Trade Center, and his daughter attended school even closer. He realized, he said later, "how vulnerable New York—and by extension, all of Western Civ—actually is. I took my city, and those homely, arrogant towers, for granted. It's actually all as transient and ephemeral as, say, old newspapers."[31] For Spiegelman, 9/11 and the fear of the city's destruction provided the jolt that finally made this "rootless cosmopolitan" a "rooted cosmopolitan." He finally realized (thinking of Jews who couldn't make themselves leave Berlin when they had a chance) what it means to be tied to a home. The vision of the towers falling, and of future attacks on New York, pervades the book. George Bush is seen with a hammer; in the background his wrecking crew is taking down the Statue of Liberty. Fire licks the bottom of some of the pages, shaped like the twin towers; the demons of a "crazy lady" who lives on his block are unleashed and erupt into the city, tumbling skyscrapers down and flinging people to their death.[32]

The visceral power of the experience made Spiegelman long for genuine literary or visual imagery to make sense of the event. Much of what he found was offensive. Beneath a cartoon panel showing the billowing smoke of September 11 behind a poster for Arnold Schwarzenegger's *Collateral Damage,* Spiegelman notes, "Oddly in the aftermath of September 11th, some pundits insisted that irony was dead." And he offers a jab at architectural deconstructionists: "If not for all the tragedy and death, I could think of the attack as some sort of radical architectural criticism." He includes a panel of a frustrated painter on Canal Street trying to capture on canvas the falling towers: "The damned model had moved."[33]

But even as Spiegelman mocks the misuse of the tragedy and pillories a culture fascinated and politically stunted by the imagery of death and destruc-tion, he recognizes his own immersion in and inspiration from that culture. In one series of panels, Spiegelman and his wife search for their daughter, Nadja, at Stuyvesant High School, a few blocks from Ground Zero. When he hears that a plane has flown into the Pentagon the image in his head comes from a 1962 Topps Gum trading card series called Mars Attacks. The series of fifty-five cards sold for five cents a pack in candy stores, much like baseball cards. The series told the story—rooted in H. G. Wells's *War of the Worlds* but inspired by a gen-eration of popular science fiction—of a Martian invasion that destroys most of the world, until humans somehow mount a counterattack. Children needed to collect all fifty-five cards to reach the redemptive ending. Discontinued because of criticism of their graphic imagery, the cards quickly became collectors' items, today garnering thousands of dollars for the full set. They also inspired a film of the same name. For Spiegelman, who "loved those Mars Attacks cards" and spent twenty years working for Topps, the sly point was a powerful one: the imagery we call on to comprehend horrific events is as often as not the commercial camp product of our disaster-obsessed culture.[34]

The fractured storytelling and self-consciousness of *In the Shadow of No Towers* eloquently portrays Spiegelman's desperate effort to wend his way through the contradictions of the aftermath of 9/11 and to find imagery to match his mood and the political moment. Rather than stand high above the world and rant that popular culture is taboo and disaster imagery has no place in a post-9/11 world, Spiegelman searches out imagery that can offer "solace." He finds little in literature, in all of the well-meaning poetry written after 9/11. Indeed, "the only cultural artifacts that could get past my defenses to flood my eyes and brain with something other than images of burning towers were old comic strips; vital, unpretentious ephemera from the optimistic dawn of the twentieth century."[35] Their very transience—they were dailies, effectively expected to be destroyed by the next day's paper and the next strip—made them "just right for an end-of-the world moment." He finds humor in historical strips that deal humorously with disasters of all types—fireworks going off under a July Fourth crowd, the leaning tower of Pisa falling over in a dream in the strip *Bringing Up Father,* and the painful escapades of Happy Hooligan on a camel. Misfortune and urban disaster happen, in these strips, innocently and humorously.

The most powerful image in his gallery is a full-page *Little Nemo in Slumberland* from a 1907 issue of the *New York Herald.* The dreaming Nemo is a giant climbing skyscrapers and walking down the avenues. He is lost in New York, wishing that "we could find our way back to the palace" of the invented King Morpheus. Flip, his imagined friend, comes pounding through the city, knocking down skyscrapers and starting a fire that consumes the entire city. In the last panel, Nemo cuddles with his mother, who explains that she had been calling for him but he wouldn't wake up. Little Nemo's dream is about love for the great city, even if Flip does stomp a few of the skyscrapers. It is a play structure for a young, dreaming mind. Spiegelman seems to be offering a welcome mat to artists and writers to reenter the New York destruction genre that he recasts as a celebration of the city.

Little Nemo in Slumberland, 1907, reproduced in *In the Shadow of No Towers,* 2004

Skycaptain and the World of Tomorrow, 2004

Back to Normal: The Resilience of the Disaster Theme

If culture makers needed any inspiration to return to the theme of the city's end, policy makers, politicians, and scientists helped by creatively imagining horrible destruction arriving in New York. Blowing up a chlorine tank, spreading pneumonic plague throughout the city, bombing the Holland Tunnel, releasing a "suitcase" nuclear bomb in Times Square or dirty bombs in the subway, attacking the Indian Point nuclear power plant, launching a terror attack in Shea Stadium, destroying the Brooklyn Bridge—the list of scenarios offered up to a frightened public went on forever. The city, state, and federal governments contributed with mock terror attacks, reports of unreadiness, and plans for evacuation.[36] The Bush administration played the fear card like a good Hollywood screenwriter. Plots were floated, terror alerts were raised, headline fonts were enlarged, nervous New Yorkers were quoted. And then holes would begin to appear in the stories. The attack was not imminent; it was only in the planning stages, or a passing comment by a man on the streets of Cairo. In July 2006, just as the Bush administration was in the midst of a counteroffensive to rescue its final two years from utter political disaster, it announced that a plot to bomb the Holland Tunnel in order to flood lower Manhattan had been foiled. As it turns out, none of the suspects was in the United States, and there were no real plans, only words. Such "truth-based" scenarios provided fodder and inspiration for popular culture makers.

On the other hand, when a real disaster of sorts hit—a blackout that struck New York and a large part of the Northeast in August 2003, just a month before the second anniversary of 9/11—the experience taught the city and nation new lessons. The almost universal calm that accompanied the blackout was in stark contrast to reactions to the 1977 blackout, the worst in the nation's history; that episode had led to utter chaos in the city, with looting, riots, and arson taking over whole neighborhoods. The city was far less fragile than it had seemed after 9/11.[37] Similarly, when a man blew up his Upper East Side home in the summer of 2006 rather than let his wife have it in their divorce settlement, the disaster registered for a day or two, inspiring more jokes about the value of Manhattan real estate than concerns about the possibilities of post-9/11 catastrophe. Disasters that struck other people—New York is nothing if not a catalogue of daily pain, violence, crime, and collapse—became, once again, entertainment for everyone else.[38] As in the good old bad old days, New York had about a minute to be concerned with threats and daily disasters.

Or people had a couple of hours to watch it on the screen. Though film-makers made forays to other cities, the power of New York as the locus of the culture's destructive fantasies was remarkably resilient. After that brief era of editing out the twin towers, or avoiding destruction in and of New York, Americans rushed back to that theme with gusto. The films came at an accelerating pace: *Spider-Man* and *Spider-Man II* (2002 and 2004), *Batman Begins* (2005); *Skycaptain and the World of Tomorrow* (2004); *The Day After Tomorrow* (2004); *Superman Returns* (2006); *X-Men: The Last Stand* (2006), television shows *10.5* (2004), *Category 6* (2004), and *Heroes* (2006), to name just a few. Perhaps the finale to several years of battling over whether or not to show New York's destruction, or to show the twin towers, came in a fluffy comedy in the summer of 2006, *Click,* starring Adam Sandler as a man who gets a "universal remote" that allows him to fast-forward through his life. For just a brief second, in a scene set in 2021, we see the skyline of the city two decades from now. At the tip of lower Manhattan stands not one Freedom Tower (based on the initial design by David Childs after control had been wrested from the architect Daniel Libeskind) but two. A feeling that the site needed twin towers to "restore" the skyline and deny the terrorists victory seemed to have found a supporter in Hollywood.

Filmmakers and artists did not necessarily slip back into pre-9/11 conventions as they returned to destroy New York. For many artists and directors caution still reigned. For example, Steven Spielberg, in his *War of the Worlds* remake in 2005, expressly chose not to picture the destruction of New York because, as he acknowledged, "the shadow of 9/11" followed him during the making of the film. Perhaps mindful of how the lovingly crafted flights through a submerged and abandoned New York in *A.I.* romanticized the city as a ruin, *War of the Worlds* studiously avoided picturing New York's destruction. The screenwriter David Koepp has said that he and Spielberg agreed on a few principles, including "One: no destruction of famous landmarks. Two: no unnecessary beating up of New York City." The only hint of post-9/11 fears comes from the young daughter of the protagonist as she watches the aliens launch their destruction: "Is it the terrorists?"[39]

But the film nevertheless draws attention to the absence of New York. Alien machines planted deep in the earth thousands of years earlier awaken and explode out of the earth to begin their rampage . . . in New Jersey. Soon, Ray Ferrier (Tom Cruise), a dock operator who lives in the shadow of the Goethals Bridge, across from Staten Island, flees as the bridge is torn apart and the robots head toward the river and, inevitably, New York. But we see nothing of the city's demise. As the sky lights up with fire, the robots come over a hill, presumably having conquered New York, and the fight is on. This sensitivity to 9/11—or astute calculation—may be disappearing: Spielberg has said he intends, in 2008, to remake the 1951 *When Worlds Collide*.[40]

The End of the World as We Know It: Environmental Fears and the End of New York

The shackles restraining American culture from one of its favorite activities—imagining new ways to demolish New York—were quickly shattered. Just a year or two after 9/11, new themes began to emerge. The most powerful of these was global warming, which scientists unanimously predicted and right-wing politicians stridently repudiated. Natural disaster, and the subgenre of climate change, has always been a popular theme—as we have seen in works as diverse as *Deluge,* the *Twilight Zone* episode "The Midnight Sun," *Meteor,* and *Deep Impact.* All these dramas demonstrate the persistent fear that natural forces on the earth or beyond will end New York's fragile existence.[41]

In the early years of this century, natural disaster became environmental disaster, caused by human action, or inaction. Some earlier works had hinted at human culpability. But now the movies and stories showed humans provoking not degradation—not a natural, steady state of decline—but a dramatic shift in the earth's fortunes that would lead to cataclysmic shifts in the earth's atmosphere.

"In this unearthly light many tall structures of the metropolis, which had as yet escaped the effects of undermining by the rushing torrents in the streets, towered dimly toward the sky, shedding streams of water from every cornice. Most of the buildings of only six or eight stories had already been submerged, with the exception of those that stood on high grounds in the upper part of the island." This is an excerpt from the astronomer Garrett P. Serviss's 1912 novel *The Second Deluge.* The disaster is inevitable; the best humans can do is to recognize the coming calamity and be resourceful enough to survive. That scene, minus the biblical overtones, and with the addition of human environmental depredation as the root cause, could have been a summary of a scene from the 2004 film *The Day After Tomorrow.* The makers of that film consciously launched it into the global warming fracas and the 2004 election.[42] The story is built on a scientific theory that global warming would lead not to a steady warming and gradual melting of glaciers but rather force a tipping point, causing rapid cooling and the onset of an ice age.

Waters rush through the canyons of Manhattan in *The Day After Tomorrow,* 2004. As the ice age rapidly sets in, survivors try to get inside the New York Public Library

To establish his catastrophe as worldwide, the director Roland Emmerich piles in an assortment of disaster scenarios—hurricanes, tornadoes, ice age. Devastation hits every corner of the globe. And yet Emmerich comes back, as filmmakers always do, to New York City. The city's destruction brings it all home in a horrible—and horribly beautiful—frozen dream.

The climax of the destruction is a fifteen-minute disaster spree that begins with the flooding of New York.[43] The waves sweep into Manhattan and gush down the avenues—an image eerily reminiscent, even to the ground-level camera angles, of the clouds of dust and debris bursting through those canyonesque streets on 9/11—spinning people and cars and buses, bringing an oil tanker to rest in front of the New York Public Library. And then, just as quickly, temperatures drop and everything enters a deep freeze. The skyscrapers crackle as they are turned into upstanding icicles. In an homage to the Statue of Liberty's iconic place in the fictional destruction of New York—toppled and buried in *Planet of the Apes,* ruined in Harrison Cady's images, nearly submerged in *A.I.*—an arriving rescue party trudges by that frozen landmark, which just hours before had been chest high in water. The disaster is as beautiful as a new snow.[44]

The screenplay allows Emmerich to destroy the city but avoid the hellish fires of his previous films, such as *Independence Day.* Like a neutron bomb, the successive weather "events" of rising water and rapid deep freeze kill thousands but leave buildings standing. Perhaps this reflects a leftover fear of offending New York's post-9/11 sensibilities. Although there are some frightening scenes of floods overtaking people on the streets of Manhattan, the buildings do not fall. Indeed, the city is largely intact, even as water and ice envelop and freeze it.

The ending offers a hopeful vision: thousands upon thousands of New Yorkers escape to the rooftops of the skyscrapers and are saved. (Thank goodness for those boxy modernist skyscrapers with their flat roofs, perfect places for survivors to assemble and be rescued by helicopter.) And the city itself remains beautiful, locked in a light blue embrace of ice. Perhaps there is the smallest suggestion, as in Stephen Vincent Benét's "By the Waters of Babylon," that someday the ecological damage that created the deep freeze will recede and New York can be rediscovered. But this is beneath the surface of the story. The culmination of the movie is the rescue and the flight southward, to the warmth of Mexico. New York is left behind.

In reviews of *The Day After Tomorrow,* irony returned with a vengeance. Tad Friend, in a cheeky *New Yorker* piece about the film, notes, "If you're planning to depict an attack on New York City in a disaster film, you need to bring your A game." Roland Emmerich had brought his skills to New York's destruction previously in the alien invasion films *Independence Day* (1996) and *Godzilla* (1998). Reviewing the recent entries in the New York disaster film competition, Emmerich told Friend: "You don't want to repeat the same images. And you want to avoid the mistakes they made, the parts that don't look convincing. . . . We didn't want to go over the edge and have people laughing."[45]

The critical reaction was a telling cultural turning point. The press and audiences were strong and vocal but judged the film on its own merits (or lack thereof). The *New York Post* reviewer, in a piece headlined "Apocalypse Wow," panned it as "brain-freezing fun," but without reference to 9/11: "This is mindless popcorn fun for moviegoers who get a vicarious thrill . . . and have a high pain threshold for tin-eared dialogue."[46] Viewers who flocked to the movie in the first weekend recognized how things had changed. A man interviewed about the movie while he was waiting in line on opening night noted, "If people were squeamish, they wouldn't all be out here like this, going crazy over this movie."[47]

A month later a different kind of environmental disaster hit the screens, with the arrival in June 2004 of the highly praised sequel to *Spider-Man*. Critics were impressed that a summer blockbuster film chose to emphasize the darker sides of the superhero story: Peter Parker's inability to commit to Mary Jane, and his fury at the obligations of his spectacular abilities as Spider-Man. In frustration, he decides to abandon his superhero life. The result is that the city falls into a kind of 1970s decline, with criminal activity increasing exponentially ("Crime jumps 75%!" screams the *Daily Bugle* headline). But a much larger danger is suddenly unleashed. Peter's friend Harry Osborn, whose father, Norman (unbeknownst to his son, the evil Green Goblin), was killed in the first film, has embarked on a venture with Dr. Otto Octavius to harness the power of nuclear fusion. At the launch of this new force—at which Dr. Octavius makes fun of a nervous Peter Parker: "Dear, Mr. Parker thinks I'm going to destroy New York!"—something goes radically wrong and the scientist is transformed into a villainous machine, with four huge metal tentacles. He scales buildings, robs a bank, and unleashes havoc on the city. But worse is yet to come: he makes a deal with Osborn to acquire more of the material used to unleash the new power, tritium, and makes his way to a crumbling warehouse on the Hudson River where he hopes to achieve the most massive fusion reaction ever. The reaction creates a powerful magnet that begins to draw everything in the city toward it. Cabs and lampposts are pulled down the avenues toward the reactor. If it is not stopped,

Eric Drooker, "Turtle Island" and "Woman Under a Street Lamp," in *FLOOD! A Novel in Pictures*, 1992

WORST-CASE SCENARIO
Unless greenhouse-gas emissions are curbed, warns James Hansen of NASA, global temperatures could climb 2 to 3 degrees Celsius by 2100. "The last time the earth was that warm, sea levels were 80 feet higher than today." Such a rise, which could take hundreds of years, would leave little of Manhattan but the skyscrapers.

The administration "cherry-picked"
THE SCIENCE ON CLIMATE CHANGE,
"just like it cherry-picked the intelligence on
WEAPONS OF MASS DESTRUCTION,"
says Paul O'Neill.

What climate change could bring to the island of Manhattan: "While Washington Slept," *Vanity Fair*, 2006

the entire city will be drawn into the black hole of the reactor. Despite the enormous potential for total destruction, the city is, of course, saved.[48]

The fear of global warming proved fertile ground for a variety of culture makers. Hurricane Katrina, which hit New Orleans at the end of August 2005, fueled the global warming debate in several ways. Katrina raised the fear of more frequent and more violent hurricanes, which could devastate coastal cities. But it also offered dramatic images of what global warming would mean: flooded coastal cities as waters rise. Though New Orleans is a unique case in the United States—a city that sits below the water line, artificially protected by a system of levees—its submersion sent scientists, journalists, and artists scurrying to picture the future of their cities. Katrina also revealed the utter impotence of the federal and state governments either to prepare for the hurricane by building up adequate levees or to respond adequately to disaster.

Images of New Orleans in a future of continued global warming and rising waters were soon paired with visions of a flooded New York. They appeared in *Harvard Magazine,* in *Vanity Fair,* on the History Channel, and in newspapers.[49] The image of New York under water appeared in former vice president Al Gore's 2006 movie *An Inconvenient Truth.* One of the most powerful images of the film shows the impact of melting Arctic glaciers through a satellite view of New York if the ocean level were to rise just a few feet. The edge of Manhattan would be at Broadway, with the World Trade Center memorial site deep under water. While seeking to sound a loud alarm about the threat of global warming, the filmmakers wanted to avoid being marginalized for hyperbole. The shrinking of Manhattan Island—to roughly its dimensions of the eighteenth century before a succession of infills widened the island significantly—was a good choice: dramatic and suggestive of far greater tragedy (say, if the ocean levels rose ten feet) without overwhelming audiences with apocalyptic imagery. In an escapist disaster movie, audiences demand drama and realism; in a documentary, accuracy and caution win out.

No such caution is seen in the visionary paintings of Alexis Rockman, an artist who has spent a decade imagining and painting a submerged New York, a future environmental wasteland. In his work, Central Park is half tropical jungle, half arctic glacier, ringed by decaying skyscrapers; Times Square and Washington Square are submerged with palm trees growing out of the buildings' windows. The culmination of this decadelong exploration is *Manifest Destiny,* completed in 2004. In an eight-by-twenty-four-foot mural first exhibited in the Brooklyn Museum of Art, Rockman painstakingly depicts a panoramic view across the East River to Brooklyn in the year 5000, after three millennia of global warming and environmental degradation. (By choosing to take in the view of the borough he saw from his childhood home on the Upper East Side, Rockman offers one of the few New York destruction fantasies focusing on boroughs other than Manhattan.) The water has risen by eighty-two feet, submerging one-third of the shoreline of Manhattan looking across to the skyline of Brooklyn.[50] The glaciers have long ago melted and the waters have risen near the top of the Brooklyn Bridge. Brooklyn is entirely submerged, save a few landmarks of the past peeking above the water, such as the tower of the Williamsburg Savings Bank.

Rockman's images were inspired by Thomas Cole's angry denunciation of industrialization and urbanization in his *Course of Empire* series and the moralistic string of popular fantasies of New York's end seen throughout this book. Rockman also has on the wall of his studio the cover of *Amazing Stories* magazine from 1929, showing the Woolworth Tower collapsing under the onslaught of glaciers that have overcome New York in "The Sixth Glacier." He follows a long series of artists—including Art Spiegelman—who grew up enthralled by science fiction and especially the end–of–New York genre.

But to see *Manifest Destiny* and Rockman's earlier works simply as high-art versions of *Amazing Stories* misses what a close examination of the paintings reveals: they are remarkably accurate portraits of the city, as well as carefully researched visions of what future ruin might look like. Collaborating with architects, historians, and global warming scientists at Columbia's Earth Institute, Rockman offers a detailed slice through the coast of Brooklyn as it might look three thousand years from now. The depth of the riverbed, the layers of sediment, infrastructure tunnels, birds and sea creatures that would survive and those that would emerge from a new environment—all can be carefully observed. And the painting goes further: it imagines buildings yet to emerge in the twenty-first century (such as a revision of the Manhattan Bridge by Santiago Calatrava, and the New York Nets Stadium, which is only now being planned), as well as future, vain efforts to stop the rising waters, such as a levee running around the perimeter of the island. Those lie deep under the water, a laughable effort of a civilization unwilling to make the deeper changes to stem global warming.

Just as Rockman intends, a child would appreciate the image and might even giggle with enjoyment at the futuristic creatures, and the mess of it all.[51] But the artist also means for the work to be a warning about our current misuse of the earth. Though he loves disaster movies, Rockman is more in line with Chesley Bonestell and his 1950s images of nuclear attacks on the city—lush, attractive, even beautiful, but also as accurate as possible. Indeed, Rockman calls *Manifest Destiny* a "very traditional history painting."[52] This is a history painting for the future: global deluge caused by global warming, he suggests, will be our history if we cannot change our ways. The oil barrel—a cause of global warming—floats along, providing a haven for the creature that would surely persist: the cockroach. New York, once the exemplar of civilization, now becomes its graveyard. Beneath the waters lies a necropolis, a dead city that was unwilling or unable to curb its consumption and pollution. Tunnels and an oil tanker, a stealth bomber and a submarine—these are all that remain of the grand vision that animated this city.

Welcome Back, King Kong

If you were worried about New York's future in the aftermath of 9/11, you could take heart in late 2005: just like old times, the city was being destroyed at a theater near you. The best thing for New York might have been the sight of King Kong tramping through the streets of Manhattan on his way to a fateful appointment at the top of the Empire State Building. For if there is one thing that symbolizes New York's preeminence, it is that so many still want to imagine the city's end.[53]

Rather than bemoan the degradation of our insensitive culture, perhaps we should celebrate these fantasies. New York has been destroyed for so long that it is somehow reassuring to see the tradition continue. Even as we watch New York being demolished in a darkened screening room, we are already anticipating the aftermath—not the postapocalyptic landscape, but the scene after the lights go up. What we crave from these tense Hollywood films of menace and devastation is, in fact, reassurance that the city has survived. For New Yorkers, that means walking out of the movie theater and into a still extant, and robustly alive, city of New York. For those beyond the city, we expect the relief of watching that skyline behind David Letterman, as reliable as ever.[54]

It is important to remember that New York has always been better at celebration than at fear. New York has always prided itself on humming—tickertape parades down Broadway, the tall ships at the Bicentennial, that memorable V-J Day kiss caught by Eisenstaedt in Times Square—these are New York's emotional landmarks.

All this life explains why we continue to destroy New York in books, on canvas, on movie screens, and on computer monitors: because it is so unimaginable for us, in reality, not to have this city. We have played out our worst fears on the screen and in our pulp fiction because, as the city's oracle, E. B. White, wrote in the shadow of the atomic bomb: "If it were to go, all would go—this city, this mischievous and marvelous monument which not to look upon would be like death."[55]

Embracing these fantasies of the city's destruction is a reaffirmation of New York's greatness. Colson Whitehead's paean to New York in *Colossus of New York,* which appeared two years after 9/11, is a beautiful essay, reminiscent of White's "Here Is New York." It studiously avoids any direct mention of 9/11, although there are the briefest of hints of the new world in which he is writing. Referring equally to the city's builders and to the children in the sandbox he is

Alexis Rockman, *Washington Square*, 2004

observing, Whitehead writes, "What they build cannot last. Fragile skylines are too easily destroyed."[56] But at heart the book, which comprises thirteen stream-of-consciousness chapters, is an embrace of New York's fragility. "No matter how long you have been here," he writes in the first pages of the book, "you are a New Yorker the first time you say, That used to be Munsey's, or That used to be the Tic Toc Lounge. . . . You are a New Yorker when what was there before is more real and solid than what is here now." The city's cultural and social changeability, what Schumpeter might have called its social creative destruction, is its beauty. New Yorkers, Whitehead writes, love to know that "some lovely destruction is going on nearby. They secretly relish the violence done to their neighborhoods and old haunts because after they're gone they can brag about witness to the heyday." Owning New York means surrendering to its rapid change, and the threats it constantly survives.[57]

So the makers of American popular culture flirt with causing real disaster

Tom Cruise running through a startlingly empty Times Square in *Vanilla Sky*, 2001

Joel Meyerowitz, *West 46th St., NYC*, 1976. Digital archival print, Joel Meyerowitz, 2004

if they move their sets and canvases to other cities. When New York is no longer destroyed—on film, in flight-simulator software, in video games, paintings, and books—that will be a sign that the city no longer dominates America's, and the world's, imagination. And if New York is no longer the setting of our worst fears, then it may no longer be the home of our greatest hopes.

And that would be the beginning of the city's end.

The Korean artist Atta Kim's eight-hour-exposure photographs of Times Square and Fifth Avenue show a city utterly devoid of people, like the city Harry Belafonte finds in *The World, the Flesh, and the Devil,* or the Times Square Tom Cruise sprints through in *Vanilla Sky.* The lights are on, the Coke sign is illuminated, the traffic lights are working. But there are no people. If you take a photograph in an instant—say 1/250 of a second—the city is filled with life. But expose it for eight hours and you realize the people can be made to disappear. Over eight hours, any individual will leave virtually no mark on the film or digital chip. It's as if she were never there. Only the buildings, stationary for those eight hours, remain. It is almost a mystical suggestion here—the ghosts of the city can be conjured if you leave the lens open long enough. But also: the city is fragile. Its people, who seem to course down the avenues all hours of the day, could disappear in an instant.

There continues to be anxiety and uncertainty about New York. The city is no longer an invulnerable porcupine of skyscrapers. Instead, the city has been rediscovered as a fragile community—a community built on a delicate mix of people and buildings, the solace of anonymity and the thrill of cosmopolitanism, what Jane Jacobs famously called "organized complexity" in her classic study *The Death and Life of Great American Cities.* Only from beyond the five boroughs, in the hinterlands, does the city appear chaotic.[58]

This new uncertainty brought New Yorkers together in empathy and concern in the months after 9/11. But uncertainty could also lead to a pulling away from public life, New York's enduring justification for being, and a mimicking of the fortress mentality that has rolled across the country. It might remind New Yorkers again of the precariousness of their place, its indispensability to a personal and national identity. It might make New Yorkers want to defend the city even more, by starting an era of unprecedented creativity.

The city that never sleeps because of fear of airplanes, fear of bombs, might again become a city that never sleeps because it is too busy creating and telling, building and imagining, eating and singing. Jonathan Larson's words in the musical *Rent* could only have been written in New York: "The opposite of war isn't peace, it's creation!"[59]

When E. B. White wrote his soaring lines in 1949—"New York is to the nation what the white church spire is to the village—the visible symbol of aspiration and faith, the white plume saying the way is up!"—New York had not seen anything like the attack we experienced on September 11.[60] On that day, our fantasies and nightmares were made real. We now wait nervously for the next plume.

Still, I think White was right. New York will remain the way up for us all, the home of our ideals, and the place to which the world looks, for ideas, for success, for art, and for a new start.

Notes

1. Beauty and Terror

Epigraph. Mary Oliver, *Blue Pastures* (New York: Harcourt Brace, 1995).

1. I wasn't the only one: a review of Flight Simulator from 1988, the year I graduated from college, noted that not only did version 3.0 allow you to "fly in formation," but you could also "chase your lead plane right between the towers of the World Trade Center"; http://www.mobygames.com/game/dos/microsoft-flight-simulator-v30/adblurbs. Philip Petit's walk took place on August 7, 1974 (just before Richard Nixon's resignation, incidentally).

2. A. O. Scott, "Pinned Under the Weight of 9/11 History," *New York Times,* August 9, 2006. Scott writes, "It was impossible to banish the thought, even in the midst of that day's horror and confusion, that the attacks themselves represented a movie scenario made grotesquely literal. What other frame of reference did we have for burning skyscrapers and commandeered airplanes? And then our eyes and minds were so quickly saturated with the actual, endlessly replayed images—the second plane's impact; the plumes of smoke coming from the tops of the twin towers; the panicked citizens covered in ash—that the very notion of a cinematic reconstruction seemed worse than redundant. Nobody needed to be told that this was not a movie. And at the same time nobody could doubt that, someday, it would be."

3. Joaquin Miller, *The Destruction of Gotham* (New York: Funk and Wagnalls, 1886), 213.

4. Jacob Riis, *How the Other Half Lives* (New York: Charles Scribner's Sons, 1890), 229.

5. My focus is on the work of American artists, although I make references to foreign artists, writers, and filmmakers. The years leading up to 9/11, and the years since, have brought a rapid globalization of the New York disaster genre. Some of the most widely seen fictional images of New York's destruction are found in Japanese bootleg videos, Egyptian anti-American pamphlets, European video games, and even Al Qaeda adherents' drawings. Ted Burrows, "Utopian and Dystopian Visions of New York," unpublished manuscript.

6. I am especially indebted to two excellent recent books: Kevin Rozario, *The Culture of Calamity: Disaster and the Making of Modern America* (Chicago: University of Chicago

Press, 2007), and Nick Yablon, *American Ruins: An Archaeology of Urban Modernity, 1830–1920* (Chicago: University of Chicago Press, forthcoming, 2009). Rozario writes, "I have come to wonder if dominant American ideas of progress would even be imaginable without disasters." Rozario, *Culture of Calamity,* 3.

   7. Susan Sontag, "The Imagination of Disaster," in *Against Interpretation* (New York: Farrar, Straus and Giroux, 1966), 224.

   8. Don DeLillo, *White Noise* (New York: Viking, 1985), 66. See Rozario's discussion of the novel in *Culture of Calamity,* 1–2.

   9. Slavoj Žižek, *Welcome to the Desert of the Real! Five Essays on September 11 and Related Dates* (London: Verso, 2002). The attack on the World Trade Center, as I will discuss in the last chapter, was "libidinally invested" in a way another disaster would not be, because of our own submerged fear of the threats prompted by our own global economic hegemony.

   10. William Langewiesche, *American Ground: Unbuilding the World Trade Center* (New York: North Point, 2002). Quoted in Leon Wieseltier, "A Year Later," *New Republic,* September 2, 2002.

   11. This sense of amazement was heard in the NORAD (North American Aerospace Defense Command) headquarters on 9/11. "Is that real-world?" one air traffic controller asks. "Real-world hijack," says another. "Cool!" responds the first. See Michael Bronner, "9/11 Live: The Norad Tapes," *Vanity Fair,* September 2006, 262.

   12. Authors of a number of works in recent years have addressed the centrality of disaster in American life, but none has argued for the centrality of New York as I do here. See especially Steven Biel, *American Disasters* (New York: New York University Press, 2001); Carl S. Smith, *Urban Disorder and the Shape of Belief: The Great Chicago Fire, the Haymarket Bomb, and the Model Town of Pullman* (Chicago: University of Chicago Press, 1995). On Los Angeles, see Mike Davis, *Ecology of Fear: Los Angeles and the Imagination of Disaster* (New York: Metropolitan, 1998). Clearly many other cities, including London, have been destroyed on screen and in print, some with now lengthy traditions. London's goes well back in time to such novels as Richard Jefferies's *After London* (1885) and Graham Greene's *Ministry of Fear* (1943), and to the present, with such films as *28 Days Later* (2002), *Dirty War* (2004), and *V for Vendetta* (2005).

   13. Oswald Spengler and Charles Francis Atkinson, *The Decline of the West* (New York: Knopf, 1926), 2: 98, 99. Quoted in Peter Conrad, "Necropolis Now," *Observer,* May 16, 2004.

   14. Paul Virilio, *Ground Zero* (New York: Verso, 2002), 82.

   15. See especially Paul S. Boyer, *When Time Shall Be No More: Prophecy Belief in Modern American Culture* (Cambridge: Belknap Press of Harvard University Press, 1992).

   16. See Max Page, *The Creative Destruction of Manhattan, 1900–1940* (Chicago: University of Chicago Press, 1999).

   17. Rev. Jerry Falwell suggested a somewhat different version of this on September 12, 2001. Calling on long-standing conservative views of New York's debased moral milieu, Falwell declared, "I really believe that the pagans, and the abortionists, and the feminists, and the gays and the lesbians who are actively trying to make that an alternative lifestyle, the ACLU, People for the American Way, all of them who have tried to secularize America. I point the finger in their face and say, 'You helped this happen.'" For a discussion of this see Gustav

Niebuhr, "After the Attacks: Finding Fault; U.S. 'Secular' Groups Set Tone for Terror Attacks, Falwell Says," *New York Times,* September 14, 2001.

18. E. B. White, "Here Is New York," in *Essays of E. B. White* (New York: Harper and Row, 1977), 123. Originally published in *Holiday* in 1949.

19. Nicodemus Havens, *Wonderful Vision of Nicodemus Havens Wherein He Was Presented with a View of the Situation of the World, after the Dreadful Fourth of June 1812 and Shewing What Part of New York Is to Be Destroyed* (Boston: Coverley Jr., 1812), 9. The microform of this book was viewed at New York University's Bobst Library.

20. Ibid., 8.

21. Ibid., 10.

22. Thomas F. De Voe, *The Market Book, Containing a Historical Account of the Public Markets in the Cities of New York, Boston, Philadelphia and Brooklyn, with a Brief Description of Every Article of Human Food Sold Therein, the Introduction of Cattle in America, and Notices of Many Remarkable Specimens. In Two Volumes* (New York: B. Franklin, 1862, rpt. 1969 as vol. 1 of *American Classics in History and Social Science*), 83. See Joel Rose, *New York Sawed in Half: An Urban Historical* (New York: Bloomsbury, 2001).

23. Edward Robb Ellis, *The Epic of New York City* (New York: Coward-McCann, 1966).

24. Kenneth T. Jackson, "The Capital of Capitalism: The New York Metropolitan Region," in *Metropolis, 1890–1940,* ed. Anthony Sutcliffe (Chicago: University of Chicago Press, 1984).

2. "Horrors Were Their Delight"

1. José Martí, "New York Under the Snow," rpt. in *Writing New York: A Literary Anthology,* ed. Philip Lopate (New York: Library of America, 1998), 277. Martí wrote this piece while living in New York and organizing the Cuban independence movement. It was published in the Buenos Aires periodical *La Nación* on April 27, 1888. The piece opened like this: "Never in this century has New York seen a storm like the one on March 13. The day before, a Sunday, had been rainy, and the insomniac writer, the ticket seller at the railway station, and the milkman on his cart making the rounds of the sleeping houses at dawn could hear the wind that had descended upon the city whipping in fury against the chimneys and in even greater fury against rooftops and walls, taking off the roofs, demolishing shutters and balconies in its path, clutching at trees, carrying them off, and pitching down the narrow streets with a howl, as if caught in a trap. The electrical wires snapped by its passage sputtered and died. The telegraph lines that had so often withstood it were wrenched from their posts. . . .

"When New York was like an Arctic plain and night was falling with nothing to light it up, and fear was everywhere; when the generous mailmen fell face down, numb and blind, defending the mail sacks with their bodies; when families, gripped by mortal terror, tried in vain to open blocked doors in their search for a way out of houses that had lost their roofs; when the fire hydrants, like the rest of the city, lay beneath five feet of snow, hidden to even the most faithful hand—a raging fire broke out, tinting its snowy surroundings with the colors of dawn, and bringing down three tenements in as many gulps." José Martí, *José Martí: Selected Writing,* ed. and trans. Esther Allen (New York: Penguin, 2002), 225–31.

2. David M. Scobey, *Empire City: The Making and Meaning of the New York City Landscape* (Philadelphia: Temple University Press, 2002).

3. See Nick Yablon, *American Ruins: An Archaeology of Urban Modernity, 1830–1920* (University of Chicago Press, forthcoming 2009), on the long-standing belief, especially in writings of southern intellectuals, of the insistence that New York would fall into ruin of its own. Yablon in particular cites Edmund Ruffin's dreams of such an end in his *Anticipations of the Future* (1860), which can be found at http://delta.ulib.org/cgi-bin/handlers/handle2?call=8660.9465.

4. Thomas J. Vivian and Grena J. Bennet, "The Tilting Island," *Everybody's Magazine,* 1909, 385, 388, 383, 389.

5. *Everybody's Magazine* was founded in 1899 and, under the leadership of editor John O'Hara Cosgrave, was one of the major investigative (or muckraking, depending on your political perspective) journals. It featured some of the key writers of the era, including Upton Sinclair (who wrote about the meat industry in 1906), Ambrose Bierce, and Lincoln Steffens. The magazine slowly declined in the 1920s and was discontinued in 1929. For a good summary see http://www.spartacus.schoolnet.co.uk/USAeverybodys.htm.

6. Henry James, *New York Revisited* (New York: Franklin Square, 1994), 34; originally published 1906 in *Harper's Monthly.* This section is derived from my book *The Creative Destruction of Manhattan, 1900–1940* (Chicago: University of Chicago Press, 1999).

7. See "Le Corbusier Scans Gotham's Towers," *New York Times Magazine,* November 3, 1935.

8. Le Corbusier, *When the Cathedrals Were White* (New York: Reynal and Hitchcock, 1947), 45. Also see Nathan Silver, *Lost New York,* expanded ed. (Boston: Houghton Mifflin, 2000), 11.

9. Le Corbusier, *When the Cathedrals Were White,* 45.

10. See Joseph A. Schumpeter, "The Process of Creative Destruction," chapter 7 of *Capitalism, Socialism, and Democracy* (1942; New York: Harper and Row, 1976).

11. The population of New York City grew from 2.33 million in 1910 to 7,891,957 in 1950. See George Lankevitch, *A History of New York City* (New York: New York University Press, 1998), 146.

12. "The Building of New York," *Architecture* 56 (1927): 324, quoted in Robert A. M. Stern, Gregory Gilmartin, and Thomas Mellins, *New York 1930: Architecture and Urbanism Between the Two World Wars* (New York: Rizzoli, 1987), 19.

13. See http://www.barrypopik.com/index.php/new_york_city/entry/new_york_will_be_a_nice_town_when_its_finished/ for a history of the uses of this line.

14. William Dean Howells, *Their Wedding Journey* (Boston: Houghton Mifflin, 1871), 27.

15. Ann Douglas, *Terrible Honesty: Mongrel Manhattan in the 1920s* (New York: Farrar, Straus and Giroux, 1995), 17.

16. "The Vanishing of New York's Social Citadels: Four Great Establishments on Fifth Avenue That Have Unwillingly Given Up the Ghost," *Vanity Fair* 25 (October 1925): 51, quoted in Stern, Gilmartin, and Mellins, *New York 1930,* 20.

17. Gutzon Borglum, "Our Ugly Cities," *North American Review* 228 (November 1929): 548–53, quoted in Stern, Gilmartin, and Mellins, *New York 1930,* 19.

18. One response to those urban disasters was to put it all on stage. At Coney Island's amusement parks, on the hour, visitors could view a reenactment of a tenement house fire. See Lynn K. Sally, *Fighting the Flames: The Spectacular Performance of Fire at Coney Island* (New York: Routledge, 2006).

19. "A Lurid Prophecy: What a Colored Preacher Predicts Will Happen in New-York," *New York Times,* July 31, 1891.

20. "Here Is the Warning," *New York Times,* January 18, 1902. The announcement was also in the *New York Daily Tribune.*

21. "End of the World in Six Years," *New York Times,* January 17, 1894.

22. "A False Alarm," *New York Times,* May 10, 1903.

23. "Will Destroy New York. Connecticut Prophet Says Great Earthquake Will Arrive in August," *New York Times,* May 30, 1907.

24. "Connecticut Prophet," letter to the editor, *New York Times,* June 2, 1907.

25. "Cannot Crush the New York Spirit," letter to the editor, *New York Times,* June 4, 1907.

26. See Morton Keller, *The Art and Politics of Thomas Nast* (New York: Oxford University Press, 1968).

27. The scandal left urban legends of corruption for the ages: A quarry in Sheffield, Massachusetts, was to deliver $1,250 worth of marble, but by 1867 it had cost $220,000. It is said that the $300,000 allotted to carpeting, had it actually been used to buy carpeting at the going rates, could have paid to carpet all of Central Park. See "Priceless: Historic Preservation and the Valuing of Space," chapter 4 of Max Page, *The Creative Destruction of Manhattan* (Chicago: University of Chicago Press, 1999).

28. *New York Times,* July 7, 1889.

29. For a description of the threatening class battles, see William Dean Howells, *A Hazard of New Fortunes* (New York: Harper and Brothers, 1890).

30. Joaquin Miller, *The Destruction of Gotham* (New York: Funk and Wagnalls, 1886), 7, 8.

31. See *The Columbia Encyclopedia,* 6th ed. (New York: Columbia University Press, 2000); and *Dictionary of American Biography* (New York: Scribner's, 1930).

32. Miller, *Destruction of Gotham,* 17.

33. Ibid., 213, 212.

34. Ibid., 215, 213. In J. A. Mitchell's *The Last American,* a visitor from Persia in the year 2951 comes upon the ruins of New York and seeks to understand what happened to the "mehrikans." What follows is a long critique of contemporary New York, including its derivative culture, its excessive wealth and poverty; for ancient New Yorkers, the visitor is told, "horrors were their great delight." The remains of this once great civilization will, with irony magnified in our own time, be taken to the anthropology museum in Teheran. As a side note, it is "frightful climatic changes which swept the country like a mower's scythe" and did the city in. See J. A. Mitchell, *The Last American: A Fragment from the Journal of Khan-Li* (New York: Frederick A. Stokes, 1889).

35. Jacob Riis, *How the Other Half Lives* (New York: Charles Scribner's Sons, 1890), p. 229.

36. Garrett P. Serviss, *The Second Deluge* (New York: McBride, Nast, 1912).

37. Ibid., 133.

38. Ibid., 368, 370. See a further discussion of *The Second Deluge* in Nick Yablon, *American Ruins.*

39. Ignatius Donnelly, *Caesar's Column: A Story of the Twentieth Century,* ed. Walter B. Rideout (1890; Cambridge: Belknap Press of Harvard University Press, 1960).

40. Donnelly gives a sense that the city is almost beyond help. As it stands in 1988, it is a version of hell. But when the oppressive power is overthrown, a new, perhaps even more vicious power takes over. The only answer is to flee. And yet, while Donnelly describes in detail the vision of a better place Welstein and his followers will create in remote Africa, the success of the project is far from assured. In the meantime, guards with Gatling guns will have to monitor the narrow pass that protects the new community.

41. Donnelly, *Caesar's Column,* 256, 259.

42. Ibid., 277, 281.

43. Ibid., 282, 290.

44. Sacvan Bercovitch, *The American Jeremiad* (Madison: University of Wisconsin Press, 1978).

45. *Dictionary of American Biography,* 369–71.

46. William Jennings Bryan, speech delivered at the Democratic National Convention, Chicago, July 9, 1896. See http://historymatters.gmu.edu/d/5354/ for the text of the speech and an audio recording made by Bryan in 1921.

47. Donnelly, *Caesar's Column,* 3.

48. Information on Cady can be found at http://artarchives.si.edu/exhibits/cadyharr/cadydadr.htm.

49. Of course, the creation of such an image requires absence—leaving off any ink from the paper. So in those parts of the print, there literally is no building there at all.

50. The roots of the new fears lie in the shifting power arrangements in Europe after 1871 and the rise of American imperial efforts at the end of the century. See Yablon, *American Ruins,* chapter 3.

51. Arthur Dudley Vinton, *Looking Further Backward. Being a Series of Lectures Delivered to the Freshman Class at Shawmut College* (Albany, N.Y.: Albany Book Co., 1890).

52. Ibid., 122, 83.

53. Ibid., 77, 83, 98.

54. David M. Kennedy, *Over Here: The First World War and American Society* (New York: Oxford University Press, 1980).

55. Ibid., 37.

56. Ibid., 66, 67.

57. Ibid., 114.

58. Ibid., 36.

59. Eugene Griffin, *Our Sea-Coast Defences* (New York: G. P. Putnam's Sons, 1885), 13.

60. H. G. Wells, *The War in the Air: And Particularly How Mr. Bert Smallways Fared While It Lasted* (1908; Lincoln: University of Nebraska Press, 2002), 1, 258.

61. Dave Duncan, introduction to Wells, *The War in the Air,* ix.

62. H. G. Wells, *The War in the Air: And Particularly How Mr. Bert Smallways Fared While It Lasted* (Harmondsworth, England: Penguin, 1967), 7, 8.

63. See James Sanders, *Celluloid Skyline: New York and the Movies* (New York: Knopf, 2001), 388.

64. Wells, *War in the Air* (2002), 117, 116.

65. Ibid., 154.

66. Ibid., 210–11. See Mike Davis, "The Flames of New York," *New Left Review* 12 (2001), for a discussion of this book.

67. J. Bernard Walker, *America Fallen! The Sequel to the European War* (New York: Dodd, Mead, 1915).

68. Ibid., 104–5.

69. Ibid., 111.

70. "How Germans Might Capture New York; General Francis V. Greene Describes Imaginary Invasion and Levying of Tribute on Our Multi-Millionaires," *New York Times,* February 21, 1915.

71. For a discussion of the obsession with imagining future ruins and the "mood of the 'future anterior'" see Nick Yablon, "The Metropolitan Life in Ruins: Architectural and Fictional Speculations in New York, 1909–19," *American Quarterly* 56, no. 2 (2004), 308–47.

72. George Allan England, *Darkness and Dawn: Illustrated* (1912; New York: Avalon, 1965).

73. Ibid., 19, 20, 56.

74. Ibid., 20, 21, 28–29.

75. Ibid., 74, 87.

76. "Romance of a Depopulated New York," *New York Times,* February 8, 1914.

77. England, *Darkness and Dawn,* 41.

78. Boilers on the roof come crashing through the entire Met Life Tower: "Both of them expected nothing but that the entire structure would collapse like a card house and shatter down in ruins that would be their death. But though it swayed and quivered, as in the grasp of an earthquake, it held." Ibid., 102.

79. Ibid., 111, 129.

80. Van Tassel Sutphen, *The Doomsman* (1905; New York: Harper and Brothers, 1906). New York gains the name "Doom City" in this book. "The city did not suffer from any general and organized conflagration, as was the fate of Philadelphia and St. Louis and New Orleans. The destiny of the Metropolis was decided in a different way; already it had passed into the keeping of the Doomsmen. . . . In effect then, the highly civilized North American continent had relapsed within the brief period of ninety years into its primeval estate." Ibid., 10.

81. England, *Darkness and Dawn,* 132.

82. Ibid., 177, 182.

83. Ibid., 185, 189.

3. Utopian and Dystopian Fantasies

Epigraph. Oswald Spengler, *The Decline of the West,* trans. Charles Francis Atkinson (New York: Knopf, 1926), 2: 99.

1. The first commercial radio stations with regularly scheduled broadcasts were heard in 1920. WWJ, then known as 8MK, went on the air in Detroit in August. KDKA debuted

in Pittsburgh in November with the results of the presidential election. Listen to the first radio broadcast in 1920 at http://www.kdkaradio.com/pages/15486.php.

2. Beverly Gage, "The First Wall Street Bomb," in *After the World Trade Center: Rethinking New York City,* ed. Michael Sorkin and Sharon Zukin (New York: Routledge, 2002), 47. See also Beverly Gage, *The Day Wall Street Exploded* (New York: Oxford University Press, 2008).

3. W. E. B. Du Bois, "The Comet," in *Darkwater: Voices from Within the Veil* (1920; New York: AMS Press, 1969), 257, 56.

4. Ibid., 259, 263.

5. Ibid., 266.

6. Ibid., 269, 270.

7. Ibid., 271.

8. Upton Sinclair, *The Millennium: A Comedy of the Year 2000* (New York: Seven Stories, 1924).

9. Ibid., 67.

10. Ibid., 229.

11. This is the thesis of Ian Buruma and Avishai Margalit, *Occidentalism: The West in the Eyes of Its Enemies* (New York: Penguin, 2004). See also Mike Davis, "Flames of New York," in *Dead Cities, and Other Tales* (New York: New Press, 2002), 13, 15, who notes that Sayyid Qutb, who would become the "major philosopher of radical Islamism," found his voice through disgust with the New York he experienced after disembarking from a boat in 1948.

12. Federico García Lorca, *Poet in New York* (1932; New York: Grove, 1955). Quoted in Davis, "Flames of New York," 3.

13. From a 1931 interview, found in *Columbia World of Quotations* (1996), http://www.bartleby.com/66/86/36786.html.

14. Quoted in Davis, "Flames of New York," 3.

15. Elsewhere in the novel, the skyscrapers "go up like flames, in flames, flames." John Dos Passos, *Manhattan Transfer* (Boston: Houghton Mifflin, 1925), 253. And Jimmy Herf declares, "But what's the use of spending your whole life fleeing the City of Destruction?"

16. This is written on Rosenberg's 1929 *The Call for Margins,* Smith College Art Museum.

17. James N. Rosenberg, *50 Lithographs* (New York: Abrams, 1964).

18. Rosenberg wrote that "In the afternoon of October 28, 1929, the terrible day when nine million shares were slaughtered on the New York Stock Exchange, I rushed to [printmaker] George Miller's place and made my lithograph Dies Irae." See http://www.loc.gov/exhibits/goldstein/goldcity.html. See also Rosenberg, *50 Lithographs.*

19. The writer Stephen Vincent Benét would play on this image as well, in his "Notes to Be Left in a Cornerstone": "And for money and the lack of it many died, / Leaping from windows or crushed by the big truck. / They shot themselves in washrooms because of money. / They were starved and died on the benches of subway stations. Stephen Vincent Benét, *Burning City: New Poems* (New York: Farrar and Rinehart, 1936), 7.

20. Vivian Sobchack sees this era as generally hopeful: "The positive image of the 1930s has its roots in the earlier urban and technological visions of Futurism and Modernism." See Vivian Sobchack, "Cities on the Edge of Time: The Urban Science-Fiction Film," in *Alien Zone II: The Spaces of Science Fiction Cinema,* ed. Annette Kuhn (New York: Verso, 1999).

21. There is some debate about whether Siegel and Schuster proposed a Superman figure in 1933 or 1934. For a good timeline, see http://www.collectortimes.com/~comichistory/Hist1.html. But in June 1938, *Action Comics* no. 1 came out, with a figure in the now familiar blue and red costume, holding a car over his head.

22. E. B. White, "Here Is New York," in *Essays of E. B. White* (New York: Harper and Row, 1977), 122. Originally published in *Holiday* in 1949. This and the following four paragraphs were adapted from Max Page, "Crashing to Earth, Again and Again," *New York Times,* April 23, 2006. Used with permission.

23. F. Scott Fitzgerald, "My Lost City," rpt. in *Writing New York: A Literary Anthology,* ed. Phillip Lopate (New York: Library of America, 1998), 578.

24. James Sanders, *Celluloid Skyline: New York and the Movies* (New York: Knopf, 2001), 98.

25. This is truly an international work. The English writer's story centered on Britain is transferred to the American cinema. But the American version of the film has long been lost; only in 1987 was an Italian-dubbed version rediscovered, complete with new clips inserted, including a scene where an Italian calendar has been placed on the wall when Martin is seen marking the passing days. Some have speculated that with the arrival in 1933, the year the film was issued, of the Hays production code, sharply restricting Hollywood's subjects, that RKO found it had an unusable film on its hands. See http://imdb.com/title/tt0023938/.

26. See http://www.sfw.org/filmdeluge.html.

27. The other great urban disaster film of the 1930s was Twentieth Century–Fox's *In Old Chicago* (1937), which had an astounding $1.8 million budget. Most of that budget was spent on a remarkable half-hour of destruction following the infamous kick by Mrs. O'Leary's cow in 1871.

28. Parry Edmund Stroud, *Stephen Vincent Benét* (New York: Twayne, 1963).

29. Charles A. Fenton, *Stephen Vincent Benét: The Life and Times of an American Man of Letters, 1898–1943* (New Haven: Yale University Press, 1958), 357.

30. Benét, *Burning City,* 3, 9.

31. Ibid., 72.

32. Ibid., 75.

33. Ibid., 76, 77.

34. Ibid., 80.

35. "By the Waters of Babylon" first appeared in 1937 in the *Saturday Evening Post* as "The Place of the Gods." Stephen Vincent Benét, "By the Waters of Babylon," in *Selected Works of Stephen Vincent Benét* (New York: Farrar and Rinehart, 1937), 476.

36. Ibid., 475, 477, 478, 480, 481.

37. Ibid., 481, 482, 483. In a letter to a Harvey E. Fisk, Jr., Benét wrote that the misspelling of Lincoln's name was deliberate: "I thought he probably saw a sign with a piece cut out—like this—LI COLN. Or possibly that the name of the folk-hero had become a little slurred by time as well. Sincerely, S. V. Benét." Letter signed on stationery of Thomas Carr Benét, NYC, with envelope postmarked January 6, 1938, viewed at www.biblio.com on August 25, 2006, since removed.

38. Guglielmi uses the threat to this landmark as a wake-up call to Americans, to "bring home his fears over the spread of fascism, symbolized by the remains of a suit of medieval armor—a trope used by left-wing political cartoonists during the thirties—ensnared by

the bridge's cables." Gerrit Lansing, "Surrealism as a Weapon," in *Surrealism USA,* ed. Isabelle Dervaux (New York: National Academy Museum, New York, and Hatje Cantz, 2004).

39. Quoted in "Guglielmi's First," *Art Digest* 13 (November 15, 1938), 20.

40. O. Louis Guglielmi, "I Hope to Sing Again," *Magazine of Art* 37 (May 1944), 175, quoted in Lansing, "Surrealism as a Weapon."

41. Lansing notes, "It is possible that Guglielmi was, in part, responding to America's neutrality policy." Lansing, "Surrealism as a Weapon," 35, n. 18.

42. Guglielmi's 1941 *Panic in Brooklyn* is far more direct in its terror. It portrays an empty street in Brooklyn, although it has the feel of the main street of a small town. A line of brick stores and a diner at the corner frame the image. But in the foreground is a glass container which covers two huddling women. The white curves of airplanes in the sky and the indications of an unseen bombing behind the brownstones indicate that the attack has begun.

43. Orrin E. Dunlap, Jr., "Message from Mars," *New York Times,* November 6, 1938.

44. Charles Higham, *Orson Welles: The Rise and Fall of an American Genius* (New York: St. Martin's, 1985), 124; Hadley Cantril, with Hazel Gaudet and Herta Herzog, *The Invasion from Mars: A Study in the Psychology of Panic* (Princeton: Princeton University Press, 1940), 28. The text of the broadcast is reproduced in Cantril's book, 3–44.

45. Cantril, *Invasion,* 31.

46. "Radio Listeners in Panic, Taking War Drama as Fact," *New York Times,* October 31, 1938.

47. Cantril, *Invasion,* 34, 41.

48. Quoted ibid., 47.

49. Alice V. Keliher, "Radio 'War' Fear Stirs Educators," *New York Times,* November 6, 1938.

50. "Screen News Here and in Hollywood," *New York Times,* November 2, 1938; "Radio Listeners in Panic."

51. In a *Fortune* magazine poll, 50 percent of respondents said that radio was the medium freest from prejudice; only 17 percent ranked newspapers at the top.

52. Cantril, *Invasion,* 153, 161, 162; Keliher, "Radio 'War.'

53. *New York World-Telegram,* November 2, 1938, quoted in Cantril, *Invasion,* 202.

54. Cantril, *Invasion,* 205.

55. Barbara Leaming, *Orson Welles: A Biography* (New York: Viking, 1985), 159; "Radio Listeners in Panic."

56. Leaming, *Orson Welles,* 159. To be sure, some could not imagine New York destroyed, especially by Martians. One listener began by believing the show to be a real news report. But then "I heard the announcer say he was broadcasting from New York and he saw a Martian standing in the middle of Times Square and he was tall as a skyscraper. That's all I had to hear—just the word Martian was enough even without that fantastic and incredible description. . . . I knew it had to be a play." Some "checked" by looking out the window: "I went to the window and looked over to New York. I didn't see anything unusual there either, so I thought they hadn't gotten there yet." Cantril, *Invasion,* 91.

57. In one of the many spoofs of the *War of the Worlds* fiasco, Welles is sent to Mars in a *Superman* issue from the 1950s ("Black Magic on Mars"). Upon arriving, Welles realizes that the Martians are planning an invasion and sends a warning—real this time—back to earth.

Unfortunately, because of the memory of *War of the Worlds,* no one heeds his call, except for Superman. See E. Nelson Bridwell, *Superman, from the Thirties to the Eighties* (New York: Crown, 1983), 213.

58. Gordon Kahn and Maxwell Shane, screenplay for *S.O.S. Tidal Wave,* Republic Pictures, 1939, 89, 90, 91, 92.

59. Ibid., 97, 98.

60. Ibid., 102.

61. Frank S. Nugent, "The Screen: At the World Cinema," *New York Times,* June 22, 1939.

62. Bridwell, *Superman,* 54, 131, 193. A 1942 strip includes Lois Lane and Clark watching a film based on the DC comic strip *Superman,* about a huge robot tramping through Metropolis. Clark has to distract Lois during the scenes that reveal Superman's secret identity! Bridwell, *Superman,* 146–52.

63. As we shall see, this motif of a new weapon that could undermine the strength of the steel skyscraper and bring it crashing down would be borrowed almost exactly in the 1949 *King of the Rocketmen* serial.

64. Those mechanical monsters were brought back, with remarkable similarity, in the 2005 film *Sky Captain and the World of Tomorrow.*

65. "Book Notes," *New York Times,* December 27, 1932.

4. "Falls Rome, Falls the World"

1. George R. Stewart, *Earth Abides* (New York: Random House, 1949), 71–72.

2. See Paul Brians, *Nuclear Holocausts: Atomic War in Fiction, 1895–1984* (Kent, Ohio: Kent State University Press, 1987).

3. See Mike Davis, *Ecology of Fear: Los Angeles and the Imagination of Disaster* (New York: Metropolitan, 1998).

4. "Might-Have-Been," *Time,* February 12, 1940, 44.

5. The film *Spider-Man 2* (2004) was to play on this theme as well: in an abandoned warehouse on Gotham's shoreline, an evil genius assembles a machine that soon threatens to explode and destroy the city.

6. Ironically, one of the first newscasts reporting on the dropping of the bomb used Denver as an illustration of scale: "It would be the same as Denver, Colorado, with a population of 350,000 persons, being there one moment, and wiped out the next." But very quickly, the comparisons came to focus on New York. See Paul S. Boyer, *By the Bomb's Early Light: American Thought and Culture at the Dawn of the Atomic Age* (New York: Pantheon, 1985), 5.

7. Robert Jay Lifton and Greg Mitchell, *Hiroshima in America: Fifty Years of Denial* (New York: Putnam, 1995), 302. Quoted in Michael Quinn Dudley, "Sprawl as Strategy: City Planners Face the Bomb," *Journal of Planning Education and Research* 21, no. 3 (2001): 53.

8. Boyer, *By the Bomb's Early Light,* 351.

9. "1945 Cassandra," *New Yorker,* August 28, 1945, 16.

10. Gregory Corso, "Bomb," in *Gasoline* (San Francisco: City Lights Books, 1958).

11. Pat Frank, *Alas, Babylon* (New York: Lippincott, 1959), 28. "Some would survive, but they will largely be mutated. They'll give birth to freaks or supermen or telepaths." Frank

also writes: "If an atomic-powered taxi hit an atomic-powered streetcar at Forty-second and Lex it would completely destroy the whole Grand Central area." See John Wood Campbell, ed., *The Astounding Science Fiction Anthology* (New York: Simon and Schuster, 1952), 16.

12. Francis Vivian Drake, "Let's Be Realistic About the Atom Bomb," *Reader's Digest,* December 1945, 109.

13. See, for example, Harold R. Hinton, "Atom Bomb Force in Big City Argued," *New York Times,* February 16, 1946.

14. David B. Parker, "Mist of Death over New York," *Reader's Digest,* April 1947, 7–10.

15. Philip Morrison, "If the Bomb Gets Out of Hand," in *One World or None: A Report to the Public on the Full Meaning of the Atomic Bomb,* ed. Dexter Masters and Katharine Way (New York: McGraw-Hill, 1946).

16. Morrison, "If the Bomb Gets Out of Hand," 3; Edward L. Glaeser, "Urban Colossus: Why New York Is America's Largest City," *Federal Reserve Bank of New York Economic Policy Review* 11, no. 2 (2005).

17. Ralph Eugene Lapp, *Must We Hide?* (Cambridge, Mass.: Addison-Wesley, 1949).

18. Ibid., 81, 84.

19. John Lear, "Hiroshima, USA," *Collier's,* August 5, 1950, 65; William L. Laurence, "H-Bomb Can Wipe Out Any City, Strauss Reports After Tests; U.S. Restudies Plant Dispersal," *New York Times,* April 1, 1954.

20. For information on Bonestell, see Ron Miller, *The Art of Chesley Bonestell* (London: Paper Tiger, 2001).

21. Lear, "Hiroshima, USA."

22. Parker, "Mist of Death over New York," 10.

23. "First Daytime Air Raid Drill Ties Up City," *New York Times,* October 23, 1942.

24. Ibid.

25. Arthur Brown, *What Happened on June 15?* (New York: Provisional Defense Committee, 1955). On the experience of civil defense in the United States and Europe see Lawrence Vale, *The Limits of Civil Defence* (Basingstoke: Macmillan, 1987).

26. Philip Wylie, *Triumph* (Garden City, N.Y: Doubleday, 1963), 123–24.

27. The hydrogen bomb was being developed at the time, and would finally be detonated in a test on November 1, 1952. Newspapers showed the new power of the H-bomb first and foremost using images of New York, with the two generations of nuclear weapons imposed on the same scene. The mushroom cloud of the A-bomb spreads around eight hundred yards across but appears rather contained in its effect. But the H-bomb seems to encompass the entire city in its destructive embrace, as it would in reality. (There is an odd similarity between the hydrogen bomb's shell-like appearance and the sense of New York encased in glass, like a snow globe, in one of the earliest *Superman* comics.) See Richard Rhodes, *Dark Sun: The Making of the Hydrogen Bomb* (New York: Simon and Schuster, 1995).

28. "The 36 Hour War," *Life,* November 19, 1945, 27–35.

29. E. Nelson Bridwell, *Superman, from the Thirties to the Eighties* (New York: Crown, 1983), 215. This attack was prevented by a warning from, of all people, Orson Welles.

30. Harryhausen photographed scenes of contemporary New York and projected them onto small screens. Then he put the beast between the images, so that it appears to be walking—and crashing—through the streets of the city. This was a vast improvement over the

King of the Rocketmen series, as well as the previous year's *Captive Women,* which managed only unconvincing background murals to indicate locations in destroyed New York.

31. *Godzilla,* the 1956 American adaptation of the 1954 Japanese *Gojira,* evokes a similar feeling: the atomic bomb, the films suggest, have awakened not only the worst in humans but the worst in nature. While Hollywood was eager to play on the fears of nuclear disaster, and explored the issue in hundreds of films, it was far more likely to produce films that underscored the need for military preparedness, civil defense, and vigilance against communists. So when *Godzilla* was brought to American moviehouses, many of the overt antinuclear elements had been cleansed.

32. W. D. Herrstrom, *The Third World War and International Suicide* (Faribault, Minn.: Bible News Flashes, 1951).

33. Billy Graham, *Revival in Our Time* (Wheaton, Ill.: Van Kampen, 1950), 75, 70. Los Angeles was a serious contender for the title of Sin City, as Graham made clear in a sermon in the city on September 25, 1949, two days after President Truman revealed news of the first Soviet atomic test: "I particularly believe this applies to the city of Los Angeles—this city of wickedness and sin, this city that is known around the world because of its sin, crime and immorality."

34. Ibid., 69. Graham opened his May 15, 1957, sermon in Madison Square Garden, part of his vast New York revival of that year, with the same scriptural passage.

35. Herrstrom, *The 3rd World War,* 16–17.

36. See Thomas J. Sugrue, *The Origins of the Urban Crisis: Race and Inequality in Postwar Detroit* (Princeton: Princeton University Press, 1996).

37. William Fielding Ogburn, "Sociology and the Atom," *American Journal of Sociology* 51, no. 4 (1946): 270, 272. See also Donald and Astrid Monson, "How Can We Disperse Our Large Cities?" *American City*, December 1950 (part 1) and January 1951 (part 2).

38. Laurence, "H-Bomb Can Wipe Out Any City."

39. Lee E. Cooper, "Asks Better Plan to Disperse Cities," *New York Times,* May 12, 1950.

40. Ogburn, "Sociology and the Atom," 271.

41. Lapp, *Must We Hide?* 159; Matthew L. Wald, "R. E. Lapp, 87, Physicist in Cold-War Debate on Civil Defense," *New York Times,* September 10, 2004.

42. Lapp, *Must We Hide?* 143, 159.

43. Ibid., 148, 75, 84–85, 162–63, 157. The resonance of Lapp's words to the contemporary world is startling: "In the streets of America talk is heard of a *preventive* war. There are some who argue that we should attack while we still have a-bomb supremacy. . . . Remember that vanquished people do not feel kindly disposed toward the conqueror, especially in a war where atomic bombs are used. A preventive war might well be long drawn out and very destructive. . . . We are witnessing today a clash of ideologies" (174–75).

Dispersal became public policy, through a crucial series of federal government policies that urban historians now recognize as having remade the urban landscape: the Housing Acts of 1949 and 1954, the Highway Act of 1956, and the urban renewal projects designed to rid cities of blight and create highways that would move people from their safe, distant homes into the still-crucial center of cities.

Project East River was the largest of all the studies. It was so named because its planning ideas were based on a scenario of atomic bombs dropped over the East River. The devastation posited in the study lent credibility to their claims that dispersal was required to save the city.

44. Charles Grutzner, "City Folk's Fear of Bombs Aids Boom in Rural Realty," *New York Times,* August 27, 1950; "A-Bombs on a U.S. City," *Life,* February 27, 1950.

45. Lapp, *Must We Hide?* 51.

46. Parker, "Mist of Death over New York," 9.

47. Richard Foster, *The Rest Must Die* (Greenwich, Conn.: Fawcett, 1959), 7. Another story that pictures an underground, postapocalyptic New York is Albert Stockvis, "The Coming Destruction of New York City" (Cleveland, 1957). In this short pamphlet, Stockvis prophesies the fate of New York City in A.D. 6000 and beyond. In 6000, he predicts, "fiery bodies of unusual brightness" (comets? asteroids?) appear in the sky and are followed by "columns of fire rising skyward" (volcanic eruptions?). As the "waters of the ocean and rivers" rise, the "earth trembles" and "hot vases of thousands of degrees" (volcanoes?) start fires that wipe out 85 percent of the residential quarters, destroy nearly all means of communication, damage public buildings beyond repair, and burn millions of people alive. If this isn't enough, "an air attack of enemy nations" blankets the city with bombs, killing millions. Those New Yorkers who survive this catastrophe, Stockvis foresees, will rebuild a city "comparable to no other city in the world." By A.D. 7000 it will have "annexed the city of Philadelphia and all territory between New York and Philadelphia. It will be "scattered over five former states of the former U.S.A., covering millions of acres of land. But this New York will be an unreal city. The unreality of the houses and buildings will be no more than facades. . . . Two different New Yorks will exist. There will be the old New York on the surface, with the New York underground where it will be forced to recede" (23). Stockvis then goes on to describe this subterranean metropolis in detail: "Anyone desiring to visualize this underground city on a small scale, can find concrete proof of its being in Radio City on Fifth Ave. and its neighborhood in the New York of 1957. There one can take escalators to floors with passages lined with stores of all kinds, offices, barber shops and restaurants—an underground city of its own, entombed in the bowels of the earth" (24).

49. Foster, *The Rest Must Die,* 132, 131.

49. Ibid., 175.

50. Ibid., 148, 175.

51. Frederik Pohl, "The Knights of Arthur," in *The Frederik Pohl Omnibus* (London: Victor Gollancz, 1966), 106.

52. The British film *The Day the Earth Caught Fire* was released the same year with a similar theme to that of "Midnight Sun." Simultaneous H-bomb detonations from the Soviets and the Americans have sent earth out of its orbit and headed straight toward the sun.

53. For another description of the lawlessness of the postapocalyptic city see Pohl, "The Knights of Arthur."

54. Judith Merril, *Shadow on the Hearth* (Garden City, N.Y.: Doubleday, 1950). The novel was made into a television program called *Atomic Attack* on ABC in 1954.

55. "Over the Hills and Far Away?" *Commonweal,* September 29, 1950, 596.

56. Edward A. Conway, "A-Bomb over Manhattan," *America: National Catholic Weekly Review,* July 22, 1950, 413.

57. See Tom Vanderbilt, "City Without Fear," *New York Times,* April 24, 2003. "House Subcommittee of the Committee on Government Operations, Civil Defense," Washington, D.C., 85th Congress, 2nd session, 1958.

58. Some have suggested that Groeteschele, played by Walter Matthau, is modeled on Herman Kahn (1922–83), a military strategist and founder of the Hudson Institute, who argued that atomic war is survivable. See http://en.wikipedia.org/wiki/Fail-Safe_(1964_film).

59. It is an open question how much Jacobs's focus on safety was derived from the language of civil defense and the fear of nuclear attack. But clearly, she transposed this fear into the older fear: fear of crime.

60. E. B. White, "Here Is New York," in *Essays of E. B. White* (New York: Harper and Row, 1977), 121, 33. Originally published in *Holiday* in 1949.

61. Ibid., 132.

5. Escape from New York

1. Robert Venturi, *Complexity and Contradiction in Architecture* (New York: Museum of Modern Art, 1966), 102.

2. Jonathan Schell, *The Fate of the Earth* (New York: Knopf, 1982).

3. Ibid., 47–48, 52.

4. Robert Buchard, *Thirty Seconds over New York,* trans. June P. Wilson and Walter B. Michaels (New York: Morrow, 1970). This novel recalls Arthur's *Looking Further Backward* (1890), about a Chinese attack on the city. Roald Dahl, *James and the Giant Peach, a Children's Story* (New York: Knopf, 1961).

5. Tom Wicker, "The Hardest Truth," *New York Times,* December 16, 1983.

6. Jennifer Leaning and Langley Carleton Keyes, *The Counterfeit Ark: Crisis Relocation for Nuclear War* (Cambridge, Mass.: Ballinger, 1984).

7. Edward Zuckerman, *The Day After World War III* (New York: Viking, 1984), 105–6, 15.

8. Buchard, *Thirty Seconds over New York,* 216–18.

9. Billy Joel, "Miami 2017 (Seen the Lights Go Out on Broadway)" (1976). In 1978 Mick Jagger of the Rolling Stones added, in "Shattered": "Rats on the West Side, bedbugs uptown / What a mess! This town's in tatters / I've been shattered." See David Brooks, "The Bursting Point," *New York Times,* September 4, 2005.

10. Kenneth Jackson, *Crabgrass Frontier: The Suburbanization of the United States* (New York: Oxford University Press, 1985), 217.

11. See Joshua Freeman, *Working-Class New York: Life and Labor Since World War II* (New York: New Press, 2000); Frederick F. Siegel, *The Future Once Happened Here: New York, D.C., L.A., and the Fate of America's Big Cities* (New York: Free Press, 1997); Robert Fitch, *The Assassination of New York* (London: Verso, 1993); George J. Lankevich, *American Metropolis: A History of New York City* (New York: New York University Press, 1998). This discussion of New York's economic troubles is drawn from Max Page and Eve Weinbaum, "The City That Workers Built," *Reviews in American History* 29, no. 3 (2001): 433–40.

12. Brent Haydamack, Daniel Flaming, and Patrick Burns, "Los Angeles Labor Market Strengths and Weaknesses," http://www.economicrt.org/summaries/la_lm_strengths_weaknesses_synopsis.html.

13. Susan Sontag, "The Imagination of Disaster," in *Against Interpretation* (New York: Farrar, Straus and Giroux, 1966), 213.

14. Quoted in Robert Moses, "Are Cities Dead?" *Atlantic Monthly,* January 1962.

15. Quoted in David Brooks, "The Bursting Point," *New York Times,* September 4, 2005.

16. Quoted in "Episcopal Bishop Paul Moore Jr., 83, Strong Voice on Social and Political Issues, Dies," *New York Times,* May 6, 2003.

17. Jason Epstein, "The Last Days of New York," in *The Fiscal Crisis of American Cities: Essays on the Political Economy of Urban America with Special Reference to New York,* ed. Roger E. Alcaly and David Mermelstein (New York: Vintage, 1976).

18. Richard J. Whalen, "A City Destroying Itself," *Fortune,* September 1964; Richard J. Whalen, *A City Destroying Itself: An Angry View of New York* (New York: William Morrow, 1965), 13.

19. Whalen, *A City Destroying Itself,* 14, 15, 17, 18. Jacob Riis had spoken of the "waves" of immigrants flooding New York at the turn of the previous century; Garrett Serviss's *Second Deluge* and the films *Deluge* and *S.O.S. Tidal Wave* were among the many visions of New York's death by water.

20. Stewart Alsop, "The City Disease," *Newsweek,* February 28, 1972.

21. One particular fear in nuclear disaster planning was that the rural counties where millions of New Yorkers had fled would greet African-Americans and other minorities not with open arms but with guns. Indeed, in 1980 FEMA studied the reception problem when black and Hispanic residents headed out to the suburbs and rural areas. FEMA found, not surprisingly, that there would be problems. "How are you going to keep those people there [in Ulster County, New York] from shooting the people coming in?" a reporter asked Bardyl Tirana, the codirector of the Defense Civil Preparedness Agency in 1978. His reply was simply, "That's tough." The greater danger was not a nuclear attack in suburban areas but that the urban crisis—understood as minorities and the poverty and crime they allegedly brought with them—would migrate to the suburbs. The social chaos of nuclear war's aftermath was seen to be worse—or least more imaginable—than the nuclear attack itself.

Perhaps FEMA planners decided that this wouldn't be such a problem after all. For in their scenarios they imagine that the bulk of the 20 percent who voluntarily choose not to leave the city would be "drug addicts, terrorists, and doomsayers." (Many of the rest would be hopelessly sentimental pet lovers.) Part of the urban crisis was the sense, among many middle-class whites, that minorities, the poor, and the drug addicted now truly dominated the city. In disaster scenarios, the intractable problem of drugs and crime would survive even a nuclear attack. "Those people" could not be pried free of their roosts. And it is hinted that this would not be such a bad thing. In disaster planning, FEMA reinforced the idea of the urban crisis. See Zuckerman, *The Day After World War III,* 107, 105.

22. Vincent Canby, "A Very Tall Tale," *New York Times,* July 10, 1981.

23. Richard Corliss, "Bad Apples," *Time,* July 13, 1981.

24. *The Day the Earth Caught Fire* inspired Rod Serling to produce one of most powerful episodes of *The Twilight Zone,* "Midnight Sun." The episode offered no cause for the increase in the temperature of the earth, even though *The Day the Earth Caught Fire* was clear in its antinuclear message.

25. *Fantastic Four,* no. 4 (Marvel Comics, 1962), 17–20. Thanks to Robert Grover for pointing me to this issue.

26. *Sub-Mariner,* "The Invasion of New York," no. 60 (Marvel Comics, 1973).

27. *Kamandi: The Last Boy on Earth* (National Periodical Publications, 1972), 1–4.

28. In *Captain America,* no. 193 (Marvel Comics, 1976), 2–8, an airborne chemical is released in New York City causing the residents to manifest homicidal rage. Captain America destroys the device but stands in the aftermath thinking, "I-I haven't seen anything like this since World War II. . . . The city is in a complete shambles!" All around Captain America people begin to recover from the chemical attack, their faces and bodies bloodied and broken, their clothes torn and dirtied. Buildings in the background burn and debris cover the ground around Captain America.

29. J. G. Ballard, *Hello America* (New York: Carroll and Graf, 1988), 35, 22, 16. There is a suggestion that dramatic environmental change is the root of the city's downfall in Paul Auster's *In the Country of Last Things:* a terrible winter in August is the tipping point that leads to the downfall of the city.

Kurt Vonnegut, Jr., offered a farcical tale featuring New York set back in time by environmental disaster in his 1976 novel *Slapstick.* The United States has collapsed in the wake of the "Green Death." The bridges and tunnels to Manhattan have long since been crushed, and boats will not come near the island. The island's inhabitants are isolated. The president of the United States is Wilbur Daffodil-11 Swain, his unusual name the result of his own presidential order that everyone take on a new name and a new family and community grouping. The president rules his country—or doesn't rule—from the ruins of the lobby of the Empire State Building, surrounded by an "ailanthus jungle" that used to be 34th Street. He nibbles on his declining supply of tri-benzo-Deportamil, which keeps his horrible case of Tourette's syndrome in check. He awaits his granddaughter Melody, who is making the trek from Michigan to the legendary city, like Benét's boy in "By the Waters of Babylon." "And so on," the novel ends. Kurt Vonnegut, Jr., *Slapstick; Or, Lonesome No More! A Novel* (New York: Delacorte/S. Lawrence, 1976).

30. *Diary of Philip Hone* (1845), quoted in *Quotable New York: A Literary Companion,* ed. William Cole (New York: Penguin, 1992), 50.

31. Walker Evans, "The Wreckers," *Fortune,* May 1951. See also http://www .newcriterion.com/archive/18/mar00/evans.htm.

32. Joshua Shannon, "Claes Oldenburg's 'The Street' and Urban Renewal in Greenwich Village, 1960," *Art Bulletin* 86, no. 4 (2004).

33. Gay Talese, "Panic in Brooklyn," rpt. in *Writing New York: A Literary Anthology,* ed. Philip Lopate (New York: Library of America, 1998).

34. Another film that imagines an animal out of place—Quetzalcoatl, the divine Aztec feathered serpent—mysteriously killing in the city is *Q: The Winged Serpent* (1982).

35. Where popular culture went, academic culture followed. Through the 1980s and 1990s a growing array of scholars became interested in disaster as a window into society. Some of the earliest studies—by Kai Erikson, for example—were focused on the sociology of past disasters, such as the Galveston or Johnstown floods, the Chicago fire, and the San Francisco earthquake. But steadily, academics turned their attention to the culture of disaster, to disaster movies, to the nature of ruins, to the politics of rebuilding after natural or human disasters.

Scholars in a diverse range of fields, such as Steven Biel, *Down with the Old Canoe: A Cultural History of the Titanic Disaster* (New York: Norton, 1996); Carl Smith, *Urban Disorder and the Shape of Belief: The Great Chicago Fire, the Haymarket Bomb, and the Model Town of Pullman* (Chicago: University of Chicago Press, 1995); and Eric Klinenberg, *Heat Wave: A Social Autopsy of Disaster in Chicago* (Chicago: University of Chicago Press, 2002), have shown that disasters are crucibles in which class and racial politics, understandings of nature, and attitudes toward city life are revealed and crystallized, sometimes redirecting the trajectory of a city's development. Economists such as David Weinstein have argued the opposite. Weinstein's studies of the rebuilding of Japan showed that even total war, including the attacks on Hiroshima and Nagasaki, did little to check the trajectory of Japanese cities' development. David Weinstein and Donald R. Davis, "Bones, Bombs, and Break Points: The Geography of Economic Activity," *American Economic Review* 92, no. 5 (2002): 1269–89.

Beyond the academy, Americans revealed a growing appetite for works that told the stories of past disasters, actual and imaginary, as in such works as Nathaniel Philbrick's *In the Heart of the Sea* (on the sinking of the *Essex*) and Erik Larson's *Isaac's Storm: A Man, a Time, and the Deadliest Hurricane in History* (on the Galveston Flood).

And the focus on New York's own particular disasters drew faithful readers long before 9/11. The Draft Riots of 1863, the General Slocum disaster of 1904, the Wall Street bombing of 1920—all received their chronicles in the last decade of the twentieth century.

36. There is a final irony here. To portray the effects of the meteor hitting the city, the filmmakers not only fabricated images of the World Trade Center being hit and the huge gash running up the island to Central Park. They also borrowed older images of urban disaster of a different kind. To show buildings toppling, they used stock images from the demolition of Pruitt-Igoe housing complex in St. Louis. The architectural theorist Charles Jencks has asserted that the end of modernism can be dated rather precisely to the particular hour in 1972 when that massive development, designed by the high modernist architect Minoru Yamasaki (whose later work included the World Trade Center in New York), was razed. The demise of Pruitt-Igoe after only twenty-three years was a potent symbol of the end of the vision of some modernists of massive "towers in the park." It may be too much to suggest a carefully orchestrated narrative, but the use of the demolition of a public housing failure in St. Louis as a stand-in for nature's wrath in New York is a striking, if subtle, indictment of urban renewal. Charles Jencks, *The Language of Post-Modern Architecture* (New York: Rizzoli. 1977), 9. See also David Harvey, *The Condition of Postmodernity: An Enquiry into the Origins of Cultural Change* (Oxford: Blackwell, 1989), 39.

37. Comic books, too, found New York's destruction due to natural disaster a continuing inspiration. For example, in a 2000 issue of *The Authority,* New York City is the target of an artificially generated tsunami. The waves rise above the tallest skyscraper and trap thousands under water. *The Authority,* no. 17 (DC Comics, 2000), 2–4.

38. The theme was reprised in *Superman Returns* (2006).

39. *Batman: Cataclysm* (New York: DC Comics, 1999), 316. This graphic novel has an interesting relationship to New York. There are clear references to the existing city, including subway lines, specific addresses, Dutch-sounding place names. And yet the skyline does not look at all like Manhattan's. In fact, one building looks much like Seattle's Space Needle, and there is another reference to Coit, as in San Francisco's Coit Tower. Finally, the prison island immediately calls to mind Alcatraz, in San Francisco Bay.

40. Mike Wallace uses this phrase in *A New Deal for New York* (New York: Bell and Weiland, 2002).

41. Quotations from Ken Feil, *Dying for a Laugh: Disaster Movies and the Camp Imagination* (Middletown, Conn.: Wesleyan University Press, 2005), 44, 33. *Gremlins* and *Gremlins 2* continued the campy exploitation of lovable—although incredibly destructive—otherworldly creatures. And *Mars Attacks,* a farcical parody based on a 1962 series of Topps trading cards which featured a Martian invasion of the earth, revels in urban disaster in the midst of a slapstick comedy about Martian invasion.

42. Obliteration of the Empire State Building provoked this comment on a public Web site by a user named "smartsean": "Ok, i loved that bit when the ESB got minced, but what building (or thing) do u wanna blow up the most?" Posted on imdb.com on July 13, 2006, but since deleted, presumably on grounds of taste.

43. Self-referential commentaries on classic urban disaster stories were everywhere, especially *King Kong* and *Godzilla* references. The opening scene of *Armageddon,* just before the meteorites hit the city, shows a dog rushing down the sidewalk to attack a set of plastic Godzilla statues being sold by a street vendor.

Similarly, in an unproduced screenplay, writers Anthony Bregman and Ariel Bargash feature a terrorist who carries around a doll of King Kong climbing the Empire State Building as he plans attacks on modern building projects that destroy historic buildings of the city.

44. Sontag, "The Imagination of Disaster," 224.

45. Paul Auster, *In the Country of Last Things* (New York: Viking, 1987).

46. Ibid., 21–22.

47. Ibid., 172, 1, 6, 87.

48. Madeleine E. Robins, *The Stone War* (New York: Tor, 1999).

49. *Kirkus Reviews,* June 1, 1999.

50. By Gerald Jonas, "Science Fiction," *New York Times Book Review,* August 1 1999, 16.

51. Robins, *The Stone War,* 37, 102. Robins has Tietjen interpret what he says with reference to photographs of previous disasters. Tietjen's "feeling of walking through someone else's dream increased; buildings he passed look as though they had been hit by bombs, flattened by hurricanes. Tietjen thought of photographs he had seen of Hiroshima and Beirut, London after the blitz" (65).

52. Ibid., 223, 225.

53. Ibid., 240–41, 242.

54. James Sanders has argued that the World Trade Center has had very few starring roles in American films beyond disaster movies like *Escape from New York, Independence Day,* and *Armageddon.* He cites only four: *Three Days of the Condor* (1975), *King Kong* (1976), *The Wiz* (1978), and *Other People's Money* (1991). See James Sanders, *Celluloid Skyline: New York and the Movies* (New York: Knopf, 2001); Sarah Boxer, "In Films, Twin Towers Had No Star Power," *New York Times,* February 4, 2002.

55. For a discussion of the 1933 and 1976 *King Kong* films and the significance of the architecture in each, see Sanders, *Celluloid Skyline,* 96–102.

56. *Spider-Man,* no. 16, "X-Force: Sabotage, Part 1" (Marvel Comics, 1991).

57. *Batman: Cataclysm* (New York: DC Comics, 1999), 53, 73, 316. Joan Didion, in *The Year of Magical Thinking* (New York: Knopf, 2005), 224, mentions a film script that she

and her husband, John Gregory Dunne, were writing at Christmas 1990. In the screenplay, which was never produced, a plutonium device is located in the tower of the Cathedral of St. John the Divine, though most investigators believe that it is in the World Trade Center.

58. See http://www.snopes.com/rumors/thecoup.htm. One other album, whose original album art was released—Dream Theater's *Live Scenes from New York*—also included images of a burning New York skyline, including the towers. It was recalled and repackaged after 9/11.

59. See http://www.pbs.org/wgbh/amex/newyork/peopleevents/p_petit.html.

60. Quoted in Justine Henning, "G Is for Greatness: Disaster Strikes on Sesame Street, to Wonderful Effect," http://www.slate.com/id/103401/. In Freedom Force, a computer video game released in the summer of 2001, a band of superheroes is called on to protect New York. Inevitably, they are not always successful, and one reviewer warned that players needed to "be wary of becoming too destruction-happy . . . as total disregard for public property will lose you valuable prestige points." Posted on http://www.Gamer.tv on August 9, 2001; no longer available.

61. The meaning of the coda has been much debated: the aliens speak with David and give him the opportunity to spend one more day with his mother, whom they can clone, albeit temporarily, from DNA.

62. There are a number of inside jokes on the video screens. Cruise's future wife, Katie Holmes, shows up on one screen. And on a huge television screen mounted on the Times Tower at 42nd Street a *Twilight Zone* episode is playing: "Shadow Play," which concerns a man convicted of a murder he insists happened only in his dreams. See http://en.wikipedia.org/wiki/Vanilla_Sky.

6. The Future of the City's End

1. This and the following nine paragraphs are adapted from Max Page, "On Edge, Again," *New York Times,* October 21, 2001. Used with permission.

2. On the recovery and cleanup operation see William Langewiesche, *American Ground: Unbuilding the World Trade Center* (New York: North Point, 2002).

3. Virginia Woolf, *A Room of One's Own* (1929; New York: Harcourt, 1991), 11.

4. Patrick McGeeham, "Top Executives Return Offices to Manhattan," *New York Times,* July 3, 2006.

5. José Martí, "New York Under the Snow," in *Writing New York: A Literary Anthology,* ed. Philip Lopate (New York: Library of America, 1998), 277.

6. See Ken Feil, *Dying for a Laugh: Disaster Movies and the Camp Imagination* (Middletown, Conn.: Wesleyan University Press, 2005). See also http://en.wikipedia.org/wiki/List_of_audiovisual_entertainment_affected_by_the_September_11,_2001_attacks.

7. See "Terrorist Attacks Force Video Game Makers to Purge Images of Destruction," Associated Press, September 18, 2001.

8. See Nicholas Lemann, "Crash Practice," *New Yorker,* December 17, 2001.

9. "Album Cover of WTC Blast Pulled," September 13, 2001, http://archives.cnn.com/2001/SHOWBIZ/Music/09/13/wtc.cover/.

10. Steven Jay Schneider writes, "There seemed to be a legitimate fear that images of the former World Trade Center in post-9/11 mainstream film releases would work *too* well;

that instead of conferring an additional documentary or nonfictional quality upon the mise-en-scène of the fictional story, they might well *undermine* the story's narrative and powers of illusion, leading viewers to momentarily ignore the sensuous properties of the filmic medium and reflect instead on the all-too-real consequences of the recent terrorist attacks." Steven Jay Schneider, "Architectural Nostalgia and the New York City Skyline on Film," in *Film and Television after 9/11,* ed. Wheeler Winston Dixon (Carbondale: Southern Illinois University Press, 2004), 37.

11. Anahad O'Connor, "The Claim: Violent Video Games Make Young People Aggressive," *New York Times,* August 30, 2005. O'Connor summarizes the findings of the American Psychological Association, which concluded that video games do provoke aggressive behavior among youth. But O'Connor also suggests that there is no proof of long-term dangers.

12. Anthony Lane, "This Is Not a Movie," *New Yorker,* September 24, 2001, 79. Also discussed in Kevin Rozario, *The Culture of Calamity: Disaster and the Making of Modern America* (Chicago: University of Chicago Press, 2007).

13. Leon Wieseltier, "Ruins," *New Republic,* November 26, 2001.

14. Leon Wieseltier, "A Year Later," *New Republic,* September 2, 2002.

15. Slavoj Žižek, *Welcome to the Desert of the Real! Five Essays on September 11 and Related Dates* (London: Verso, 2002), 17, 33, 16. See Rozario, *Culture of Calamity,* 9; Jean Baudrillard, *The Spirit of Terrorism* (New York: Verso, 2002).

16. A new film version of H. G. Wells's *Time Machine* was delayed from December 2001 to February 2002, although the DreamWorks studio insisted that the decision had been made on September 10, 2001. Nonetheless, a key scene, in which the moon crashes onto earth, was cut (although a brief scene of the moon breaking apart above Manhattan remains). See http://filmforce.ign.com/articles/306/306002p1.html.

17. This comment was made by Chuck Ivy at http://www.tightcircle.com/essay/twin 2001, which is no longer available.

18. See also Feil, *Dying for a Laugh.*

19. Kate Authur, "CBS Wins with a Storm," *New York Times,* November 19, 2004; Kathy Blumenstock, "Capturing the Mighty Wrath of 'Destruction,'" *Washington Post,* November 14, 2004.

20. W. G. Sebald, *On the Natural History of Destruction,* trans. Anthea Bell (New York: Random House, 2003), 9, 98.

21. Susan Sontag, *Regarding the Pain of Others* (New York: Farrar, Straus and Giroux, 2003), 110, 8.

22. Ibid., 75–76.

23. See especially Jim Dwyer and Kevin Flynn, *102 Minutes: The Untold Story of the Fight to Survive Inside the Twin Towers* (New York: Times Books, 2005), and Langewiesche, *American Ground.*

24. Don DeLillo, "In the Ruins of the Future," *Guardian,* December 22, 2001, accessed at http://www.guardian.co.uk/Archive/Article/0,4273,4324579,00.html.

25. Don DeLillo, *Cosmopolis: A Novel* (New York: Scribner's, 2003), 91–93.

26. Ibid., 97, 36.

27. Michael Cunningham, *Specimen Days* (New York: Farrar, Straus and Giroux, 2005).

28. Ian McEwan, *Saturday* (New York: Doubleday, 2005). For a discussion of several

novels that deal with 9/11, including *Specimen Days, Saturday,* and Chris Cleave's *Incendiary,* see Caryn James, "The Intertwining Legacy of Terror Attacks and Fiction," *New York Times,* August 3, 2005.

29. Art Spiegelman, *In the Shadow of No Towers* (New York: Viking, 2004), 1. Other "comix" followed the party line rather than Spiegelman's more nuanced approach. One of the first of the traditional comic books to take on 9/11, *The Amazing Spider-Man,* provided an exercise in emotional hyperbole and patriotic gore. The last chapter of *Coming Home,* a graphic novel comprising *Spider-Man* comics published in 2001 and 2002, is a graphic portrait of the destruction. Spider-Man enlists all his superhero friends to aid the firefighters in their rescue efforts. The panels are moving, but the words build toward a symphony of clichés: "Whatever our history, whatever the root of our surnames, we remain a good and decent people, and we do not bow down and we do not give up. The fire of the human spirit cannot be quenched by bomb blasts or body counts. . . . We have endured worse before; we will bear this burden and all that come hereafter, because that's what ordinary men and women do. No matter what. This has not weakened us. It has only made us stronger." J. Michael Straczynski and John Romita, Jr., *The Amazing Spider-Man: Coming Home* (London: Panini, 2002).

30. Spiegelman, *Shadow,* 10. Spiegelman implicates even the generally liberal *New Yorker* magazine in the patriotic sleepiness of America after 9/11. *In the Shadow of No Towers* began as a comic strip commissioned by the German newspaper *Die Zeit.* In the United States, an anxious press, fearing retaliation for anti-American sentiments, would not publish the strip. Only the Jewish *Forward* published it. See Spiegelman's discussion of this in an interview in *Corriere della Sera* (Milan), February 13, 2003, reprinted on http://electroniciraq.net/news/ artmusicculture/Art_Spiegelman_cartoonist_for_The_New_Yorker_resig_109-109.shtml.

31. See the interview with Spiegelman by Claudia Dreifus, "A Comic-Book Response to 9/11 and its Aftermath," *New York Times,* August 7, 2004.

32. Spiegelman, *Shadow,* 4, 8.

33. Ibid., 2, 4.

34. See http://www.marsattacksfan.com/homepage.htm.

35. Spiegelman, *Shadow,* [11].

36. New York staged a mock terror attack (a "weapon of mass destruction" in Shea Stadium) on March 14, 2004. Patrick Healy, "Mock Terror Attack Response Provides Training for Disaster," *New York Times,* March 15, 2004. An extended debate also took place about the security of the Indian Point nuclear power plant north of the city, and what the effect on New York would be of a successful attack on the plant.

37. Martin Gottlieb, "In Calm Blackout, View of Remade City," *New York Times,* August 17, 2003.

38. Randy Kennedy, "Fleeting Pathos of a New York Minute," *New York Times,* July 16, 2006.

39. Quoted in Sean Smith, "Fear Factor," *Newsweek,* June 27, 2005, http://www .msnbc.msn.com/id/8271974/site/newsweek/.

40. David McNary and Claude Brodesser, "Spielberg Tackles Other 'Worlds,'" August 29, 2005, http://www.variety.com/article/VR1117928170.html?categoryid=1236&cs=1&query= Spielberg+Tackles.

41. In a few examples, natural catastrophes are triggered by humans—such as in the *Superman* shorts of the early 1940s, in which mad scientists manage to harness comets. But

the vast majority of natural disaster films and novels have been about unstoppable natural forces that threatened the city and the world.

42. Spielberg and Kubrick's *A.I.* makes clear that climate change had been responsible for the submersion of "Man-Hattan," although that was not a central theme of the film. The television movies *Category 6* and *10.5* played on the fears of climate change. *Category 6* in particular builds on the fear—which is now gaining scientific backing—that climate change would bring about what American culture portrayed as the "the perfect storm," which would be just a regular storm in the future.

43. Eric Drooker's pictorial novel *Flood!*, originally published in 1992 (with parts published even earlier) and reprinted in 2001, is a story of the underside of the years of renewed prosperity in the 1980s. With virtually no words, it tells a story of a heartless city and society that deserves what it gets in the final of three chapters: a biblical flood to wipe away the horrors that civilization has wrought. In that final chapter, the rains fall and the city becomes steadily flooded until, on the last page, all that remains is a modern-day Noah and his ark, and the tops of the Empire State Building and the Chrysler Tower. Eric Drooker, *Flood! A Novel in Pictures* (New York: Four Walls Eight Windows, 1992). On water as a theme see Ivan Illich, *H_2O and the Waters of Forgetfulness* (London: Boyars, 1986) and Veronica Strang, *The Meaning of Water* (Oxford: Berg, 2004).

44. Peter Conrad, in an essay coinciding with the opening of *Day After Tomorrow,* notes that by flooding New York, Emmerich "ventures to undo the moral and psychological damage inflicted by 9/11. The World Trade Centre collapsed because all that aviation fuel ignited inside it. Fire, as Hitler made clear in his rant about New York, is the destroyer." Peter Conrad, "Necropolis Now," *Guardian,* May 16, 2004. One could argue, similarly, that *Sky-captain and the World of Tomorrow,* which opened just after the third anniversary of 9/11, avoided the outright destruction of the city while playing to the thrill of seeing fighter planes swooping through Manhattan's canyons.

45. Tad Friend, "Wrecked Again," *New Yorker,* May 24, 2004.

46. Megan Lehmann, "Apocalypse Wow," *New York Post,* May 28, 2004.

47. Randy Kennedy, "Hollywood Clobbers Manhattan. Again," *New York Times,* May 26, 2004, http://query.nytimes.com/gst/fullpage.html?res=9C0DE1D6143EF935A15756C0A962 9C8B63.

48. *Batman Begins* (2005) calls on one of the oldest themes of the New York destruction genre: Gotham City is destroyed because of its corrupt ways. The modern Rome "must be allowed to die" declares Henri Ducard (played by Liam Neeson), Bruce Wayne's teacher and, ultimately, enemy. But the film also plays on environmental fears of the beginning of the millennium. Instead of water overflowing the city or encasing the city in ice, the water itself is endangered. The city is to be destroyed via a poisoned water system, turning the inhabitants into hallucinating zombies who will themselves wreak destruction. Corruption and crime will be accelerated to the point where the city will simply self-destruct. Using technology designed by Wayne Industries for vaporizing the water into the air, the attacks begin in the Narrows, Gotham's island version of the Lower East Side. *Superman Returns* (2006) is not a New York destruction film, but at one point an earthquake, caused by the growth of the massive new landform in the Atlantic Ocean, opens a fault line that heads straight to Metropolis. The city rumbles, the skyscrapers shake, and the globe on the top of the Daily Planet Building topples, but the city survives.

49. *Harvard Magazine* published computer-manipulated images by Jared T. Williams showing a shrunken Manhattan after a rise of 3.5 meters in the level of the ocean—something possible in the coming century. Jonathan Shaw, "Fueling our Future," *Harvard Magazine,* May–June 2006, 40–48. See also the images of rising waters on New York in Mark Hertsgaard, "While Washington Slept," *Vanity Fair,* May 2006; Albert Gore and Melcher Media, *An Inconvenient Truth: The Planetary Emergency of Global Warming and What We Can Do About It* (Emmaus, Pa.: Rodale, 2006).

50. Linda Yablonsky, "New York's Watery New Grave," *New York Times,* April 11, 2004.

51. "I want my work to be as clear to a kid in Iowa as to an art world insider." Alexis Rockman, *Manifest Destiny* (New York: Brooklyn Museum of Art, 2005), 9.

52. Quoted in Yablonsky, "New York's Watery New Grave."

53. And the beat goes on and on. *Heroes,* launched by NBC in 2006, is centered around a future nuclear explosion that a series of "heroes" (people with unique characteristics, like the ability to paint the future—including the explosion) attempt to prevent. Early in 2007 St. Martin's Press published Alan Weisman's *The World Without Us,* which includes a chapter imagining the rapid decay of New York if the city were abandoned. And just before Christmas 2007, Warner Brothers released *I Am Legend,* starring Will Smith as a scientist who is the only survivor in New York after a virus has apparently killed off everyone in the city and perhaps the world.

54. See Rozario, *Culture of Calamity,* 9. Michael J. Apter argues that evolution has produced the powerful rush of adrenaline associated with fear, followed by a powerful sense of expansive joy when the threat—or perceived threat, as in amusement park rides or disaster movies—has passed. Michael J. Apter, *The Dangerous Edge: The Psychology of Excitement* (New York: Free Press, 1992).

55. E. B. White, "Here Is New York," in *Essays of E. B. White* (New York: Harper and Row, 1977), 132. Originally published in *Holiday* in 1949.

56. Colson Whitehead, *The Colossus of New York: A City in Thirteen Parts* (New York: Doubleday, 2003), 92.

57. Ibid., 3–4, 151.

58. This and the following four paragraphs are drawn from Max Page, "On Edge, Again," *New York Times,* October 21, 2001. Used with permission.

59. Jonathan Larson, "La Vie Bohème," from the musical *Rent!* (1996).

60. White, "Here Is New York," 123.

Acknowledgments

AMONG THE SMALLEST CASUALTIES ON 9/11 WAS AN EXHIBITION I was planning, entitled Destroying New York. Having come across dozens of fantasies of the city's end while writing my first book, a study of the cycles of real destruction and rebuilding in early–twentieth-century New York, I thought it would make a captivating exhibition to showcase the two centuries of fictional accounts of New York's end. The attacks of September 11 put this project on hold—forever, I thought at the time. I returned to it, however, as I came to believe—and others urged me to believe—that there was value in understanding how and why American culture had so consistently and persistently chose to imagine New York's end. Ironically, watching and reading the nearly endless array of narratives about New York's destruction gave me a greater love for the city than ever before.

I never fully understood the phrase I have seen in so many books—"I have acquired many debts along the way to completing this book"—until I undertook this project. During each stage of the work—research, writing, image collection, permissions, editing—I have depended on the kindness of friends and strangers to complete this work.

First and foremost, I thank the many people who eagerly shared their favorite New York disaster stories. I especially appreciate my old friend Alvin Forader, who guided me through the world of comic books; James Sanders, who offered insights based on his encyclopedic knowledge of New York films; Alexis

Rockman, who shared not only his own paintings but his enthusiasm for the subject; and Nick Yablon and Kevin Rozario, both of whom shared their scholarly work related to this topic. I benefited from the outstanding talents of a series of graduate students, first at Yale and then at UMass Amherst. Each of them—Diana Daly, Kirin Makker, David Favaloro, and Sandy Zipp—left an imprint on the book.

I also thank people who contributed something intangible but essential: their enthusiasm for the project. I especially want to note the ongoing support of Richard Rabinowitz, Vicki Levi, Ken Jackson, Jan Ramirez, Ted Burrows, Mike Wallace, Larry Vale, and Peter Farbman, as well as Jonathan Brent, who was eager to publish the book at Yale University Press. Finally, I want to thank the students at Yale and the University of Massachusetts who heard various pieces of this project in my classes about New York and American urban history.

I was told by one of my professors in graduate school that once I was a professor myself, what I would need and crave more than anything is time away from teaching, advising, and administration to do research. A Delmas Fellowship from the New-York Historical Society and the Gilder Lehrman Institute and a Healey Faculty Research Grant from the University of Massachusetts helped me conduct early research into this topic. A John Simon Guggenheim Foundation Fellowship in 2003 gave me a full year to develop the topic. I applaud the Foundation's continuing dedication to the most simple of propositions: giving scholars, artists, and writers the time and recognition they need to pursue their creative projects.

I have been fortunate to have been able to present my ongoing research and ideas in a variety of settings: the Gotham Center conference, the City Seminar at Columbia University, the Resilient City lecture series at MIT, the Out of Ground Zero lecture series at Columbia, Rutgers University (where I was invited to give the Candeub Memorial Lecture in Planning), Stanford University, the Università Ca' Foscardi di Venezia, the International City Planning History conference in New Delhi, and the NYLON seminar. I know that the book is better for all the advice I received from participants in these events.

Navigating the world of copyrights for cartoons, album covers, and film stills could have driven me mad if not for the advice of Kenn Rabin, the assistance of Annelise Finegan, and the research skills of graduate research assistant Kerry O'Grady. I especially would like to thank the Schoff Subvention Fund at Columbia University, the J. M. Kaplan Foundation, and the Guggenheim Foundation for helping to support the reproduction of images in this book, while keeping the cost of the book down. Near the end, when many mistakes and clunky phrases came closer to being published, Dan Heaton at Yale University Press and Beth Berry at UMass Amherst offered expert editing.

Finally, I have my family—Eve, Jonah, Aviva, and Ruthie—to thank for reminding me of the right way to measure the world and one's place in it: in acts of loving kindness, and the pursuit of social justice.

Illustration Credits

ABC Television, 191 top
Alexander Gallery, New York, 45
Amazing Stories Magazine, plate 5, cover of *Amazing Stories Magazine*, January 1929, vol. 3, no. 10, Frank R. Paul illustrator. Amazing Stories is a trademark of Wizards of the Coast, Inc.
Argosy Communications, 37, original artwork for "The Second Deluge" and "Finis" © 1948 by Popular Publications Inc.
Jill Bauman, 7
Bonestell Space Art, plates 12, 13
Claudio Cambon, 10, 11
CBS television, 210
Child, John, 79
Columbia Pictures, 119, 138, 170
Columbia-Tristar Pictures, 193 top
Corbis, 84
Cameron Davidson and John Blackford, 225, What climate change could bring to the island of Manhattan: "While Washington Slept" / *Vanity Fair*, May 2006. Photography © Cameron Davidson, Digital Imaging © John Blackford
DC Comics, 93, plate 15
DNA Films, 13
Dodd, Mead, 53
Eric Drooker, 224 (www.Drooker.com)
Fleischer Animation Studios. 95, 176, plates 8–10
Barney Ebsworth, plate 7
Elektra, plate 17
Epitaph Records, 206
Everett Collection, 163, 168 bottom, 173 top
Everybody's Magazine, 26
Fantastic Story Magazine, 119
Fox Television, 181
Frederick A. Stokes, 39

Hallmark Entertainment, 175

Harper and Brothers, 51

Harper's Weekly, 35

Atta Kim, plate 24

Kingfisher Press, 5

Longines Symphonette Society, 87

Marvel Comics, plates 16, 20

Ariel Meyerowitz Gallery, 230, © Joel Meyerowitz, Courtesy Edwynn Houk Gallery, West 46th Street, New York, 1976

Microsoft and Josef Havlik, 2, 3

Mizuma Art Gallery, plate 1, Makoto Aida, *A Picture of an Air Raid on New York City (War Picture Returns),* 1996. Materials: Six-panel sliding screens, hinges, Nihon Keizai Shinbun, black-and-white photocopy on hologram paper, charcoal pencil, watercolor, acrylic, magic marker, correction liquid, pencil, etc. 169 × 378 cm, CG of Zero fighters created by Mutsuo Matsuhashi, © Makoto Aida, Courtesy Mizuma Art Gallery

NBC television, 210 center

José Clemente Orozco Foundation, Clemente Orozco, curator, plate 6

Paramount Pictures, 191 bottom

Joseph Pennell, plate 3

Photofest, 73, 75, 90, 97, 99, 111–14, 118, 132, 146, 150, 158, 160 bottom, 161, 168 top, 177, 180, 188, 193 bottom, 210 top, 217 bottom, 221, 230 top, plates 14, 18, 19, 22

Random House, 128, 214, plate 21 (cover and interior images from *In The Shadow of No Towers* by Art Spiegelman, © 2004 by Art Spiegelman, reprinted with permission of the Wylie Agency, Inc., and Pantheon Books, a division of Random House, Inc.)

Robertstock.com, 107 left

Alexis Rockman, 229, plate 23

Paul Sahre, 200

Nicole Schulman, 8

Wes Sickles, 115

Small, Maynard, 55

Smithsonian American Art Museum, Washington, D.C. / Art Resource, NY, 68, James Naumberg Rosenberg (1874–1970). *Dies Irae* (October 29), 1929. Lithograph on paper, 13⅝ × 10½ in. Smithsonian Art Museum, Washington, D.C. Photo credit: Smithsonian American Art Museum, Washington, D.C. / Art Resource, NY. Permission granted by Anne Geismar; 71, Louis Lozowick (1892–1973). *Storm Clouds Above Manhattan,* 1935. Lithograph on paper, 11⅞ × 16⅞ in. Gift of Adele Lozowick. Smithsonian Art Museum, Washington, D.C. Photo credit: Smithsonian American Art Museum, Washington, D.C. / Art Resource, NY

Topps Trading Card Company, 120

Tor Books, 185

20th Century–Fox, 145

University of Nebraska, plate 4, © 2002 University of Nebraska Press, reprinted with permission

Watermill Press, 127

Westwood Studios, 205

Index

FRIENDS FREE LIBRARY
GERMANTOWN FRIENDS LIBRARY
5418 Germantown Avenue
Philadelphia, PA 19144
215-951-2355

Each borrower is responsible for all items
checked out on his/her library card, for
fines on materials kept overtime, and
replacing any lost or damaged materials.